In No Time ⎯⎯⎯⎯⎯⎯⎯⎯

Office
2000

IN NO TIME

Gunter Born

AN IMPRINT OF PEARSON EDUCATION

PEARSON EDUCATION LIMITED

Head Office:
Edinburgh Gate
Harlow CM20 2JE
Tel: +44 (0)1279 623623
Fax: +44 (0)1279 431059

London Office:
128 Long Acre
London WC2E 9AN
Tel: +44 (0)207 447 2000
Fax: +44 (0)207 240 5771

First published in Great Britain in 2000
© Pearson Education Limited 2000

First published in 1999 as *Office 2000: leicht, klar, sofort*
by Markt & Technik Buch-und Software-Verlag GmbH
Martin-Kollar-Straße 10–12
D-81829 Munich
Germany

Library of Congress Cataloging in Publication Data
Available from the publisher.

British Library Cataloguing in Publication Data
A CIP catalogue record for this book can be obtained from the British Library.

ISBN 0-130-16227-2

10 9 8 7 6 5 4 3 2 1

Translated and typeset by Cybertechnics, Sheffield.
Printed and bound in Great Britain by Henry Ling Ltd, at The Dorset Press, Dorchester, Dorset.

The publishers' policy is to use paper manufactured from sustainable forests.

Contents

2   Word – the first time   64

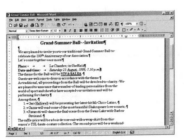

3   Word 2000 – letters and other documents   122

4   Word for professionals   182

8 Office applications combined — 364

9 The Internet and intranets and Office 2000 — 410

10 Working with Outlook 2000 **448**

11 Installation and adaptation **494**

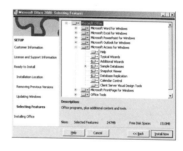

A little breakdown **550**

An initial aid for dealing with files 568

Dear reader,

This book is designed to be your travelling companion as you enter the world of Microsoft Office 2000. It will help you learn, gradually and easily, the most important of the various Office programs. In reading chapter 1, you will work through some of the basics, such as using a mouse, and understanding windows and programs. This chapter and Appendix B will explain to you why you need to use files and folders on your computer, and also how to insert a disk into the drive. Step-by-step instructions and accompanying diagrams will show you how a particular process actually works, whilst a 'breakdown service' will help you over the first hurdles.

In the following chapters you will learn about working with Word, Excel, PowerPoint and Outlook, and also some more about surfing the 'Web'. After just a few lessons you will be able to start writing your first letters and designing charts in Excel. If necessary, you can skip through various chapters in order to concentrate on a particular program. In this book you will also find various pieces of background information which will help widen your knowledge of forming letters, working with electronic mail and surfing the Internet. This book can be used with various versions of Windows and also, in a more limited way, with Microsoft Office 97.

I hope you are going to enjoy working both with Office 2000 and with my book.

G. Born

The following three pages show you how your computer keyboard is structured. Groups of keys are dealt with one by one to make it easier to understand.

Most of the computer keys are operated exactly like keys on a typewriter. However, there are a few additional keys, which are designed for the peculiarities of computer work.

See for yourself...

Typewriter keys

Use these keys exactly as you do on a typewriter.
The Enter ⏎ key is also used to send commands to your computer.

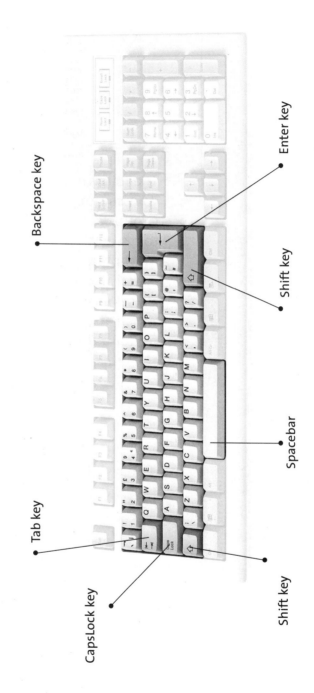

Backspace key

Enter key

Shift key

Tab key

CapsLock key

Spacebar

Shift key

Special keys, function keys, status lights, numeric key pad

Special keys and function keys are used for special tasks in computer operation. The Ctrl, Alt and AltGr keys are usually used in combination with other keys. The Esc key can cancel commands. Insert and Delete can be used, amongst other things, to insert and delete text.

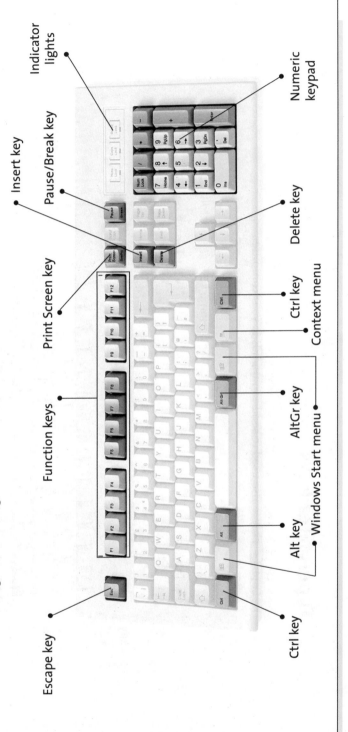

Escape key

Function keys

Print Screen key

Pause/Break key

Insert key

Indicator lights

Numeric keypad

Delete key

Ctrl key

Context menu

AltGr key

Windows Start menu

Alt key

Ctrl key

Navigation keys

These keys are used to move around the screen.

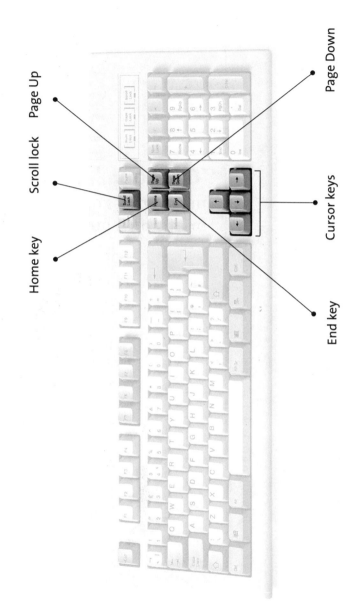

Page Up

Scroll lock

Home key

Page Down

Cursor keys

End key

'Click on...'

means press once
briefly on a button.

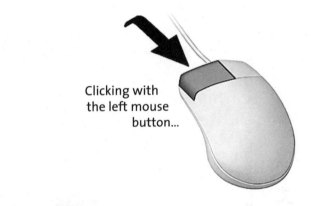

Clicking with
the left mouse
button...

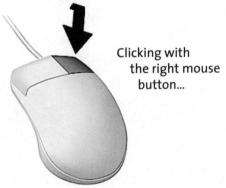

Clicking with
the right mouse
button...

'Double-click on...'

means press the left button
twice briefly in quick
succession.

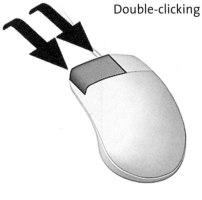

Double-clicking

'Drag...'

means click on an object with the left
mouse button, keep the button
pressed, move the mouse and thus
drag the item to another position.

Drag

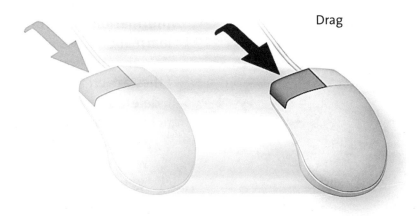

What's in this chapter?

This chapter will cover the basics of handling Windows and Office. Once completed, you will be able to start and end programs and control windows. You will know how to open, close, move and change the size of windows. You will also know how to use the Office Assistant and Help functions to find more information. You will learn about files and folders, and how they are created, deleted, copied and renamed. If you are already familiar with these topics, you may skip this chapter and proceed to the next one.

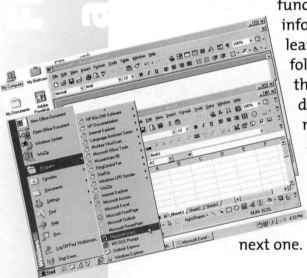

You will now learn:

What is Office?

Have you ever worked with a computer before? Are you wondering what the name 'Office' actually covers? Then read the following short overview – the details will follow later on.

Microsoft has packaged a number of separate programs under the name of 'Microsoft Office'. These programs address requirements often found in general office environments. There are several variations of the Office suite, including the Small Business Edition and the Premium Edition, which are tailored for specific requirements.

Microsoft Word	Word provides **text processing** functions in Office, in all its aspects. The program is a sort of enhanced typewriter with many convenience features. Chapters 2 onwards introduce some of its features.
Microsoft Excel	Excel is a so-called **spreadsheet**, and is also included in all variants of Office. Worksheets are used to enter data in tabular form. Calculation and analysis functions allow data to be presented in the form of reports or charts. Excel and its functions are dealt with from Chapter 5 onwards.
Microsoft Access	This program provides **database** functions. A database stores data as rows and columns. Forms for data entry and the production of reports can also be defined. Because Access is not included in all Office variants, it is not dealt with in this book.
Microsoft PowerPoint	PowerPoint is used to create **presentations.** These are either overhead sheets or slides, used for business presentations. PowerPoint can also be used to show presentations directly using a suitable projector. PowerPoint is dealt with from Chapter 7 onwards.

| Internet Explorer | Microsoft Office supports Web functions and electronic mail. All Office variants contain Internet Explorer 5.0 for **browsing web pages**. An introduction both to this program and the Internet itself will be found in Chapter 9. |
| Microsoft Outlook | Electronic mail is processed by Microsoft Outlook, which is also available in all of the Office variants. In addition, Outlook offers a **diary**, an **address book**, a **'to do' list processor** and a **contact manager**. Outlook is dealt with from Chapter 10 onwards. |

The other Office variants include applications such as FrontPage for designing Web pages and PhotoDraw for producing graphics. Because these applications are not included in all of the Office variants, they are not dealt with in this book.

Starting an Office program

Before you can start working with an Office program, the computer must be switched on and Windows must be loaded. The required program can then be started. In Windows, most programs are started with the *Start* menu. The procedure is the same for all programs – in this instance, Microsoft Word is used as an example.

A **menu** is a small window that is opened by clicking on the *Start* icon or the menu entry in a window. The menu window contains text entries that represent the commands available under that menu. Just like a menu in a restaurant, this lets you choose the options you want. An **Icon** is a small rectangular element in a window, which can be 'pressed' like the buttons of a cassette recorder by clicking on it with the mouse pointer. Such a click usually causes a program to be started or a command associated with the icon to be executed.

1 Position the mouse pointer on the *Start* icon and depress the left mouse button.

This action could also be described as: 'Open the menu by clicking on the *Start* icon'.

Windows will open the *Start* menu.

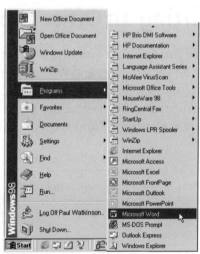

2 Move the mouse pointer on to the menu and click on the *Programs* entry.

Windows will then open another window, referred to as a submenu. Here you will see entries for programs such as *Internet Explorer*, *Microsoft Word* or *Windows Explorer* and so on, according to which programs are actually installed on your computer.

3 Click on the *Microsoft Word* entry in the *Programs* submenu.

Windows will then start the *Microsoft Word* program. A corresponding window will be opened on the **desktop**. How to use Microsoft Word is discussed in Chapter 2.

WHAT'S THIS?

Desktop is simply a term for the main Windows screen – it is the screen that is displayed when the computer is switched on. You will see on it symbols (icons) for utility functions such as the Recycle Bin and the work area you use with Windows. A double-click on the My Documents icon, for example, opens the corresponding window. Windows belonging to open applications are also displayed on the desktop.

You can start any programs listed in the menu in the same way, using the *Start* menu.

TIP

As soon as you click on a program entry in the *Start* menu or any of its submenus, Windows will start the program. A window for this program will appear on the desktop, and Windows will automatically close the menu. Menu entries and icons are usually created automatically when programs are installed.

Working with windows

The name 'Windows' derives from the way the system works – programs and functions run in separate window-like boxes. Working with Office applications, therefore, implies working with these windows. It is a good idea to become familiar with the basic elements of windows and how they are controlled. You must also learn how to open, close and change the size of windows. Fortunately, all Windows applications work in exactly the same way – once you have mastered the basics, you can deal with all other applications as well.

The *Microsoft Word* window is therefore typical of Windows programs, including other Office applications.

Title bar
Menu bar
Toolbar

Status bar

Along the top edge of the window is a so-called **title bar**, which tells you the name of the application and sometimes the name of a document.

In many windows there is a **menu bar**, with entries such as FILE, EDIT and VIEW, underneath the Title bar. These are the names of submenus with which functions can be invoked.

Office application windows also contain one or more **toolbars,** allowing frequently used functions to be accessed more quickly than with the menu.

Many windows also contain a **status bar** along the bottom edge containing more information. These are discussed in the application-specific chapters later on.

For the first example, you will need to use only the three small icons at the extreme right of the title bar. These are used to change the size of the window or close it.

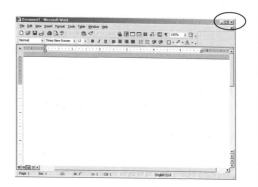

1 From an open Microsoft Word window, try placing the mouse pointer over the middle one of the three icons.

The program will display a **ScreenTip** identifying the icon's function.

2 Now click on the middle icon.

Windows enlarges the Word window to the point where it covers the entire screen. This is referred to as a **maximised** window. Note that the middle icon changes.

A double-click on the title bar changes a maximised window back to its original size and vice versa.

ScreenTip is used by many programs to display additional information about icons. Just leave the mouse pointer over the icon for a second or two, and the information is automatically displayed in a small temporary window of its own.

3 To restore the window to its original size, click on the middle icon once again.

4 Now click once on the left- hand of the three icons in the upper right corner of the screen ▄.

The window will disappear from the desktop. If you look carefully, you will find an icon for it in the **taskbar**.

5 To **reopen** the (Word) **window**, click on the icon in the taskbar.

WHAT'S THIS?

The **taskbar** is the grey block across the bottom of the desktop. Windows displays icons for most of the opened windows and programs here. If you click on one of the icons, Windows will bring the relevant application to the foreground on the desktop. In Windows 2000, clicking on the icon when the program is already in the foreground minimises it to an icon again.

Switching between windows

Windows permits you to load and execute multiple **programs** at the same time. Subsequently you can switch between programs and even move data from one application to another. As mentioned above, Windows places an icon on the taskbar for every executing program. With Office 2000, Office applications also display a list of all currently open documents. These icons can be used to switch between applications and/or documents.

1 Open the *Start* menu and click on *Programs/Accessories.*

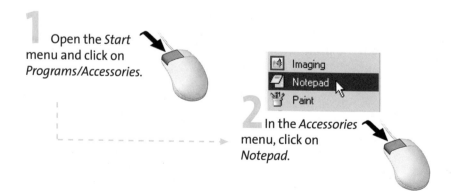

2 In the *Accessories* menu, click on *Notepad.*

17

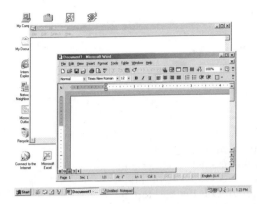

Assuming the system is still displaying the Word window, the desktop will now contain two **overlapping** windows – one for each of the active programs. You can now work with Notepad or Word without having to close either when you wish to use the other program.

3 Open the *Start* menu once more, and click on *Programs/Microsoft Excel*.

The Excel window will open in the foreground, and you will be able to work with the program.

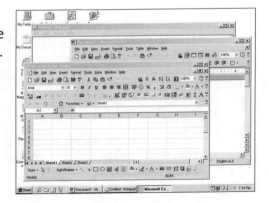

4 To use Word once again, just click on the desired document in the taskbar.

The Word window will move to the foreground, and you will be able to work with the program.

The taskbar icon for the currently active window is given a 'depressed' appearance, just like a real depressed button.

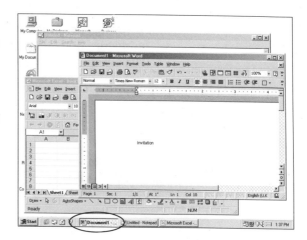

There are small differences between the various Office applications. With Microsoft Word each document has its own **application window**. Excel uses only one application window. If multiple Excel spreadsheets are open, each has a separate **document window** within the application window. Each open document has its own icon on the taskbar – clicking on this switches to the document in question.

If the desired application has an open window visible on the desktop, simply clicking on the window will bring the program into the foreground. Or you can hold down the [Alt] key and press [⇆]. Windows will then display a window listing one of the active programs. Each time [⇆] is pressed, Windows steps to the next active program. Releasing the [Alt] key selects the displayed application.

Closing a window

To keep the desktop 'tidy', it is a good idea to close windows that are no longer needed. When its window is closed, the corresponding program is terminated.

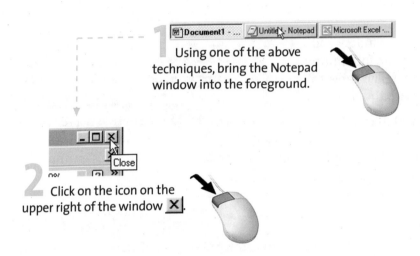

Using one of the above techniques, bring the Notepad window into the foreground.

Click on the icon on the upper right of the window.

This completely closes the application. Windows confirms this by removing the Notepad icon from the taskbar.

If a document window contains data that has not yet been saved, this dialog box will be displayed.

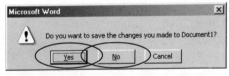

Click on *Yes* to save the data. Clicking on *No* discards any changes.

Most applications display the ☒ icon. If you want to **end a program** or **close a window**, clicking on this will be sufficient.

A **dialog box** is a window used by a program to display additional information or prompt for input. Dialog boxes are usually closed by a click on the *OK* button. Any options that have been changed will then be adopted by the program. The *Cancel* button closes the dialog box and discards any suggested changes. The elements of a dialog box are called **commands.**

Moving windows

One of the strengths of Windows is that you can work with several applications at the same time. If you find that foreground windows obscure data in the windows behind them, you can move them around on the desktop to make the data visible once more. Try this example:

1 Start Microsoft Excel again.

2 Now switch back to Microsoft Word, which should still be open from the above exercise.

If you do this correctly, you will have two windows on the desktop.

Unfortunately, these windows will overlap, and the contents of the background window will be only partly visible. You could of course close one of the windows, but simply moving it over is easier.

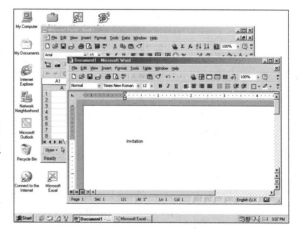

3 Place the mouse pointer on the title bar of the window you want to move.

4 Press and hold the left mouse button, and drag the window to the desired position.

Depending on settings within Windows itself, either the entire window will move or a dotted line will indicate where its new position will be.

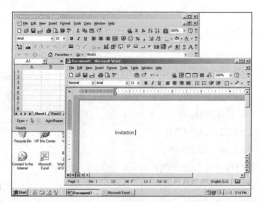

5 Once the window is in the desired position, let go of the left mouse button.

Windows will move the window to its new position. Depending on the size of the windows, it may be possible to see all of the contents on the desktop simultaneously.

Changing the size of a window

When moving windows around, you will often find that there is insufficient space on the desktop to display them. In other cases, the window is too small to permit efficient processing of the data. Earlier on in this book you have learnt how to maximise a window until it filled the whole screen or minimise it down to a taskbar icon – but window sizes can also be modified. This permits multiple applications to display data on the same desktop. For example, the Word and Excel windows can be adjusted so that both can be displayed at the same time:

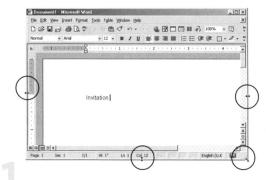

1 Rest the mouse pointer on the right edge of one of the chosen windows.

2 Now try the left edge, the lower edge, and one of the corners.

As soon as the mouse pointer is exactly over the edge of a window, the shape of the pointer changes. It is sometimes necessary to move the mouse around just a bit to see this. The new 'double arrow' symbol shows the directions in which the window's edge can be dragged to make it larger or smaller. The left and right edges can be used to change the width, the lower edge changes the height, and the corners change both while keeping the proportions of the window the same.

3 Place the mouse pointer on the edge of the window again.

4 When the double arrow appears, press and hold the left mouse button and drag the edge of the window in the desired direction.

Depending on settings, Windows either changes the window size during the dragging or shows the future window size with dotted lines.

5 Once the window is the desired size, let go of the left mouse button.

Windows will adjust the size of the window as needed.

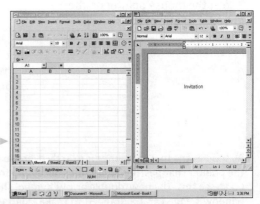

6 Repeat the above steps to place the Word and Excel windows side-by-side on the desktop.

TIP

You can make a window any size you want using this method. Dragging the edge outwards makes the window larger – 'pushing' it inwards makes it smaller. There are many other features associated with using and managing windows on the desktop that are not dealt with in this book but are covered in *Windows 98 In No Time* and *Windows 2000 In No Time* in the same series.

Scrolling in windows

What happens when there is too much data to be displayed in a window at its current size? The Word window used in the previous example can be used to explore this. If you have not yet typed anything in, Word will be showing a blank 'page' to receive new text. This page is already too big to be displayed within the bounds of the window.

1 Change to the Word window.

2 Reduce the size of the window somewhat.

This is how the smaller Word window will look. It shows a further feature of all Windows applications with adjustable window sizes – it has a **scrollbar** at the right-hand and/or the lower edges.

Scrollbars are usually found at the right and/or lower edges of a window. They allow you to change the visible content of the window. The rectangular shape in the **scrollbar** is referred to as the **scroll box.**

To display other parts of the document in the window, do the following:

1 Place the mouse pointer over the scroll box within the scrollbar.

2 Press and hold the left mouse pointer, and drag the scroll box in the desired direction.

Windows moves the data within the window to show a different part of the document.

When working on a large text item, the left scrollbar allows you to scroll through the document, while the lower scrollbar is used for displaying text batches.

> Positioning within the document by dragging the scroll box is very often too haphazard. Clicking on the scrollbar itself either above or below the scroll box moves the document up or down by exactly one page. The ◀ and ▶ icons at the end of the scrollbar move the document line by line in a vertical direction or column by column horizontally. In Microsoft Word, the vertical scrollbars ± and ∓ move the document forwards and backwards one page at a time.

Working with menus

Another common feature in Windows programs, and therefore in Office, is the way menus are used. The typical components of a window were briefly described at the beginning of the book – a menu bar will be found directly under the title bar in almost all Windows applications. Individual menus containing functions provided by the program can be opened from the menu bar.

The fundamentals of menus will already be familiar to you from the *Start* menu. To open it you click on the *Start* button. Commands can then be chosen from the opened menu. The same technique is used with Microsoft Word. If it is not currently loaded, use the instructions on the preceding pages to reload it. Then you can begin.

Move the mouse pointer over the FILE entry on the Word menu bar.

Word emphasises the selected entry, so that it looks like a selectable button.

Now click on the FILE entry on the Word menu bar.

The program will open the corresponding menu. This **Menu** contains all **commands** relevant to file handling. As soon as you click on a command, it will be executed. But more of that later.

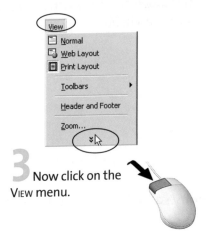

3 Now click on the VIEW menu.

This menu contains everything to do with displaying or viewing the document.

4 Now place the mouse pointer on the bottom entry in the list.

After a few seconds, or at the latest when this entry is clicked on, Office will enhance this menu with additional commands.

This is a new feature in all Office 2000 programs. Only the most frequently used commands are displayed when the menu is first opened, so as to keep it brief. As you have already seen, this menu can be extended. With previous Windows programs, menus display all available commands when they are first opened.

The most attractive feature of Windows is that most programs use identical or very similar menu names and structures. Compare the menus of Microsoft Word and Microsoft Excel, for instance. The most important entries on the menu bar and many of the commands are identical. This is a great help in learning how to use a Windows application. In many menus there is a small icon in front of the command. You will frequently find this icon in toolbars. This also helps you become acquainted with Windows and its associated applications. Wherever you are, you will find familiar features.

Is there a small tick in the VIEW menu in front of the *Ruler* command? This tick shows you that the program has been requested to display a rule across the document window.

5 Now click on this command.

Word will fade out the ruler displayed across the top of the page. If you open the VIEW menu, the tick before *Ruler* will have disappeared. If you select this command once more, the rule will be displayed once more. At the same time, the previously hidden *Ruler* command will be visible immediately the menu is opened. Office programs 'learn' the most frequently used commands and display them in menus when opened.

You have now learned the most important features of menus and how to use them. With time, you will certainly become better acquainted with the use of some of the more advanced features. Many users, for instance, prefer to call up menus and commands from the keyboard rather than by using the mouse. This is especially useful when typing text, since it isn't necessary to locate the mouse and find the pointer on

A **keystroke combination** is a technique whereby two or more keys are pressed at the same time. These are recognised by the system or the application and executed. The keystroke combinations ⎇Alt+⇧ thus means that the ⎇Alt and ⇧ keys are pressed at the same time. Keystroke combinations will be used frequently throughout this book.

the screen. You may already have noticed that many commands in the menus have underscores under one letter in the command – this lets you know which keystroke combination can be used to invoke the command.

TIP

If a letter in a menu entry is underlined, this means that the ⎇Alt key can be used in combination with this letter to execute the relevant command. If an open menu has an underlined letter in a command name, just pressing this key executes the command. In some cases an explicit sequence is given to the right of the command, such as 'Ctrl+N' alongside *New* in the FILE menu. This shows that the *New* command can also be executed without even opening the FILE menu. You merely have to press ⎈Ctrl and Ⓝ simultaneously.

Using keystroke combinations is often much faster than switching to the mouse, opening a menu and selecting a command with the mouse pointer. The following table lists some of the most common and useful keystroke combinations:

Keystrokes	Comments
⎇Alt or F10	Highlights the File entry on the menu bar. The ↵ or ↓ Arrow key will then open the selected menu.
Esc	Closes an open menu.
↵	Executes a selected command or opens a selected menu.

Keystrokes	Comments
⬅ ➡	If an entry on the menu bar is highlighted, the ⬅ and ➡ arrow keys can be used to move the highlight to other menus. If a command with a submenu is selected on a menu, ➡ will open the submenu and ⬅ will close it again.
⬆ ⬇	If an entry on the menu bar is highlighted, the ⬇ arrow will open the menu. Both keys may be used within a menu to move between commands.
Alt +letter	Pressing the Alt key together with one of the underscored letters on the menu bar opens the relevent menu. For instance Alt + ⬇ opens the File menu.

This completes the introduction to menus. Do not worry if the introduction has left you with some questions – the next few chapters will reinforce the material above with further examples and in no time at all you will be dealing with menus without even being aware of the fact.

Working with toolbars

Now just a short note on the use of toolbars. Toolbars are used in almost all Windows programs and are usually found directly underneath the menu bar. A **toolbar** consists of a bar with a number of small **icons**, or small pictures. Clicking on the icon invokes the command or function. The icon is designed to indicate the function that will be performed – a small picture of a printer identifies the print function, for example. The symbol for a diskette indicates that something will be stored on diskette. But what do the other symbols mean?

This is not a problem – Windows and the Office applications also provide assistance here. If you don't know the exact purpose of an icon, you can 'ask' the application itself.

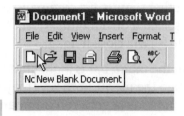

1 Place the mouse pointer over one of the icons on the toolbar.

Word will highlight the icon.

And after a moment, the program will display a **ScreenTip** with the name of the function executed by the icon. But you have already seen this much in the short introduction on how to use windows. In this example, the first icon on the standard Toolbar is selected – its purpose is to open a new, empty document. The ScreenTip displayed is the word 'New', corresponding to the same function on the FILE menu.

2 Now click on the icon.

The program will execute the command associated with the icon. In this case, it will open a new, empty document in a new window. There are no hidden secrets behind icons – they are just a productivity aid. Instead of long searches through menus, you can access common functions directly from the processing window.

Finally, a further tip for working with icons. With many toolbars, there is simply insufficient space for all icons to be displayed at once.

The Microsoft Word window on the right shows this effect. The window has been reduced in size so that there is not enough room on the toolbar for all of the icons to be displayed. The program then displays a symbol for *More Buttons*.

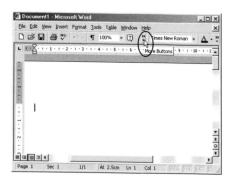

3 Click on the *More Buttons* symbol.

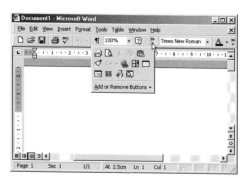

The program will display a menu containing the previously undisplayed icons. You can then select the one you want.

Once you have used one of these 'hidden' icons, most Windows applications will move it on to the visible part of the toolbar, moving one that hasn't been used into the hidden portion to make room for it. Just as with its menu structure, Microsoft Office 'learns' which toolbar icons you use most frequently. Moving and customising toolbars is dealt with in more detail in Chapter 11.

How to get help

Even those who work with Microsoft Office daily are unlikely to know all of the functions. Even after completing this book, you may still have unanswered questions.

It is not so important to know everything, but it *is* important to know where to look to find out. Office provides help functions at every stage. The ScreenTip function mentioned above is just one of these help functions. If this is not enough, you can get more detailed help. The following examples show how to invoke the help functions in Microsoft Word and the other Office applications. Taking the above example further, let us see what the *New blank document* icon in Word actually does.

Click on the HELP menu on the menu bar.

This menu provides access to the help functions.

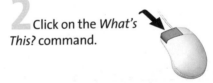

Click on the *What's This?* command.

The mouse pointer will change to look like this. This tells you that Word is in **ScreenTips** mode.

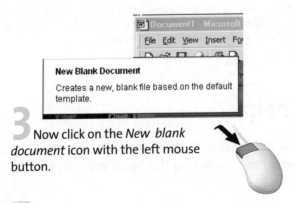

Now click on the *New blank document* icon with the left mouse button.

ScreenTips are displayed directly on the screen by the program. In contrast with the help functions described below, you do not have to select a specific topic.

Word will display another ScreenTip box with somewhat more detailed explanatory text. Do you find the text displayed by ScreenTip meaningless? Don't worry – the essential jargon is explained as you proceed through the book.

ScreenTips are not just available for icons. Repeat the above steps, but this time click on the title bar of the Microsoft Word window. A ScreenTip about changing the size of the window, as explained earlier in the book, will be displayed. Want to try another way? Remember the discussion about keystroke combinations and using menus? If you press ⇧+F1 ScreenTips are directly invoked. A question mark appears next to the mouse pointer as confirmation.

ScreenTips provide rapid help for specific functions on the screen. There are occasions, though, when the HELP menu cannot be opened. The following situation is an example:

Open the VIEW menu and click on the *Zoom* command.

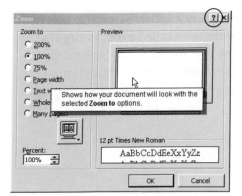

Word opens a dialog box for *Zoom*, which contains zoom factor options. Attempts to open the Help menu fail because the zoom dialog is open.

2 To call up ScreenTips, click on the **?** symbol in the top right corner.

3 Now click on the part of the screen for which you need help.

Microsoft Word (or any other Office program) will then display a ScreenTips box for the chosen element. If you want to change the scale of the display, open the *Zoom* **dialog box** in Word and click on the desired option in the *Zoom to* area. When you close the dialog box, the new zoom percentage will be used.

Options are the controlling elements in dialog boxes (for example, in the *Zoom* dialog box, the small circles, known as radio buttons). Normally mutually exclusive options are gathered into a group. Clicking on one of the options makes it active and a small black dot is added to the radio button to show this. If you then click on another option, the dot will move to show the new selection.

Now that you are familiar with the basic elements in windows, you probably want to know how to get more information about creating documents.

You may already have noticed that the Microsoft Word window on your computer differs from the ones illustrated here. You can probably also see a stylised paperclip with a speech bubble, pictured here 'sitting' on a piece of paper.

This is the Office Assistant 'Clippit', who will accompany you while you work with Office applications and give hints and tips when requested.

> **TIP**
>
> The Office Assistant was disenabled during the production of the examples used earlier, so that the significant elements and techniques could be presented in an uncomplicated way. This will usually be the case in the chapters to come. It is up to you whether you prefer to have the Assistant enabled or disenabled when working through the book. The following example shows the use of the Assistant with Microsoft Word.

Is the Office Assistant not displayed in your Microsoft Word window?

1 Click on the Microsoft Word Help icon on the Toolbar.

Word or any other Office program will display the Office Assistant icon in the document area.

2 Click on the icon for the Office Assistant.

A 'speech bubble' will appear on the display.

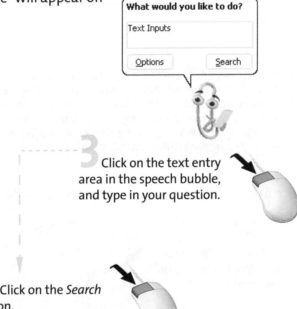

What would you like to do?

Text Inputs

Options   Search

3 Click on the text entry area in the speech bubble, and type in your question.

4 Click on the *Search* button.

The assistant will display the available help topics.

5 If none of these is appropriate, click on the *See more...* displayed at the foot of the list.

The assistant will then display a further page of suggested topics. If none of these is appropriate, the query should be reformulated.

6 If, however, one of the displayed topics seems appropriate, select it by clicking on it with the mouse.

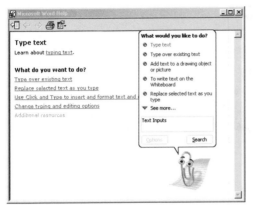

The assistant opens a dialog window with the help text displayed in it. Any items highlighted in blue are **hyperlinks** that lead to more in-depth discussions of particular topics.

If the selected item proves unhelpful, the query must be reformulated.

7 To close the speech bubble, click on the assistant again.

8 If you no longer need the assistant, click on the upper right corner of its frame to close it **X**.

Disabling the Office Assistant

The final thing you need to know about the **Office Assistant** is how to disable it. This is necessary, for instance, if you want to access help functions directly as described on the following pages.

1 Click on the *Office Assistant* icon with the right mouse button.

A **context menu** will be opened by the assistant.

Context menus are menus that can be opened by a click on the right mouse button. In such menus, programs gather together the commands that are useful in this specific context. This saves you searching through individual menus and speeds up operations with Windows and Office. You will meet context menus frequently in the remainder of this book.

2 Click on the *Hide Assistant* command to close the Assistant.

3 If you want to disable the Assistant completely, click on the *Options* command.

4 In the Office Assistant dialog box, click on the *Options* tab.

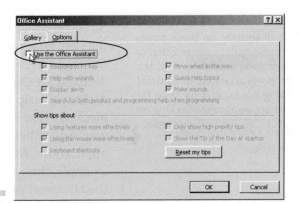

5 Clear the indicator on the *Use the Office Assistant* option by clicking on the control button.

6 Close the *Office Assistant* dialog box by clicking on the *OK* button.

If you need the Office Assistant later, click on the *Show Office Assistant* command in the HELP menu

The main function of the Office Assistant is to monitor you while you are working with Office. If you make a mistake using a command or ask a question, it will try to assemble relevant information from the help files. This saves you searching the files manually. For beginners, this can be a very helpful feature. As you accumulate experience, you are more likely to want specific help on particular topics. In this case, disable the Office Assistant and use the help files directly as in the following examples.

A program's settings are also referred to as its **properties**, and these are usually displayed in special windows called **properties dialog boxes**. In many instances, there is not enough space to display all of a program's properties at once and so a trick is used – the properties are distributed on a number of pages that are displayed as if they were cards in a card file. Clicking on the tabs changes which page is currently displayed.

WHAT'S THIS?

Check boxes are the small squares on these pages that show whether particular options are selected or not. A tick in one of these boxes indicates that the particular feature or property is active. In contrast with the options in dialog boxes, it is possible for multiple properties to be active at once. Clicking on an inactive property makes it active, and vice versa.

Do you want to use the Help window directly? Have you disabled the Office Assistant? Help is invoked in the same way in all Office applications. As an example, this is how the Microsoft Word help function is invoked:

1 Click on the Microsoft Word Help icon in the toolbar.

2 Or select the *Microsoft Word Help* command from the HELP menu.

3 A third way is simply to press the F1 key.

The application, in this case Word, will open the Help window. This is split into two parts, referred to as **panes**. The left pane contains three pages with tabs named *Contents, Index* and *Answer Wizard.* The right pane displays the actual help text.

The *Contents* page functions like the index of a book. The available topics are displayed with stylised icons of closed or open books.

4 Double-click on the icon of a closed book, to see the related items within the topic.

5 A double-click on the document icon ? opens that page in the right-hand pane.

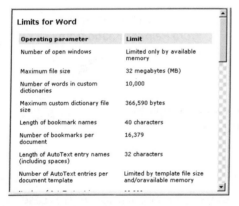

Limits for Word	
Operating parameter	**Limit**
Number of open windows	Limited only by available memory
Maximum file size	32 megabytes (MB)
Number of words in custom dictionaries	10,000
Maximum custom dictionary file size	366,590 bytes
Length of bookmark names	40 characters
Number of bookmarks per document	16,379
Length of AutoText entry names (including spaces)	32 characters
Number of AutoText entries per document template	Limited by template file size and/or available memory

The selected help text appears in the right-hand pane. You can scroll through the text using the scrollbar. Underlined text represents a hyperlink (*see above*). If you place the mouse pointer over a hyperlink, the arrow changes to a hand. One click of the mouse button will open the topic pointed to.

If you have clicked on a hyperlink or otherwise opened several different help pages, the buttons *Forwards* and *Back* let you switch between the topics easily.

You can also display help information about specific topics directly. The *Index* page in the Help dialog corresponds to the index of a book.

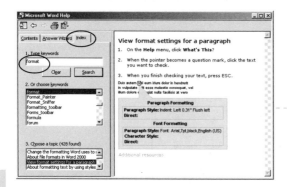

1 Click on the Index tab in the *Help* dialog box.

2 Start typing any keyword in the text entry area marked as '1. Type keywords'.

If this word is known in the index, Windows will display its related index in area 3.

3 Click in List 2. Or choose *keywords* on the term that you require and then on the *Search* button.

The topics will now appear in the lower field *3. Choose a topic (found).*

4 Click on the desired topic.

If the text is long, you can page through it using the scrollbar on the right of the screen. If the *Help* dialog box obscures other windows on the desktop, it can be resized like any other window.

The text will be displayed in the right-hand pane of the *Help* dialog box.

The Help function also lets you search for specific keywords:

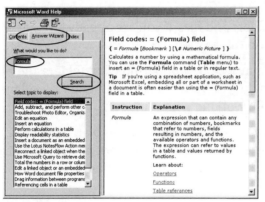

1 Open the *Help* window and click on the *Answer Wizard* tab.

2 Enter a keyword in the field entitled 'What would you like to do?'

3 Click on the *Search* button and then one of the items in the *Select topic to display* list.

The text will be displayed in the right-hand pane of the *Help* dialog box.

This concludes the introduction to the Help functions of Microsoft Office. There is more information within the Help function itself. As well as the help shipped with Office, the HELP menu and the *Microsoft on the Web* command provide access to more material on the Internet. This is beyond the scope of this book.

Folders and files

Before you start using Office applications, you must understand concepts such as drives, folders and files. If you are already familiar with these, please feel free to skip this section.

If you are a beginner, you may well be wondering what **folders** and **files** are, and what they have to do with your Office document. You will meet both terms frequently when working with Windows.

When you start Windows you will see a row of icons on the desktop. Three of these are side-by-side in a line and represent places where the computer can store things. If you click on an icon, Windows opens the corresponding window or starts a program.

My Computer

Network Neighborhood

My Documents

1 Double-click on the icon labelled *My Documents*.

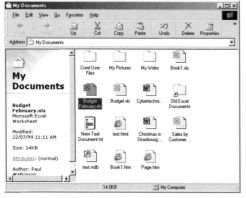

Windows will then open the *My Documents* window. This may contain icons for various files. The same is true for the *My Computer* and *Network Neighborhood* icons. These windows contain both files and other folders.

This does not bring us much further. Perhaps you are asking yourself what are files and what are they for?

Once you have written a letter, produced a drawing or a picture, created a spreadsheet, and displayed or printed it, you will probably want to keep it for potential future use. On a computer, this is called 'saving' or 'storing'. Most computer data is kept on hard disk drives or diskettes.

It is not possible to just write the characters of a letter on to a disk drive and then find them again later. A single disk may store many such letters, and each user will want to be able to find everything again. Think of the analogy of text on paper. Once produced, they are placed together in a file. Something similar happens on a computer – all of the data associated, for example, with a letter, a picture or a spreadsheet is gathered into a **file**. You could regard it as a kind of container in which a document's data is packaged. Each file has its own name and icon. The name allows the computer, and therefore yourself, to find it again. The icon helps you tell what type of file it is – text, graphics, spreadsheet, and so on.

Now we come to **folders** and their use. Another analogy from daily office life is useful. In an office, to avoid a paper snowstorm, letters and documents are collected and filed in folders. The documents kept in each folder are always related in some way – one case, one account.

The same technique is used on the computer. Files are stored on the hard drive of on diskettes. Open the *My Computer* window and then double-click on one of the drive icons within it (*see below*). Windows will open a window for the drive which shows files stored on it. Just as with a manual archive, Windows reads an index and displays the file names and some additional information.

If a drive contains hundreds or thousands of files, it may become almost impossible to find a desired file quickly. Trying to fish a letter out of a large stack of paper is very similar. Windows allows you to put individual files into folders.

All such folders are displayed by Windows using a stylised folder symbol ☐. This helps you to tell the difference between folders and files.

The illustration on the left shows the open *My Documents* window. To make things even more manageable, it contains icons for subsidiary folders with names such as *Old, My Pictures,* and so on, which could also contain files and subsidiary folders of their own.

You may use entirely your own criteria for distributing files into folders. You might decide, for instance, to keep all correspondence in a *Letters* folder and all bills in a second folder called *Invoices*.

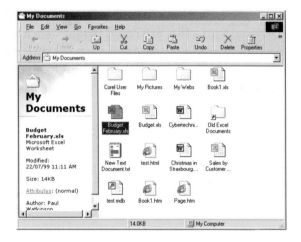

Working with files

Files and folders are stored on diskettes, hard drives or CD-ROMs.

You can create new folders in much the same way as new files with the context menu (*New/Folder* command). See 'Creating new documents' below.

49

My Computer

1 For example, open the *My Computer* window by double-clicking on the desktop icon.

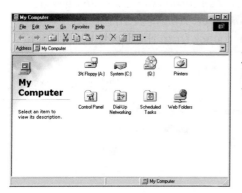

Windows will display icons for each of the drives available on your computer. The various drives are identified by a name and an icon.

2 Now double-click on the icon for the C: drive.

Windows will open a window to display the contents of the C: drive. This will include both files and folders. You can open a window for any of the folders by double-clicking on its icon.

The *Back* button on the toolbar allows you to return to the disk display or to the next higher level in a chain of subsidiary folders.

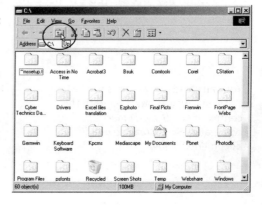

More details about your computer's disk drives can be found in 'Introduction to using files' in the Appendix. This includes information about the drive icons. If you are still not sure how to insert a diskette or perform other tasks, this is also covered in the same section.

Copying and moving

Microsoft Office documents are normally stored as files within folders on the hard drive. Older documents may no longer be needed regularly and so **archiving** them can be useful. You could copy them to **diskettes** and save the diskettes in a normal archive. The files can then be deleted from the hard drive. They can be read back from the diskette should they ever be required in the future.

Copying a file from a folder to diskette or to another folder is very easy. The first thing to check, in the former case, is that there is actually a diskette in the drive.

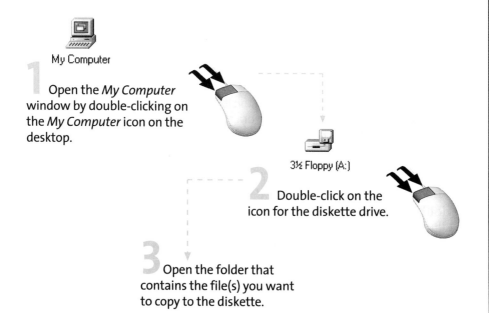

My Computer

1 Open the *My Computer* window by double-clicking on the *My Computer* icon on the desktop.

3½ Floppy (A:)

2 Double-click on the icon for the diskette drive.

3 Open the folder that contains the file(s) you want to copy to the diskette.

If the files are stored in *My Documents*, double-click on the icon of that name on the desktop. For other folders, open the *My Computer* window and then the drive, folder and subfolder as required. If this is done properly, two windows should be visible on the desktop. One is the source folder containing the files to be copied and the other is the destination folder.

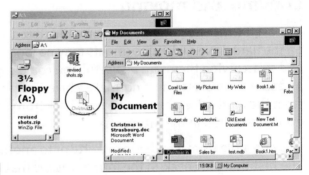

4 Position and size the windows so that they overlap a little.

5 Select the file(s) you want to copy.

6 Press and hold the left mouse button, and drag the files from the source to the destination window.

As soon as you let go of the left mouse button, the files will be copied. In the illustration, the destination is a diskette. The operation is the same when the target is another folder on the hard drive.

To **select** a file, click on it once with the mouse. If you want to select a number of neighbouring files, hold the ⬆ key after selecting the first and click on a second file. Windows will select all the files between the two. If the files you want to select are not contiguous, press and hold the Ctrl key instead.

If you drag a file from one folder to another when they are on different drives, Windows automatically copies the file. If both folders are on the same drive the file is moved, i.e. the source is deleted after the copy is successful.

You can choose between copying and moving by using the right mouse button to drag the files instead of the left. Windows will then open a context menu when you release the button, asking if you would prefer a move or a copy.

Renaming files and folders

Changing the name of a **file** is quite straightforward:

1 Click on the file to be renamed with the right mouse button.

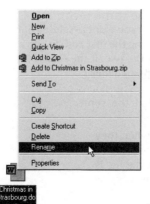

Open
New
Print
Quick View
Add to Zip
Add to Christmas in Strasbourg.zip

Send To ▸

Cut
Copy

Create Shortcut
Delete
Rename

Properties

Christmas in
Strasbourg.do
c

2 Select the *Rename* command from the context menu.

Windows will select the file by highlighting the name.

3 Press the ⬅ arrow to get the cursor to the start of the name field.

Christmas doc

Characters to the right of the **cursor** (the vertical bar in the field) are deleted with the Del key. Characters to the left of it are deleted with the ⬅ key.

4 Now just type in the new name for the file.

5 Now click somewhere else in the window, away from the icon for the file.

Windows will now use the new name. The same technique is used to rename folders.

The new name must be valid and unique, i.e. no two files in one folder can have the same name. If the file extension is displayed in the name field, make sure that the same extension is used in the new name.

Deleting files and folders

There are many ways to delete files and folders. For now, we will just explain the simplest of them.

1 Open the window containing the file or folder to be deleted.

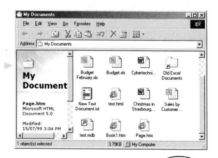

2 Select the chosen object by clicking on it with the mouse.

3 Holding the left mouse button down, drag the object across to the *Recycle Bin* icon.

As soon as you release the left mouse key, Windows will try to delete the object.

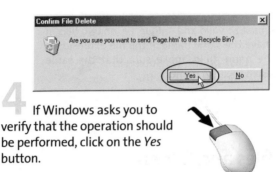

4 If Windows asks you to verify that the operation should be performed, click on the *Yes* button.

Windows will move the selected object into the Recycle Bin. The folder or file will disappear from the window it was initially in.

Emptying the Recycle Bin

Files placed in the Recycle Bin are kept for a while in case you wish to retrieve them. You will note that the icon resembles a sheaf of papers in a waste bin. Periodically, you must **empty the recycle bin.**

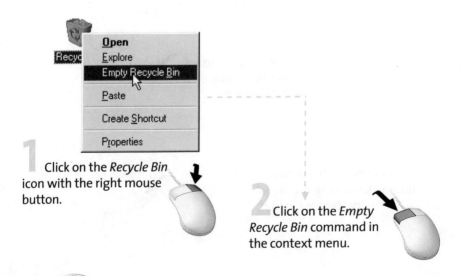

1 Click on the *Recycle Bin* icon with the right mouse button.

2 Click on the *Empty Recycle Bin* command in the context menu.

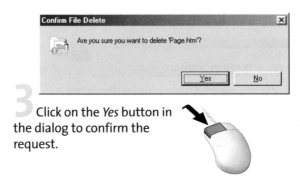

3 Click on the *Yes* button in the dialog to confirm the request.

The contents of the Recycle Bin will be deleted.

Rescuing deleted files and folders

You can retrieve files and folders that were deleted in error from the Recycle Bin, so long as you have not performed the above operation to empty it since they were deleted.

1 Click on the *Recycle Bin* icon with the right mouse button.

2 Select the *Open* command from the context menu.

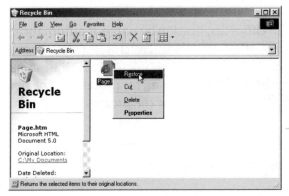

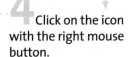

3 Click on the icon for the file or folder in the *Recycle Bin* window to select it.

4 Click on the icon with the right mouse button.

5 Select the *Restore* command from the context menu.

Windows will replace the deleted file or folder in its original position. You can then continue to work with the file as though it had never been deleted.

If you cannot find the deleted file or folder in the Recycle Bin, then its contents have been lost. Your only hope would be a separate archive copy on diskette (*see above*).

There is much more to handling files under Windows. In order to save space, retain clarity and avoid duplication, much has been left out of this book. Interested readers might care to read *Windows 98 In No Time* also published by Prentice Hall.

Creating new documents

Every time you call up an Office application by name, it automatically creates a **new document**. Both Windows and Microsoft Office offer a number of other elegant ways to create new documents. With some of these techniques, the corresponding program for processing the new document is automatically called as part of the process.

Creating a new file under Windows

The following will create a new file under Microsoft Windows without using any Office functions:

1 Open the folder that is to contain the new Office file.

2 Click on an unoccupied spot in the open window with the right mouse key.

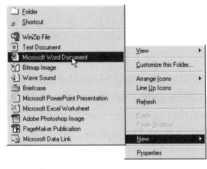

3 Select the *New* command from the context menu.

4 In the submenu, click on the desired file type, for example, *Microsoft Word Document.*

5 Enter a name for the new document.

As soon as you click on an empty space next to the file system, the new name will be assigned to the file.

If you need to create a new folder, follow the preceding steps but select *New* and then *Folder* on the context menu. Then enter the name of the new folder. You can create folders within folders to build a hierarchical data structure.

If you want to open a document file quickly, just click on it twice. Windows will automatically start the appropriate Office application and load the file into it.

Creating a new Microsoft Office document

The preceding tip describes another way of loading Office applications. Creating a new office document is just as easy – it was mentioned in passing at the beginning of the chapter, although you may not have noticed at the time.

If Microsoft Office is installed, there will be two special entries in the *Start* menu – *New Office Document* and *Open Office Document*. The latter opens a dialog box to let you select an existing Office file and loads it into the correct application. The former creates a new Office document.

1 Open the *Start* menu by clicking on the *Start* button.

2 Click on the *New Office Document* command.

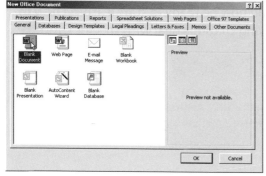

Windows will display a dialog box with a number of tabs to allow the file to be selected. Under the *General* tab you will find icons for various new but empty Office documents. The remaining tabs access new documents with more specific content, e.g. letter and fax templates.

3 Click on the required icon and then on the *OK* button.

The new file will be created and loaded immediately into the relevant Office application.

Microsoft Office also has a special toolbar – the Microsoft Office shortcut bar. This has various buttons (including ones to create new Office documents) and is displayed directly on the Windows desktop. The toolbar can be moved, resized or anchored to the edge of the screen (*see* Chapter 11).

If the special Office toolbar is not visible on your system, select *Programs/Microsoft Office Tools/Microsoft Office Shortcut Bar* from the *Start* menu. A dialog box will ask you if the toolbar should be displayed automatically every time Windows is restarted. The Microsoft Office shortcut bar is another way to access Office functions and documents quickly, but many users find it irritating while working with other Windows applications. Individual users should decide for themselves whether to display it or not.

This concludes this short introduction. You have learnt the basics of Windows operations and should now be ready to start learning how to use Microsoft Office. The following chapters deal with specific Office applications.

Test your knowledge

To ensure that you have retained the most important parts of the introduction, try answering the following questions:

1 How do you expand a window to fill the entire screen?

2 How do you end a program?

3 Name two ways of starting a program.

4 How are files named?

5 How do you copy a file or folder?

6 How is a file deleted?

7 How can you get help?

8 How do you create a new Office document?

The answers are on page 580. If you can answer the questions without any problems, you already understand the basics of working with Microsoft Windows and are ready to start learning the specifics of Microsoft Office. If you have some difficulties answering the questions, don't worry about it. You can always return to the relevant part of the introduction later. Many operations are identical from application to application, and following the steps described in the following chapters will reinforce your knowledge.

What's in this chapter?

Microsoft Word is more than a simple
replacement for a mechanical typewriter.
Naturally it can be used to enter simple
text, print it and save it in files. But you can
also tailor and customise your texts to give
them a personal flavour. This chapter will
show you how easy it is to start using the
most important Word
functions. You will also
see the first steps
towards producing text
documents.

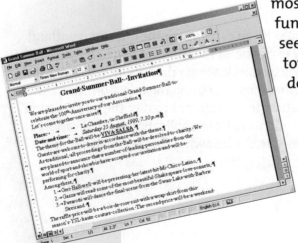

The first steps

Do you want to produce simple texts such as lists, notices and descriptions? Instead of writing these by hand or with a typewriter, you should now use Microsoft Word. Items can be saved, loaded when required, and then tailored for each occasion. You can also easily print multiple copies of documents. Before we produce the first piece of text, let us look at some of the basics of using Word. You will have seen some of this in the preceding chapter.

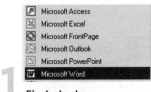

1 First start
Microsoft Word.

If you can't remember how to do this click on the *Start* button to open the *Start* menu and then click on *Programs/Microsoft Word*. Starting a program is covered in greater detail in Chapter 1. At the end of that chapter, a method of creating a document and simultaneously starting the program is discussed.

Microsoft Word opens a window, just like other Windows programs. The most important elements of a window were also dealt with in Chapter 1.

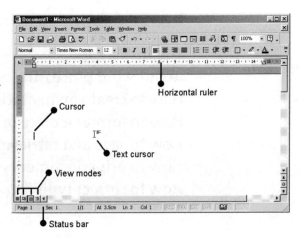

When opened, Word automatically creates a new document, which usually contains no text. The name of this document will also appear in the title bar.

The **document area** (the central portion of the window) **is used to enter text.** In the upper left-hand corner of the window you will see the **insertion point** and the **cursor.** As soon as you type a character, the insertion point moves one position to the right.

The insertion point is displayed as a vertical black blinking bar. It indicates where the next character to be typed will be placed on the screen. Insertion points are used in Windows applications wherever text is to be entered. One example of this was the procedure to rename a file in Chapter 1.

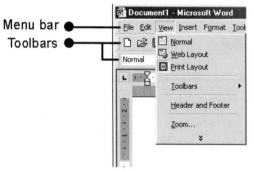

Menu bar
Toolbars

The Word **menu bar** allows you to call up the individual commands for tailoring your document.

Word's toolbars contain the buttons and elements required to save, format and print the text.

In the above illustration, the toolbars are arranged in two rows. Your screen may show them on a single row. If you want to change this by dragging the toolbar into its own row using the mouse pointer, see the section 'Using Toolbars' in Chapter 11.

If so desired, the document window can also contain displays of vertical and horizontal rules.

The meaning of the individual toolbar icons will become clear as you work through the rest of the book.

If you move the mouse pointer on to an area of the document, it changes shape into a **text cursor.** This is used in just the same way as a mouse pointer. You can select a word, text or just click. If you click on a text item, Word moves the insertion point to that point. You can then add new text or alter existing text.

Word uses the status bar to indicate exactly where you are in the document. Alongside the current page number and the total number of pages in the document, Word also displays the current column number within the line. Other boxes may contain among other things the language in use, and the number of pages during print operations.

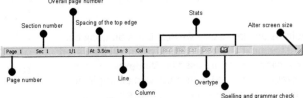

Now to start creating the document.

1 Type in the first text using the keyboard.

Here is an example of text entered into the Word document window. Try entering the same text yourself.

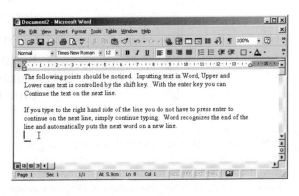

If you are not yet familiar with using the keyboard, here are a few tips about entering text:

➔ Just type the letters that make up the words. Spaces between words are entered using the ⬚ bar on the bottom edge of the keyboard

➔ By default all characters entered appear in lowercase. To enter uppercase letters, press and hold the ⬆ key and then press the desired key.

➔ If you want to enter the special characters above the row of numbers, you must also press the ⬆ key.

If you press the ⬇ key, the keyboard is switched into all capitals. All characters typed appear as uppercase. To type a lowercase character, it is necessary to press the ⬆ key. To put the keyboard back in normal mode, press Caps Lock once again.

Numbers can also be entered using the numeric pad on the right of the keyboard. This pad can also be used to control the cursor and display. Mode switching is by pressing Num Lock on the keyboard – if the 'Num' light is on, numbers can be entered.

⇥ If you hold down a key, the computer goes into repeat mode. The character is typed repeatedly until the key is released.

⇥ Some keys have three symbols on them. The first is obtained by pressing the key. The second one is obtained by pressing the ⬆ key at the same time as pressing the key. To get the third character, you must press Alt Gr before pressing the key.

A character typed in error can easily be removed with the ⬅ key.

⇥ To end a line at a particular point and **go to the next paragraph**, press the ↵ key. This key inserts a paragraph break into the text.

If you have any difficulty finding the right keys, there is an overview of the keyboard at the beginning of this book. If the symbol for the euro is missing from your keyboard, you can enter it by pressing Alt Gr and 4.

A note about paragraphs in Microsoft Word

Many new users of Word have difficulties with the concept of paragraphs. When using a typewriter, it is normal to press the ⏎ Key at the right margin to start a new line. You should never do this with Word. Just keep typing your text – Word will recognise the margin and automatically place the next word on the next lower line. Use the ⏎ key only at the end of the paragraph.

Not observing this simple rule can cause you all sorts of problems. A very simple example will suffice. Type the following text into Word. Then press the ⏎ key twice and type it in again.

The first time, press the ⏎ key at the end of each line.

The second time, don't do this. Type the piece as one paragraph, using the ⏎ key only at the end of the paragraph.

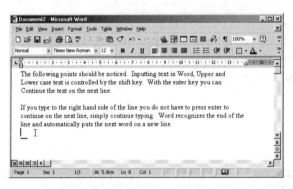

You probably think both versions look equally good. At first, you might be right. Now let us conduct a small experiment – moving the right margin a little to the left. This is quite easy to do.

In the lower left-hand corner of the document window Word displays a few icons that influence how the document is displayed. Normally, the leftmost icon *Normal View* is active, i.e. the text is displayed just as it is entered. If *Page Layout View* is active, the text appears just as it would later be printed.

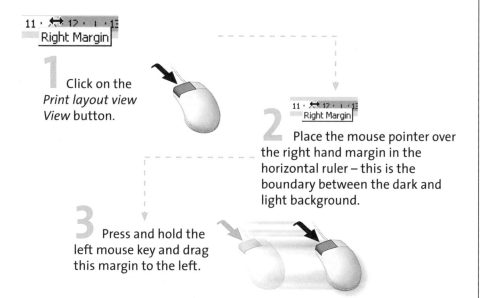

1 Click on the *Print layout view View* button.

2 Place the mouse pointer over the right hand margin in the horizontal ruler – this is the boundary between the dark and light background.

3 Press and hold the left mouse key and drag this margin to the left.

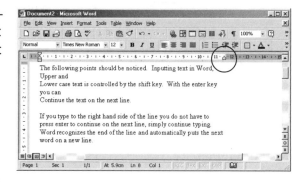

This will move the right-hand margin. The result can be seen on the right – the first paragraph looks broken up.

This is caused by the paragraph break characters. When the margins are changed, Word automatically fits text into the new borders. A paragraph break character forces Word to break the text at that point and start the next line at the left margin.

Displaying 'hidden' characters

Do you have a piece of text containing such characters? How can you find them and remove them? Word provides for this by letting you make otherwise 'hidden' characters, such as the spaces between words or paragraph breaks characters, visible on the screen.

1 Click on the *Show/Hide* icon on the *Standard* toolbar.

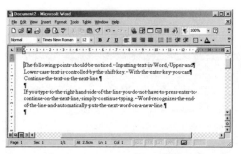

As soon as the button is active (it is displayed as 'depressed') Word will display the normally hidden characters.

Spaces between words will be displayed as dots, and each paragraph break will be displayed with the sign ¶.

`·word·on·a·new·line.¶`

Word processing

Inevitably, errors occur when entering text. Words may be forgotten, one or two characters too many may be typed, or additional text may have to be added to a draft. Many errors are found only at a later proof-reading stage. The ability to easily change an existing text is one of Microsoft Word's strengths. The following is a short overview of the techniques.

Do you still have the document created on the preceding pages? If so, it can be used as an example.

Inserting and overwriting words

Do you want to add a new word at a specific location in the text?

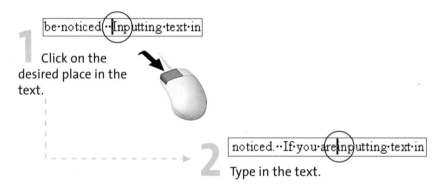

1 Click on the desired place in the text.

2 Type in the text.

Word inserts the new characters one by one at the insertion point. Text to the right of this point is shifted further right to make room.

If the text to the right of the insertion point is to be overwritten by the new text, press Ins on the numeric pad before starting to type. Word will display the symbol to indicate that it is in overtype or overlay mode. You can then type over the characters already displayed on the screen.

Deleting text

In this example, we will remove the unwanted paragraph break characters at the end of the lines in the preceding example.

·in·Word,·Upper·and[¶

1
Click on a text line immediately to the left of one of the unwanted paragraph break characters.

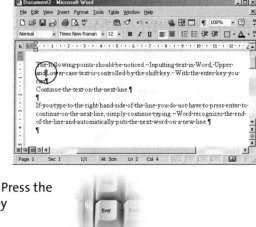

2
Press the [Del] key

Word will remove the character to the right of the insertion point. In this instance, the paragraph break character is removed and Word automatically combines the sentences into a single paragraph.

3
Press the space bar to separate the sentences by a single space.

4
Repeat steps 1 to 3 until all of the unwanted paragraph break characters have been removed.

Positioning within text

The insertion point can be positioned anywhere in the text by clicking with the mouse immediately in front of the character concerned. You may also use the **cursor keys** and certain other keys to move the insertion point around on the screen. The following describes the most important of the keys and key combinations used to move the cursor around.

Key(s)	Comment
↑	Moves the insertion point up one line in the text.
↓	Moves the insertion point down one line in the text.
←	Moves the insertion point one character to the left towards the beginning of the text.
→	Moves the insertion point one character to the right towards the end of the text.
Ctrl+←	Moves the insertion point one word to the left.
Ctrl+→	Moves the insertion point one word to the right.
Home	Moves the insertion point to the beginning of the current line.
End	Moves the insertion point to the end of the line.

Selecting text

It is often necessary to delete whole sentences or other large pieces of text from a document. One possibility is to place the insertion point at the beginning of the text and press Del until all of the characters have been deleted. It is easier and more elegant to **select** the text and then delete it.

TIP

The term 'selecting' is often encountered in Windows and its applications. You can select files, icons, folders, text or sections of graphics using the mouse. Some programs display selected objects against a coloured background, some use underscores.

Selecting is similar to applying a highlight pen to text on a piece of paper. In Word, the text cursor is dragged over the text to be selected.

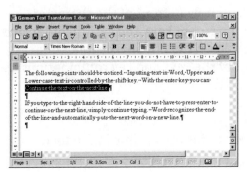

1 With the left mouse button, click on the start of the text to selected it.

2 With the mouse button still pressed, drag the mouse pointer to the end of the area to be selected.

The selected text is highlighted in black. If you now press the [Del] key, the selected text will be deleted. Or, you can type in completely new text that will wholly replace the selected text.

If you delete something in error, the key combination [Ctrl]+[Z] will undo the last change made. If a text area has been selected, all commands work directly on its contents.

To remove the highlight, click on the screen outside the selected area.

You can also select text with the keyboard. Move the insertion point to the beginning of the text area to be selected. Then press and hold the ⇧ key while you move the insertion point with the cursor control keys listed above. Word will select the appropriate characters.

Some tips about selecting text with the mouse:

To select a single word, double-click on it.
A mouse click to the left of a line selects the whole line.
A triple click on a word selects the sentence.
A quadruple click on a word selects the paragraph.
The key combination Ctrl+A selects the whole document.

This concludes the first exercises. You can now enter simple text, select it and make corrections.

Discarding documents

Just to show how it is done, we will now discard the document we used in the above example.

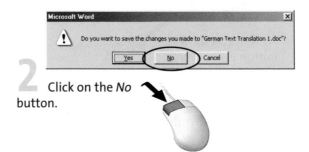

1 Click on the *Close Document* button in the upper right corner of the document window.

Word will then ask if the document should be saved.

2 Click on the *No* button.

Word will close the document window and discard the document. Saving a document is covered later in this chapter.

Creating an invitation

If you have worked through the above, it is now time to try a more concrete example. The following creates an invitation to a summer ball at a sports club, which could look something like this:

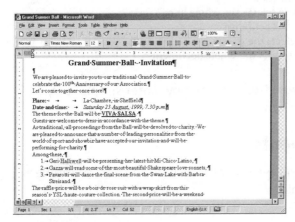

This example shows use of the major features that Microsoft Word makes available for document production. Some of the text is in a bold font, and there are underlined sections as well as bullets and numbering. The following shows how to create such a text.

Creating a new document

To start with you need a new document where you will input the relevant introductory text.

1 Click on the *New* button in the Word window.

Word will display an empty document window.

2 Type in the text for the invitation.

Enter the text as in the previous example. You do not need to worry about it having any particular structure at this point. It is only important to enter the text in paragraphs with a paragraph break character only at the real end of each paragraph.

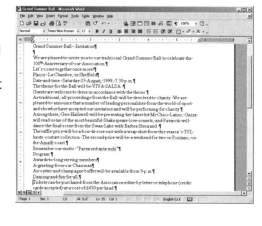

 The document contains many single-line paragraphs. If you cannot see the end of paragraph character, click on the icon displayed here to make the 'hidden' characters visible on the display.

Have you entered the text? You will probably make one or two mistakes when doing so. There are several mistakes in the text used in the examples, to show what happens. The spell checker built into Microsoft Word marks any suspicious words with a wavy line. Don't let this worry you – we will return to it at the end of the chapter. If the obvious spelling errors are disturbing, they can be corrected manually. You saw how to do this in the preceding chapter.

Moving text

Finally, the question of moving large pieces of text around in a document arises. This is particularly helpful when adapting existing documents. As sometimes happens, there is an error in the text for this example – the agenda is not in the correct order. The line announcing: 'A greeting from our Chairman' must surely come before: 'Awards to long-serving members'.

Instead of deleting the relevant lines and typing them again, it is possible to **cut** and **paste** portions of text in Windows. These are the steps necessary to move the first few lines around.

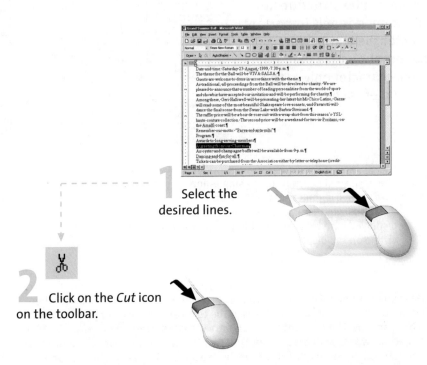

1 Select the desired lines.

2 Click on the *Cut* icon on the toolbar.

The text will be deleted from the document window. Windows stores the text in the **clipboard**.

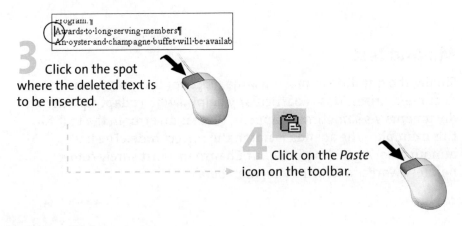

3 Click on the spot where the deleted text is to be inserted.

4 Click on the *Paste* icon on the toolbar.

Word will now insert the text from the **clipboard** into the document following the insertion point. The net effect of this operation is to move the selected text to the new position.

Windows has a special storage area known as the **clipboard**. If you select either of the *Cut* or *Copy* commands (e.g. from the EDIT menu) Windows will copy the selected text into the clipboard. The command *Paste* in the EDIT menu copies the contents of the clipboard into the current window.

Copying text

If you want to copy a piece of text (i.e. the source text should remain where it is) the process is very similar.

1 Select the text to be copied.

2 Click on the *Copy* icon on the toolbar.

Word will make a copy of the selected text and place it in the clipboard. The original text remains undisturbed in the document.

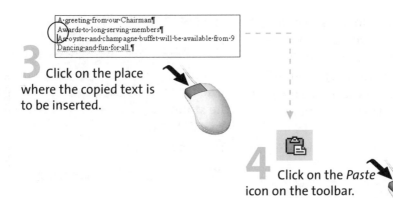

3 Click on the place where the copied text is to be inserted.

4 Click on the *Paste* icon on the toolbar.

Word inserts the text from the clipboard into the position indicated by the insertion point.

With the *Copy* function, the previously selected text remains in the document. In the illustration above, you can see that the text 'Dancing and fun for all' appears twice.

Can you remember how to undo the most recent change? Right – you need only press Ctrl+Z. Windows will immediately remove the text inserted from the clipboard.

You can copy much larger blocks of text than a single sentence and place them in the clipboard. The contents of the clipboard can be copied into the document as often as required. If you also select and copy the paragraph break character, it will be copied with the text.

The clipboard can also be used to exchange data between separate windows. For example, you can start two copies of Microsoft Word, then select text in one and copy it to the clipboard. If you then switch to the other document window, you can paste the text out of the clipboard.

Alternatives to cut and paste

Will you be using cut, copy or paste frequently? As in other areas, Word allows you to call up these functions in several ways. With most Windows and Office applications, the three icons used in the preceding pages are available in the standard toolbar. At first, it will be more convenient to use these for calling up the functions. It can be useful, however, to be aware of the alternatives.

This button removes the selected text from the document and places it in the clipboard. *Cut* in the EDIT menu serves the same purpose. The key combination Ctrl+X is even more convenient.

This button copies the text into the clipboard – the original in the document is undisturbed. If the toolbar is not visible, the EDIT menu's *Copy* command does the same thing. Or, in this case, Ctrl+C.

The clipboard is the last of the three inserts. This stores cut or copied images or data from either the *Cut* or *Copy* options. The same effect is achieved by Ctrl+V or the *Paste* command in the EDIT menu.

The clipboard is not just for text. Graphics and other objects can be selected in other programs and transferred to the clipboard for use in other documents.

> In Chapter 1 you saw how it was possible to move or copy files and folders from one window to another. This drag-and-drop technique naturally also works within Word. You can move a selected piece of text by pressing and holding the left mouse button while you move the mouse pointer to the destination. If you use the right mouse button for this operation, Word opens a context (shortcut) menu to ask if the text should be moved or copied. Because many beginners find this technique difficult, it is recommended that the above techniques be used at first.

Formatting the document

Have you corrected the text in the invitation? It doesn't yet resemble the example shown at the beginning of the chapter. This has been formatted – some of the text is bold, the heading is in the centre, and some items are numbered. Microsoft Word offers many formatting options that you are about to see.

Justifying text horizontally

In many documents the text always begins at the left-hand margin. However, this is not always appropriate. Heading lines, for instance, are often centred. This is very easy in Word.

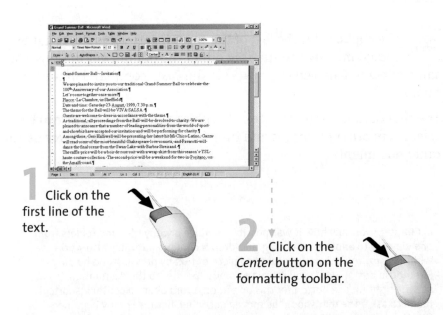

1 Click on the first line of the text.

2 Click on the *Center* button on the formatting toolbar.

Word will centre the text on the line in the middle of the page.

Do you need different alignment on one or more selected lines? This is just as easy. There are a number of other icons on the formatting toolbar to make Word use different horizontal justifications.

 The *Align Left* button causes each selected line to start at the left margin. If the text reaches the right margin, the next word is automatically shifted to the next line. Because the lines are of differing lengths, this is referred to as 'unjustified'. It is the normal form used in most documents.

Text is aligned to the left margin and not justified.

Use the *Center* button to place the text equidistant from the left and right margins. This is often used for headings.

Text is centred.

The *Align Right* button aligns the end of each line to the right margin, while the beginning of the lines have a ragged appearance. Unless you are creating Hebrew or Arabic documents, this feature will probably only be useful when adding addresses or dates to the head of a letter.

Text is aligned to the right margin and not justified.

If the *Justify* button is used, text is aligned to both the left and right margins. If necessary, space will be added between the words so that all lines are the same width.

Justified   text.

Alignment is performed for the selected text or the current paragraph. If you ended each line by pressing the *Enter key*, Word will treat each line as a separate paragraph. You observed this behaviour at the beginning of this chapter. This makes alignment difficult, because each individual line has to be aligned separately. As you can see once again, it pays to enter text in whole paragraphs.

Changing the font size

When creating a document, you will soon need different font sizes. In the sample invitation, the heading line should be in larger characters to give it some prominence.

1 Select the text of the first line.

2 Click on the arrow next to the *Font* box on the toolbar.

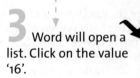

3 Word will open a list. Click on the value '16'.

4 Click somewhere near the text to remove the selecting.

The invitation's heading will now appear larger.

Various specialist jargon is used when discussing the formatting of text. The size of characters is not referred to as 'character size' or 'character height' but **font size.** The numbers refer to the font size in **points**. A point is a measurement just like a millimetre. The larger the value, the larger the characters. By default, Word uses a 10-point font.

Changing the type of font

Documents are printed using character sets referred to as **fonts**. These describe the appearance of each individual character in great detail. You will have seen different fonts in use everywhere – a newspaper page looks very different from a supermarket poster. Yet another unmistakable font is familiar from the 'Wanted' posters in Western films. Fonts can be as individual as companies – see the Cola manufacturers, for example.

Simple documents are normally written in the Times font, known under Windows as 'Times New Roman'. The Helvetica font – known as 'Arial' under Windows – is commonly used for headings. Courier has the appearance of typewriter text, because each character is exactly the same width.

The **font** can be set directly from a list item on the formatting toolbar, just like the size.

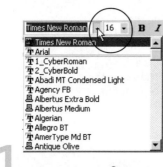

1 Click on the arrow at the end of the font box on the toolbar.

Find the desired font in the list and click on its entry.

If a segment of text was selected, Word would now display and print it in this font. If nothing was selected, Word would note the chosen font and use it for any text typed subsequently.

You should be cautious about using multiple fonts in a single document. Mixed fonts do not always look aesthetically pleasing and the readability of the document can be impaired. For this reason, we will leave the sample invitation in Times New Roman.

Bold, italic and underlined text

As well as changing the size and font, you can also select bold, italic or underlined text. There are three buttons on the formatting toolbar for this purpose:

B   This button formats the marked text with **bold** characters.

I   Click on this button to format the selected text in *italics*.

<u>U</u>   This button formats text with <u>underlines</u>.

These three can be combined as required, so that text could appear in bold, underlined italics. Some of the text on the sample invitation will be formatted in this way.

Hopefully the sample invitation is still available in the document window.

Now try formatting the remaining text on the invitation in bold, underlined italics.

You can also remove the unnecessary blank lines below the heading at the same time. Here is a step-by-step guide:

1 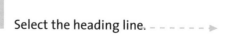 Select the heading line. - - - - - - ▶

2 Click on the icon. **B**

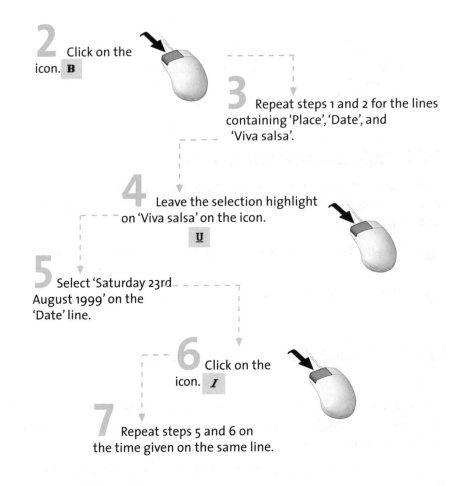

3 Repeat steps 1 and 2 for the lines containing 'Place', 'Date', and 'Viva salsa'.

4 Leave the selection highlight on 'Viva salsa' on the icon.

U

5 Select 'Saturday 23rd August 1999' on the 'Date' line.

6 Click on the icon. **I**

7 Repeat steps 5 and 6 on the time given on the same line.

The result should now look something like this:

TIP If you want to assign any or all of these attributes as the text is typed, just click on the desired button(s) and type the text. The formatting currently in use can be seen from the 'depressed' appearance of the button.

You can see that using bold, italic and underlined text in Microsoft Word is not difficult.

If you want to remove one of these attributes from a piece of text, just select it and click on the button once more. If the button no longer has the 'depressed' appearance, the attribute has been removed.

If you select a segment of text, the operation works on all of the selected text. If the insertion point is on one word, the operation works on that word only.

Those who prefer using the keyboard might find the following key combinations somewhat quicker:

[Ctrl]+[⇧]+[B] **Bold**

[Ctrl]+[⇧]+[I] *Italic*

[Ctrl]+[⇧]+[U] Underlined

There is more information about formatting in Chapter 3.

Using columns

This is a suitable point to discuss a topic with which many Word users often have to struggle. In many documents, there are tables or lists that have to be arranged in columns.

As an example, here is an extract from a telephone list. The individual entries have been aligned in columns by adding spaces – the technique that most users intuitively use.

Surname	Forename	Telephone¶
Mitton	Jonathan	3465¶
Watkinson	Paul	9987¶
Fox	Richard	1243¶
Smith	John	6734¶
Billard	Simon	8412¶

Despite some effort, the entries in the list are slightly misaligned and the list is really unusable. With some patience, this can be corrected, but the surprise comes when the list is printed. Everything is shifted around again by differing amounts.

Aligning lists by inserting blanks is almost impossible. During the earlier discussion it was noted that individual characters within a specific font have different widths. This causes small shifts in the length of words and lines that are especially noticeable when printed. With a typewriter, the font (or typeface) is usually Courier, in which all characters have the same width. With this font, it is possible to construct aligned lists by typing spaces.

Before you begin to experiment with the Courier font in Microsoft Word there is a much more elegant solution, which is also often used with typewriters. The sample invitation can also be used to demonstrate this. The place and time can be aligned to the same column.

1 Click after the word 'Place'.

2 Press ⬱ twice.

3 Click after the phrase 'Date and time:'.

4 Press ⬱ once.

Word will insert tab characters into the document.

This causes the text on the right to be pushed inwards.

The tab stops Word uses are, as with a typewriter, predefined in fixed positions. If a single tab character is insufficient, press the ⟨↹⟩ key twice. Word will shift the text each time to a predefined position.

Using ⟨↹⟩ saves you the effort of typing lots of spaces. It also ensures that the text is always aligned to the correct columns.

Setting and clearing tab stops

The predefined tab stops often require you to use multiple tab characters to align lists. It is also often necessary to position tab stops at a specific place on the line. Word allows you to set your own tab stops.

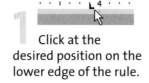

Click at the desired position on the lower edge of the rule.

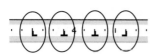

Word will indicate the new tab stop position with a tab marker. The shape of this mark tells you what form of tabulation (left-aligned, right-aligned, centred, etc.) it implies.

93

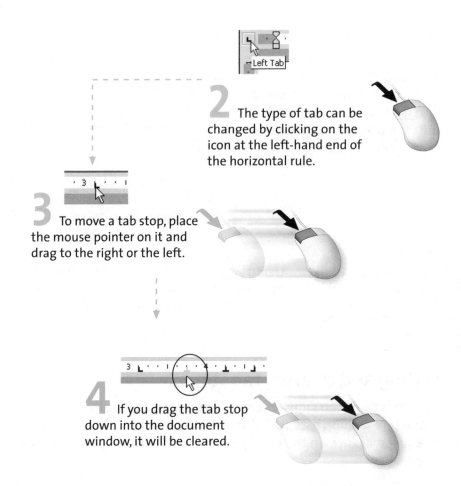

2 The type of tab can be changed by clicking on the icon at the left-hand end of the horizontal rule.

3 To move a tab stop, place the mouse pointer on it and drag to the right or the left.

4 If you drag the tab stop down into the document window, it will be cleared.

Tab stops will be used in subsequent chapters for aligning columns within a table.

Listing and numbering

Two more formatting options are still missing: listing and numbering items in a document. In the sample invitation, the main events are numbered, i.e. each line is preceded by an ascending number. In contrast, the highlights of the summer ball are simply listed without numbers. Both are very easy to do in Word.

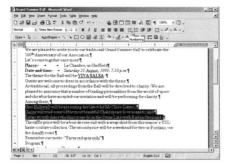

1 Select the lines/paragraphs that are to be numbered.

2 Click on the *Numbering* button on the toolbar.

Word will now insert a number in front of each of the selected lines.

3 Click on another part of the document window to remove the selection highlight.

4 Now select the lines that are to form the bulleted list.

95

5 Click on the *Bullets* button on the toolbar.

6 Click on another part of the document window to remove the selection highlight.

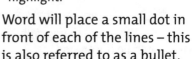

Word will place a small dot in front of each of the lines – this is also referred to as a bullet.

The text will be shifted somewhat to the right to make room for the preceding number or bullet. If there is more than one line in any paragraph, succeeding lines in that paragraph will be indented to align with the text in the first line. This is also referred to as a hanging indent.

Adjusting line length

Another aspect of formatting is setting the line length. Word starts each line at the left margin and places as many words as will fit on the line until it hits the right-hand margin. It then continues placing words on the next line, and so on. But how does it know where the margins should be?

One possibility was discussed at the beginning. The edges of the page are visible as shaded bars at both ends of the horizontal rule.

Right Margin

In page layout view, you can drag the edge of the shaded bar and thus move the margin. By default, the document margins are changed, but left and right margins can also be set for individual lines of text.

 In the horizontal rule there are small triangles at the left and right ends.

These triangles are also known as indents. Using the left and right lower indents, you can set the left and right margins for the first line in every paragraph. The upper indent on the left sets the left margin for subsequent lines in the paragraph. This is called a first line indent. We will now use an indent marker to move the right-hand edge of the text somewhat to the left.

1 Select all of the text in the document.

You can do this with the mouse by dragging it across all of the text. It is quicker to use Ctrl+A.

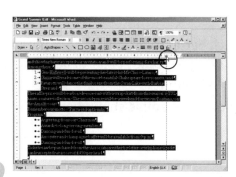

2 Point to the right indent and drag it to the left.

Word will display a vertical line to show where the margin would be in the document.

By default, the indents change the margins only for the current paragraph or for the selected text. If you want to change margins for the document, the whole document must be selected before performing the operation.

Pulling the indent to the left reduces the line width. Word will adjust the text accordingly and flow the words within each paragraph into more lines. The result is a narrower text area.

Both the left and right margins can be adjusted in this way.

Paragraph spacing

The last significant topic under formatting is paragraph spacing. It is common to see Word users spacing paragraphs by simply pressing the Enter key twice. This provides an adequate space between the paragraphs, and all Word users occasionally do it this way – especially when writing letters.

```
Dear·John¶
¶
Today·I·wanted·you·to…¶
```

The technique should not be used in longer documents, however. Pressing Enter twice produces an empty paragraph. If a page break occurs at this point, perhaps when the document is later edited, it is possible to have a page beginning with a blank line.

It is much better to terminate each paragraph normally and let Word apply a chosen separation both before and after the paragraph.

The following example shows how this is done.

```
Dear·John¶

Today·I·wanted·you·to…¶
```

In the sample invitation, there is only standard line spacing between the individual paragraphs.

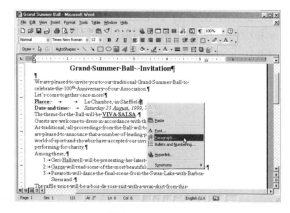

1 Click on a paragraph with the right mouse button.

2 Windows will display a context menu. Click on the *Paragraph* command.

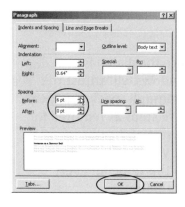

On the page with an *Indents and Spacing* tab, Word offers you the chance to set vertical spacing between paragraphs in the *Spacing* group.

3 Try setting the *Before* field, e.g. to 6 pt.

4 If desired, you can also set the *After* box.

99

The *Before* and *After* boxes define how large the vertical separation will be between the paragraphs in question, the one before it, and the one following it.

5 Close the *Indents and Spacing* dialog box by clicking on *OK*.

Once the dialog is closed, Windows will adjust the paragraph spacing. Repeat these steps as required for the rest of the document. The version illustrated here has this done for every paragraph.

The preceding steps showed you the most important functions for formatting a document. There are many more features available in Word, and they are described in the help files.

When proof-reading longer documents, e.g. book manuscripts, it is often very useful to use double or triple spacing between lines so that hand-written notes can be made wherever required. The following key combinations set these options for a paragraph or piece of selected text very quickly and conveniently:

Ctrl + 1   single-line spacing

Ctrl + 2   double-line spacing

Ctrl + 5   1.5-line spacing

Saving and retrieving documents

Have you produced a sample invitation as described above? If so, you can save it in a file for future use. At any point in the future, such a file can be reloaded, customised and printed. The following shows how this is done.

Saving a Microsoft Word document for the first time is quite simple:

1 Click on the *Save* icon on the toolbar.

If the document is new, a dialog box entitled *Save As* will appear.

On the left of the dialog box there will be a list of places where the file can be saved. You can click on any one to select it.

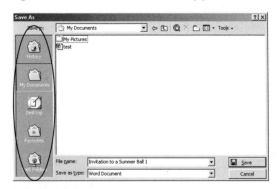

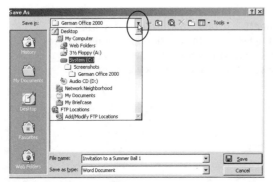

The *Save in* field allows you to select a specific drive and folder for the file to be saved in. A click on the arrow icon opens the list. A chosen drive or folder is opened by double-clicking on its icon.

The sample document will be saved in the *My Documents/Letters* folder. This subfolder does not yet exist, so it will be necessary to create it.

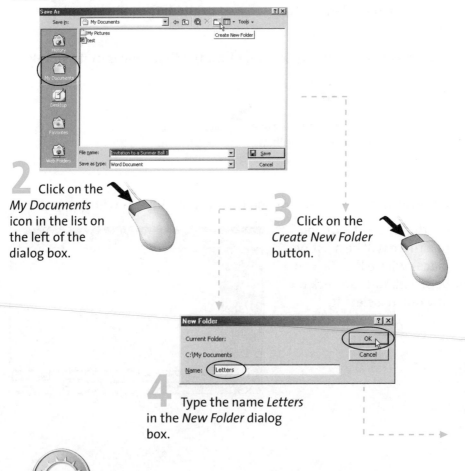

2 Click on the *My Documents* icon in the list on the left of the dialog box.

3 Click on the *Create New Folder* button.

4 Type the name *Letters* in the *New Folder* dialog box.

5 Click on *OK* to close the dialog.

Word will create a new folder and open it automatically.

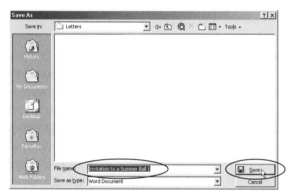

6 Enter the file name in the field of the same name.

7 Click on the *Save* button.

Word closes the dialog and saves the file in the desired folder. The filename will be whatever you specified with the *.doc* extension added automatically.

You do not need to specify the *.doc* extension explicitly. As long as *Word Document (*.doc)* is selected in the *Save as type* list, Word will use the *.doc* extension.

You will find other file formats available in the *Save as type* list. If you select *.txt* Word will save the document as a simple text file. This causes the loss of the document's formatting, however.

If you want to save a document for which there is already a file on disk, just click on the *Save* button. Word will save your changes without issuing any prompts for more information.

Ending Word

Has the document been saved? If you wish, you can end the Word application. You may remember how to do this from the discussion at the beginning of the book – click on the icon in the extreme upper right-hand corner of the Word window. Really experienced users will also know that the key combination Alt+F4 closes the current window.

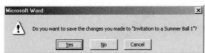

You have no need to worry about losing changes made to open documents when closing Word. If you have made changes but have not saved the document, Word will open a dialog box to ask if you wish to save the changes, discard them, or go back to processing the document.

Reloading a document

Have you closed Word? Excellent; now we can look at how to reload an existing document. Do you know where the document was stored?

1 Restart Word. ----> **2**
Click the *Open* button in the Standard toolbar.

The *Open* dialog box appears in which you can select a file and file storage location.

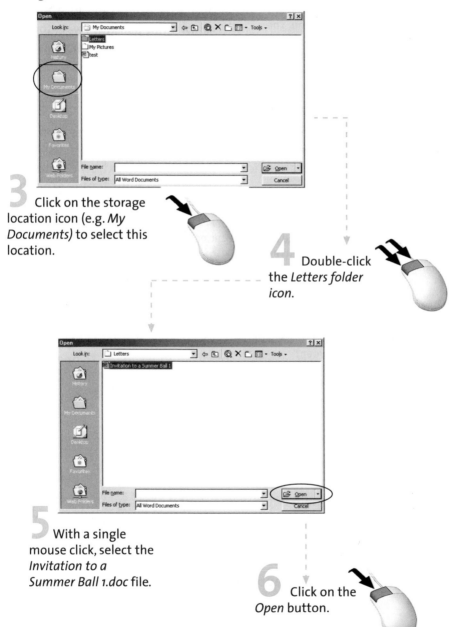

3 Click on the storage location icon (e.g. *My Documents)* to select this location.

4 Double-click the *Letters folder icon*.

5 With a single mouse click, select the *Invitation to a Summer Ball 1.doc* file.

6 Click on the *Open* button.

Word now loads the document and displays it in the document window. You can browse the document using the window scroll bars (*see also* Chapter 1).

(*see also* Chapter 1).

In many cases you can avoid using the *Open* dialog box to load an existing document.

When you open any application FILE menu, this often lists the names of the last four files to be processed. A mouse click on the one you want is all that is needed to load one of these 'documents'.

<u>1</u> C:\...\Invitation to a Summer Ball 1
<u>2</u> C:\...\Invitation to a Summer Ball 1
<u>3</u> C:\...\Invitation to a Summer Ball
<u>4</u> A:\Invitation to a Summer Ball

E<u>x</u>it

The only problem might be in selecting the correct entry as word sometimes lists an entry more than once. In this case, a document with the same name has been saved in different folders, but there is not enough room in the Menu list to display the full folder/filename. So you may have to experiment a little to find the correct document.

Loading a document directly from Windows is even faster. If a document file is listed in a folder window, load it by double-clicking on it. Windows starts Word and causes the document file to be loaded.

Printing documents

'Only trust what is down in black and white'. This saying is still valid in the computer age. To send out your invitation you have to print it. I shall now take you through all the instructions for getting to know this process.

In Word, as in other Office applications, printing a document is very simple.

1 In the standard toolbar, click on the button shown on the left.

Word now prepares the output data for the printer. While this is proceeding, watch the stylised printer icon in the status bar.

TIP

Have you selected the *Print* button by mistake? If so double-click the printer icon on the status bar. Word cancels the output to the printer.

For a multipage document, you will see how many pages have already been sent to the printer.

TIP

The document to be printed is sent to the printer by Windows in the background. This allows you to continue working in Word or another application while printing is in process. If you experience any difficulties when printing, please consult the Appendix. There you will find several tips for sorting out printing problems.

Using Print Preview

For proofing a document, a printout is most helpful. Errors are easier to see on the printed page than on a computer screen. You will probably notice that some of your colleagues need ten or more test printouts before they get an even half satisfactory end result. To approve the page layout, however, there is a smarter way to go about things.

WHAT'S THIS?

Layout is a printer's term for the build-up of a page. The layout determines the arrangement of the various elements and graphic items on the page.

Use **Print Preview** to obtain a quick overview of the layout. By doing so you will spare both your purse and the environment by using fewer natural resources.

107

1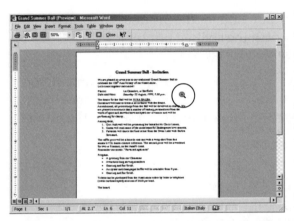

Click the *Print Preview* button on the standard toolbar.

Word opens a preview window showing the document reduced in size. The mouse cursor takes the shape of a magnifying glass. A click on the document increases the document size to 100%; a second click reduces it back to the previous size.

Using the Zoom pull-down list on the preview toolbar you can set any desired degree of magnification. The *One Page* and *Multiple Pages* buttons permit the style of display to be toggled.

2 **Close**

To close the preview, simply click on the *Close* button on the preview toolbar.

Word then changes back to displaying the document as usual in either normal or page layout view.

Print options

Having read the above description, you are now aware of the basic printing technique. We should now examine briefly the use of various printing options. Let us suppose you have created a multipage document and would like to print several pages, or perhaps you would like to print more than one copy.

1 In the FILE menu select the *Print* command or press the Ctrl+P key.

Would you like to print specific single pages?

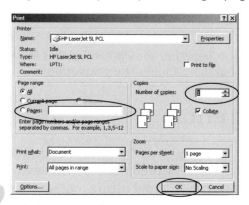

2 Click on the *Pages* option button in the *Page range* section.

3 Enter the numbers of the pages to be printed in the adjacent input field.

The page numbers can be separated by semi-colons (e.g. 5; 7; 8 will print pages 5, 7 and 8). Or you can enter a range of pages in the form 2-3 in the *Pages* box. To print only the current page, tick the *Current page* button. If you had selected part of the document before opening the *Print* dialog box, the *Selection* button becomes available.

Would you like to print more than one copy?

4 Set the desired number of copies with the *Number of copies* spin-arrows.

5 Click on the *OK* button to start printing.

Further settings can be made via the *Properties* and *Options* buttons. When necessary, use online Help to find out more about the various options.

Typos and spelling errors

Hand on heart, who can claim honestly never to make mistakes when working? However, every mistake on a printed page is mercilessly and inexorably recorded for posterity. To avoid future mockery then, you should place your trust in the help Word can provide. The program offers spell checking of a special kind.

At this point I would like to go into the basic functions of spell checking. Actually, you will already have met the spell checker, provided you have worked through the previous pages.

AutoCorrect

Favourite sources of error are letters typed in the wrong order, and missed capitals at the start of sentences. Here Word can step in to correct errors as you type.

1 Open a new Word document with the *New* button on the standard toolbar.

2 For test purposes now type in 'teh', 'adn', and 'wre'.

The result is here to see. Hmm, what's happening?

teh··adn·wre¶

If everything is working as it should, in the Word window you will instantly see the words 'The', 'and' and 'were'. The first word on the line is even furnished with an initial capital letter.

Word and many Office programs have an AutoCorrect function, which supervises your keyboard input and automatically corrects certain frequently occurring errors. This is also the reason for the capital letter at the start of the sentence, or why Word automatically replaces the 1/2 digit combination with the ½ character.

If the AutoCorrect function corrects something that you do not wish to be corrected, it is no use just retyping the same sequence of characters. Word will stubbornly continue to use the same replacement sequence. But all is not lost. Simply press the key combination Ctrl+Z to undo the last replacement. Word then suspends the AutoCorrect function for that input and displays the text in the form in which you typed it. In Word you can specify the words to be supervised by the AutoCorrect function. This is one way to customise Office to your personal needs. Further details on this are available in Chapter 11.

'One thing less to worry about' you are now thinking. But AutoCorrect does not take care of everything. The purpose of AutoCorrect is to detect and correct *typical* typing errors. When working with Office you will therefore find that AutoCorrect ignores many input errors.

111

> | September |
> The·20th·Sept¶

Spelling and grammar checking as you type

No need to lose heart here either. The grammar and spelling checker built into Office gives you a helping hand as you enter your text.

1 Load the document with the invitation.

2 Insert a small spelling mistake in the text.

For example, I have changed the word 'Place' to 'Placce'.

> **Grand·Summer·Ball·--·Invitation¶**
> ¶
> We·are·pleased·to·invite·you·to·our·traditional·Grand·Summer·Ball·to·celebrate·the·100th·Anniversary·of·our·Association.¶
> Let's·come·together·once·more!¶
>
> **Placce:·** → → La·Chambre,·in·Sheffield¶
> **Date·and·time:·** → *Saturday·23·August,·1999,·7.30·p.m.*¶

If everything goes to plan, you will now see places in the document that Word has marked with a wavy line.

Simultaneously, Word displays the Spelling and Grammar Status icon on the status bar.

Underlined words in the document indicate possible errors. In the case of the word 'Place', the matter is obvious.

3 Click on the error-underlined word with the right mouse button.

Word opens a shortcut menu in which you can click on the correction you want.

4 Click on the replacement word you select from the proposed list in the shortcut menu.

The shortcut menu shows the spelling which Word thinks is correct. Sometimes Word suggests several terms, separated from the remaining commands by a horizontal line. Selecting one of these causes Word to make the corresponding correction.

But what happens, for example, with the name of the singers invited to the party, Ms 'Halliwell' or 'Barbara Streisand', which are also indicated as wrong.

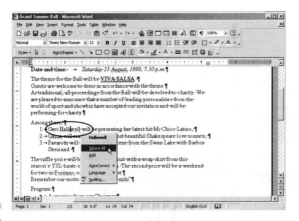

5 Right-click the word 'Halliwell'.

6 Select the *Ignore All* command in the shortcut menu.

From now on, the word will be accepted as a correct spelling in the current document, even if the spell checker cannot suggest a spelling. If you use the same word in a new document, however, it will again be marked as wrong.

> For frequently occurring words you should select the *Add* command in the shortcut menu. Word then records the word in question in its current spelling in a user-defined dictionary. These dictionaries are likewise used for spell checking.

Foreign language checking

Now we come to the subject of foreign words in documents. Office cannot unconditionally differentiate between foreign words and spelling mistakes. Consequently, such words will be marked as wrong. This may affect you considerably when you include foreign language texts or quotes in a document.

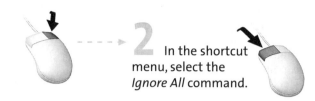

1 Right-click a foreign term (e.g. 'Parva').

2 In the shortcut menu, select the *Ignore All* command.

From now on, within the current document, the term is categorised by Word as correctly written. The default underlining of other errors continues in the current document.

To be sure, you thereby dispense with the help that Word can offer here. Are you sure that the foreign text is correctly written? No? Then just ask Office for help. The **spelling and grammar checker** supports **various languages** as well as English. Therefore, proceed as follows:

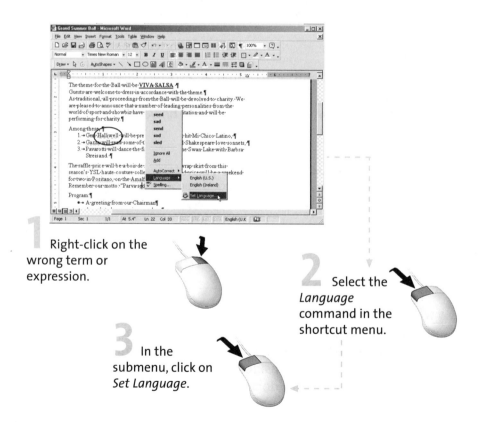

1 Right-click on the wrong term or expression.

2 Select the *Language* command in the shortcut menu.

3 In the submenu, click on *Set Language*.

Word uses the dictionary of the chosen language to check the selected text. If, after setting the language, no error is shown, you can be sure that the expression is spelt correctly.

When Office is installed, spelling and grammar checking while typing is automatically switched on. If you load an existing document that has not yet been checked, the checker will in that case indicate many errors in the text. After a certain number of errors, Word suggests that the spelling and grammar checker should be switched off. The same thing can also be recommended if the spell-checker simply annoys you. In the Tools menu click on the *Options* command.

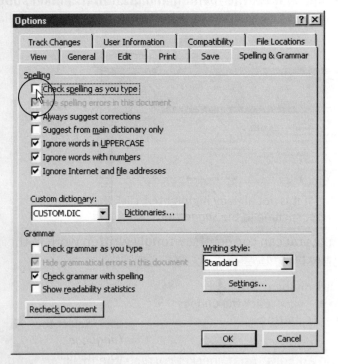

On the *Spelling & Grammar* tab you must then click the *Check spelling as you type* check box to deselect it. The underlining will then be blanked out.

Spelling and grammar checking on demand

Did you switch off spelling and grammar checking while typing? Then Word gives you the opportunity to have text checked by the **spelling and grammar checker** at any time.

1 Click the *Spelling and Grammar* button on the standard toolbar.

Discovered spelling mistakes are then displayed in a dialog box. To correct them, proceed as follows:

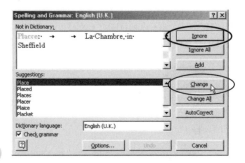

2 If it is not already highlighted, click the correct spelling in the *Suggestions* list.

Alternatively, you can correct the wrongly written word in the *Not in Dictionary* text window.

3 Click the *Change* button.

The spelling and grammar checker corrects the misspelt word.

4 If the word is not misspelt, click the *Ignore* button.

The wrongly marked word will then be bypassed.

As well as simple misspelling correction, the spelling and grammar checker provides various options, which you call up using the dialog box buttons.

With the *Change All* button you can instruct the checker to correct every occurrence of a word in a document.

In order to tell the checker to ignore every occurrence of a term in the document, select the *Ignore All* button.

If you want to **record** the term in the **Custom dictionary**, click on the *Add* button.

If you frequently misspell a word, click on the *AutoCorrect* button. Both the misspelt and correct term will then be added to the table of words to be autocorrected. After this, Word corrects such terms as you type.

Language change for the spelling and grammar checker

Are you processing a document containing expressions in a foreign language? If so, the spelling and grammar checker will display such expressions as errors.

Here an Italian term has been detected, which is 'foreign' to an 'English' dictionary.

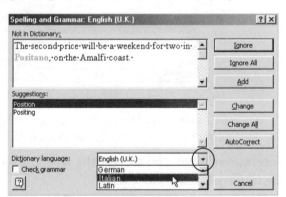

In this case set the desired language in the *Dictionary language* box.

As soon as you click the *Change* button, the spell checker checks the term against the selected dictionary and either accepts the spelling or signals a further error.

If you make a mistake using the spell checker, click on the *Undo* button. The checker goes back to the last error location in the document and reinstates the original term. You can use the *Undo* button repeatedly to reverse various corrections.

Grammar checking

The spelling and grammar checker is a pretty big work tool just to detect obvious spelling mistakes. Also it cannot detect missing words or words with a mistaken meaning. The checker does, however, have the ability to analyse the grammar of an individual sentence against set criteria.

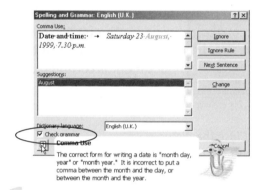

For this purpose, tick the *Check grammar* check box.

In this case you will be shown the result of the grammatical analysis. You will receive additional correction suggestions.

While spelling mistakes are marked in red, the grammar checker marks critical passages in green.

2 Correct the mangled passage in the *Grammatical error* text box, or highlight the suggested correction.

3 Click the *Change* button to take up the correction.

With the other buttons you can ignore the correction, bypass the grammatical rule or pass on to check the next sentence.

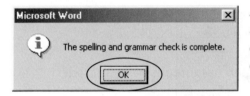

As soon as this dialog box appears, the spelling and grammar checking of the document is complete.

4 Close the dialog box with the *OK* button.

Further details about spelling and grammar checking are available with the application *Help* utility. In chapter 11 you will learn how to handle AutoCorrect entries.

Test your knowledge

You have now encountered the most important Word functions for creating simple text documents. You can format, save, print and reload a document. To check your knowledge, you should answer the following questions. The answers are on page 581.

1   How do you save a document under a new name?

2   How do you create a document in which the lines are centrally justified?

3   How can a text passage be changed to a bigger font?

4   How can the spacing between paragraphs be increased?

5   What is there to note about the right margin when entering text?

6   How do you move a text passage within a document?

In the following chapters you will learn about further functions used in Word.

What's in this chapter?

After learning the basics of Microsoft Word it is time to start using the program as a workhorse for the daily grind. What about turning out letters, a stylish telephone list or an invoice? With the right approach this will be no big problem. In some instances, Word even offers support in the form of task-specific templates. Here you will find all you need to know about using these templates. In the process, you will also learn how letters are correctly formatted and fine-tuned in Word.

Let's write a letter

The most frequent use for Word is almost certainly the production of letters. Many companies use pre-printed form letters to speed the process. The disadvantage of this is that as soon as a detail such as the company's address or telephone number changes, the printed form letters have to be thrown away. Therefore more and more users are starting to use Word to produce the forms themselves. Below you will find out how letters are written in Word and how in some cases they can be based on form letters.

Loading a document template

We will begin with a simple letter, and then adapt it step by step to our needs. The basics of working with Word were covered in the previous chapter. Are you ready for more advanced word processing with Word?

1 Start Microsoft Word.

You could now (as if using a typewriter) type in the text of the letter laid out appropriately. However, you should leave the job of formatting the letter largely to Word, by using one of the letter templates provided.

The first thing you need is a clean sheet. Perhaps you remember from Chapter 2 how to open a blank sheet using the *New Blank Document* button? Unfortunately that method is of little use here; you need to **use a ready-made letter form**. To do this, execute the following steps:

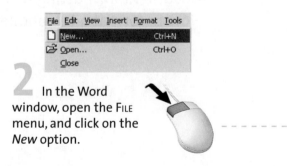

2 In the Word window, open the FILE menu, and click on the *New* option.

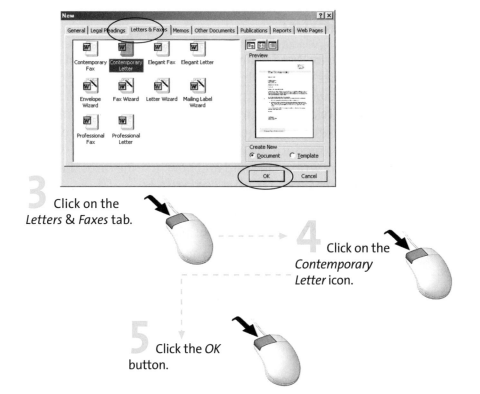

3 Click on the *Letters* & *Faxes* tab.

4 Click on the *Contemporary Letter* icon.

5 Click the *OK* button.

Microsoft Word now creates a new page, which already contains a complete, prepared letter template.

You need only insert the necessary recipient and return address details and type in the body of your letter. The document is finished.

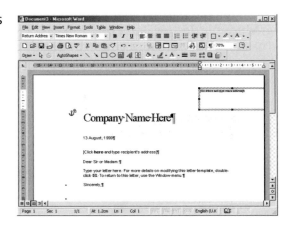

Adding the letter text to the template

Have you completed the above steps? If you have, the Word window should display the letter structure. At various places in the document you are invited to enter text.

As soon as you click on such a place, Word surrounds it with a hatched border. These are **boundary frames**, which make it easy to position text freely on the page.

[Click here and type return address]

An insurance claims report will serve as an example, in which a worried colleague is reporting an accident. Execute the following steps to produce the desired letter on the basis of the template.

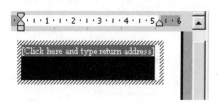

1 In the letterhead at the top right click the return address section.

2 Enter your return address in the frame.

The result might then look something like this. Leave the left alignment unchanged, and use several lines.

11·August,·1999¶

3 Now select the company name line.

4 Type in your company name. if it is a private letter, remove this line by pressing the ⌦(Del) key.

[Click **here** and type recipient's address]¶

5 Click the line with the recipient's address.

Designs·Inc¶
188·Long·Lane·Rd·¶
Sheffield¶
S4·8GA¶

6 Type in the recipient's address.

Dear·Sir·or·Madam:¶

Type·your·letter·here.·For·more·details·on·modifying· this·letter·template,·double-click·⊠.·To·return·to·this· letter,·use·the·Window·menu.¶

Sincerely,¶

7 The template offers the default formula 'Dear Sir or Madam' and salutation 'Sincerely'.

127

There is a catch to **entering** the **recipient's address**. If you press the ⏎ key at the end of the first line, the cursor automatically 'jumps' out of the boundary frame to the next section. To avoid this difficulty when entering the address, at the end of each line use the ⇧+⏎ key combination. Word then inserts a line break instead of a paragraph break. The text continues in the next line, the paragraph marker remains unchanged. Line breaks are marked by a small bent arrow.

8 Now complete the entries for 'Your name' and 'Job title' at the bottom.

In a private letter, simply select the job title line and remove it by pressing the Del key. If you make a mistake while completing or deleting lines, undo your action by pressing the Ctrl+Z key combination or the Undo ↰ button.

9 Click on 'Click here and type your name'.

10 You can type in 'Your name.' and 'job title.' if required.

The text is displayed in bold whenever the original text has bold formatting.

11 You can click on the **B** button, to undo the bold formatting.

12 Enter a blank space and then type 'Damage Report'.

The result should then look something like this.

13 Now select the section containing the letter and enter your own text.

Dear·Sir·or·Madam:¶

Damage·Report¶

We·would·like·to·draw·your·attention·to·the·ever·increasing·problem·of·damaged·l·files;·we·would·therefore·suggest·that·before·files·are·brought·to·us·they·are·checked.¶

Yours·faithfully,¶

Paul·Watkinson¶
Graphic·Design¶

14 Finally add your company name again underneath the 'type your name' and 'type job title' lines.

Remember that for a private letter, you can also remove the lines relating to your job title.

15 Now click the bottom line.

Here you can enter a slogan or erase the line.

16 Now click the 🔍 button.

Your letter should now look like the adjacent illustration, in page layout view.

TIP

How to work in page layout view was covered in Chapter 2.

If required, this letter can now be saved in a file, and also printed. What do you think of the result?

As you see, letter-writing is very easy in Microsoft Word. By using a predefined template you obtain an instant, preformatted letter form, which needs only to be adapted to your needs. It couldn't be simpler, could it?

TIP

In the *New* dialog box Word offers **templates for different types of document**. As well as letters, you can also create faxes, CVs, memos, brochures and reports among other things. Simply load the relevant template and complete it as you wish. You have just covered the necessary steps in the above pages.

Creating a letter template

Do you find the templates supplied with Word to be unsuitable, or maybe frustrating? You will probably quickly find that for each new letter you have to make adaptations to the selected letter template.

⇨ It is annoying having to enter your sender details afresh each time. Your address is constant, and could easily be part of the template.

⇉ If you use printed letterhead stationery, you have to delete the entry in the template letterhead each time. This means a great deal of adapting must be done.

⇉ The layout used in Word letter templates is not to everyone's taste. True, Word offers a variety of templates, but not all are necessarily suitable for the intended purpose.

If you write few private letters, you can perhaps live with these Word restrictions, but to set up and save a template for your own letters is a sensible thing to do. This will not only reduce the frustration factor, but ensure that the layout will be tuned to your needs, whether you use printed letterheads or not.

Preparing your own letter template

In view of these restrictions, the Word document templates lead only a shadowy existence in my own case. Very early on, I set up my own templates for the most important documents (private letter, business letter, invoice, fax etc.). This is not particularly difficult to do. Therefore I recommend you to make your own templates according to the following steps.

TIP

For private letters the formatting of the template is broadly unrestricted. In business correspondence, letters should be formatted to A4 size. Word has default values for width (8.5") and height (11"). A letter formatted to these standards follows with the illustrated layout. Obviously, the page had to be compressed for reasons of space. An A4 sheet is 210 mm wide and 297 mm long, with a 1" top and bottom margins. Word sets minimum margins for letters at 1.25" for the left margin and 1.25" for the right margin. For the font size, a minimum of 10 points is specified. Both header and footer are set at 0.49" from the edge. The first line contains a name or the means of delivery (e.g. Registered). The last line is reserved for the (not highlighted) postal place name. Further components of the letter are reference and subject blocks, greetings, salutation, signature and enclosures blocks. These components are separated by a specified number of empty lines. Since paragraph markers are not printed, empty lines are marked in the following diagram by small dots. There are no rules determing the format of the footer.

CyberTechnics

620 Attercliffe Rd.
Sheffield
Tel 0114 2431000

CyberTechnics 620 Attercliffe Road Sheffield

Mark Kemp
Design Inc
188 Long Lane Rd
Sheffield

S4 8GA

Your Ref	Your Messages	Our Ref	Our Messages	Telephone number	Date
		P.W		0114 2438795	13 August 1999

Invoice number 002045

Dear Mr Kemp

Re Design Printouts

Thank you for your payment received 12th August 1999, however the amount is £25.50 short due to the fact that you have taken off the 10% discount that we had already included in the price.

Yours sincerely

Paul Watkinson

Enclosures

Bank connection D2   Account No 14789   BLZ 300 700 00

If you need a non-standard template, simply leave out the corresponding elements. For example, if you print on printed company letterheads, leave out the steps defining the letterhead. If you don't need the bank details, leave the footer out. You could also leave out the lines with the 'Your Ref' text. Instead, at the right margin insert the text, 'Place, the Date' in the relevant line. In this way, you can very quickly create individual templates.

Now execute the following steps, and enter the text with your address, etc. in appropriate places. Then you will have your own template for letters.

1 In the Word window, click on the *New* button, to load a new, empty document in which to create the template.

2 On the Word standard toolbar, click on the *Show/ Hide* button.

This toggles the display of hidden paragraph end markers.

You could also adapt a Word-prepared template. This throws up various problems however, since Microsoft uses certain techniques for creating document templates. I have therefore decided to create the letter template starting from an empty document.

3 In the bottom-left corner of the document window, click the *Print Layout View* button.

4 Select the first paragraph marker in the document.

5 Set the font to 'Times New Roman' and the font size to 10 points.

These preliminaries help you with the next steps. For example, the switch to *Print Layout View* causes the horizontal and vertical rulers to be displayed. The font style and size settings ensure that the text will print in sensibly sized letters. If you prefer, you could increase the font size from 10 to 11 or even 12 points. Personally I prefer 10 point, since this is adequate for most letters.

Setting page margins

While Word sets margins to DIN-standard (the original German abbreviation of *German Industry Standards*) by default, you should check these for safety's sake before starting to format a document.

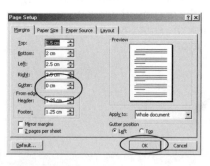

1 In the FILE menu, select the *Page setup* command.

2 In the *Margins* tab, set the *Left* and *Right* margins or accept the default ones.

3 Close the tab with the *OK* button.

The settings as displayed correspond to DIN 5008. The 1.25" left margin means that the address when printed will be visible from a window envelope.

To create the letterhead

In principle you could now type in the letterhead and insert the other elements in the layout. However, at this point I would like to bring in a brief preliminary consideration. On the one hand, a letter contains some components (such as the sender's address), which never or very rarely need changing. Here it would be good if you could **protect** such components from **unintentional alteration**. Word offers both headers and footers for document pages. When you type normally on a page with a header or footer, these are not altered. We shall now put this knowledge to good use.

There are no standard rules regarding headers. You can therefore have a left-aligned or centred address. In this example the address will be at the top right.

1 In the VIEW menu, select *Header and Footer*.

Is this command missing from your view menu? Then click the symbol at the bottom of the menu ⌄ . Word then displays the less frequently used commands for this menu.

Now you can form the letterhead with company name and return address.

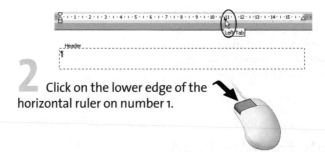

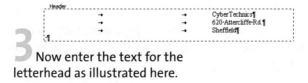

2 Click on the lower edge of the horizontal ruler on number 1.

This sets a tab stop at this position. Now when you press the ⇥ key, the text cursor jumps to the predefined tab stop. This is helpful if, for example, you want to arrange text at the upper-right margin of the letterhead.

3 Now enter the text for the letterhead as illustrated here.

Each new line is shifted to the the same position on the right by pressing the ⇥ key.

4 Select and format each line.

The letterhead might then look as pictured on the right.

→ **CyberTechnics¶**

→ 620·Attercliffe·Rd.¶
→ Sheffield¶
→ Tel·0114·2431000¶

The header should have a depth of 4.5 cm.

The telephone number has been added on a separate line. Also, the lines have been formatted with different font sizes.

To create the address block

Now is the time to **position** the **address block**, so that both the sender and recipient details will be visible in the window of the envelope. According to Word default values, the left margin is to be set at 1.45" and the right margin at 1.25". The top and bottom distance is set at 1".

In an empty Word document, the left margin of the letter template is already set at 1.25". We need now only insert a few empty lines, which move the sender details down to the upper edge of the address block.

Using a boundary frame, you can set the position of the address block to match exactly the window envelope you are using with the paragraph format dialog (*see* Chapter 2). For practical considerations, however, we will use a technique that makes sure that the address details (even given inexact folding) show in the envelope window, but in some cases differ from the Word default values by several millimetres. Furthermore, the sender details are positioned here in the window. If you want to be more precise, a tip for adjusting a text area for an address block is given below.

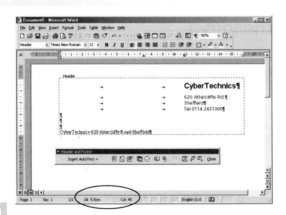

1 Press the ⇧ key a few time, until the (approx.) measurement 'At 5.3 cm' appears in the status bar.

The vertical distance measurement can vary a little, depending on the font size.

What is important is that the minimum distance from the top edge is reached.

2 Now type in the sender details. ------► **3** Format the sender details to an 8 point font with underlining.

With these three steps, you have arranged the sender detail in the letterhead so that it will later be visible in the envelope window. Consequently you have saved yourself the need to write it on the

> TIP
> The remaining lines for the address details have been ignored here, because these lines must be located in the document body. However, by including the sender address in the document header, we have ensured that this is protected against unintentional change.

envelope. If you use envelopes printed with sender details, leave the line with the sender details empty.

Completing the footer

The footer of a letter is often used to list bank connections or other details such as directors names. To make use of this area, proceed as follows:

1 In the Header and Footer toolbar, click the *Switch Between Header and Footer* button, or brow down to the bottom of the page.

Word now displays the footer. To make the arrangement of text in the footer easier, a table should be inserted. A table has rows and columns. You can insert text in each table cell. Thus text can easily be arranged in columns. To insert a table, the following steps must be followed:

2 In the standard toolbar, click the *Insert Table* button.

Word opens a **palette** for **selecting the size of table**. Each box in the palette represents a table cell.

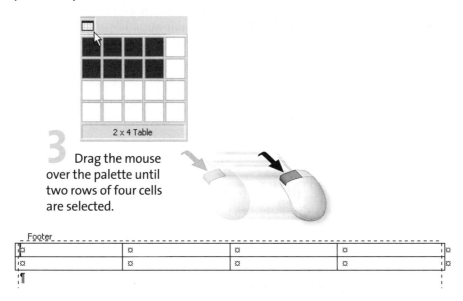

3 Drag the mouse over the palette until two rows of four cells are selected.

When you release the mouse button, Word inserts a table into the footer. The lines outlining the table are rather annoying. These lines shall now be removed.

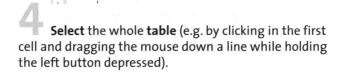

4 **Select** the whole **table** (e.g. by clicking in the first cell and dragging the mouse down a line while holding the left button depressed).

139

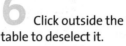

5 On the formatting toolbar, click the *Outside Border* button and then on *No Border*, as illustrated.

6 Click outside the table to deselect it.

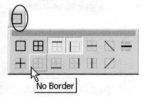

Windows now removes the solid black lines from the table and replaces them with faint gray lines (called **gridlines**). These give only a hint of the table structure and disappear when printed.

| CyberTechnics¤ | Attercliffe Rd¤ | Sheffield¤ | S9·3QS¤ | ¤ |
| ¤ | ¤ | ¤ | ¤ | ¤ |

7 Now click in each cell of the table and enter the desired text for the footer block.

8 When the footer block is complete, close the Header and Footer display by clicking the *Close* button on the Header and Footer toolbar.

Word now shows you the text input area in the document window. The text you just inserted in the header and footer blocks is seen in greyed-out style.

Because of the table cell structure, data in the footer block can easily be arranged and formatted. If you do not need the footer block, bypass the above steps or leave the table empty.

Folding marks wanted?

Pre-printed forms and letterheads often feature folding markings. This facilitates folding and insertion into envelopes, and also hole-punching for filing. Wouldn't it be great if your letter template was provided with such marking? Just execute the following extra steps:

 Double-click at the top of the document on the greyed-out text of the header.

Word changes immediately to Header and Footer edit mode. This only works, however, when a header already exists.

 In the standard toolbar, click the *Drawing* button.

141

Word now displays the drawing toolbar (usually at the bottom of the window).

3 Click the *Line* button.

While this button displays as 'pressed', you can **draw lines in the document.**

4 Now click with the mouse at the left edge of the paper, about 10.5 cm below the top edge.

5 Hold down the mouse button, and draw a short horizontal line.

When you release the mouse button, Word inserts a short black line at the left edge. This is the position of the fold mark, i.e. the letter must be folded here for insertion in the envelope.

Accurate positioning of this mark with the mouse to the prescribed offset is almost impossible. So now perform the following additional steps.

1 Click on the line with the right mouse button.

2 Click on the *Format AutoShape* option, and its dialog box opens.

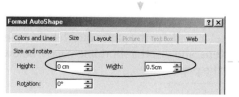

3 In the *Size* tab, set the *Height* to 0 cm and the *Width* to 0.5 cm.

4 Switch to the *Layout* tab and click on the *Advanced* button.

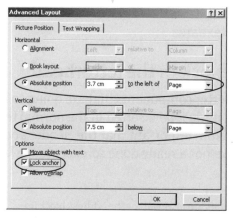

5 In the *Horizontal* section, select, the *Absolute position* option button and set the position to 3.7 cm 'to the left of Page'.

6 In the *Vertical* section, select the *Absolute Position* option and set the position to 7.5 cm 'below Page'.

143

7 Activate the *Lock anchor* control box.

8 Close the dialog box by clicking the *OK* button.

With this technique you have positioned the upper fold mark at the left edge. Step 7 is important, as it anchors the line to a fixed position on the page.

1 To set a mark for the paper punch hole, repeat the above steps, and insert a short line 11.5 cm below the top edge of the paper.

2 If needed, you can insert a second marker line 17.5 cm from the top edge.

3 Then click the *Close* button in the Header and Footer toolbar.

Word returns to the document text area.

Inserting the address block in the letterhead

The address block is one of the letter components that are going to be continually modified. Therefore it must be inserted in the normal text area. For the next step, it is therefore important that the Header and Footer mode is ended. If you have not already done so, execute the last step in the previous section.

According to the standard rules, nine lines are reserved for the address block (in which the first line details the mode of delivery). In the current outline, however, the sender details were inserted in the header. The remaining lines are for the mode of delivery, special instructions, the company name or form of address, and the street and place names. In some languages addresses, street and town names can be separated by an empty line, but in English they are not separated.

By creating the sender detail in the header block of the letter outline, the first line of the text area already begins at the correct position in the address block. Since the sender details are already present, up to eight lines remain for the address details.

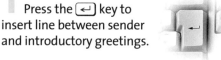

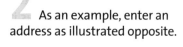 As an example, enter an address as illustrated opposite.

1 Press the ⏎ key to insert line between sender and introductory greetings.

If you enter address details in the template, it will later be immediately clear what should be entered in what line. The letter writer need only click on a line of text and then replace or overtype the text; the formatting will remain intact.

Town names can be all uppercase. Or you can separate the town name with an empty line. The country code (UK, I, CH) is not required for addresses within a country. It is only to be added perhaps on a separate line after the postcode if the letter is for another country.

Using an address block boundary frame

Some users prefer to insert a movable address block in the letter. I have not used this technique, since many users have experienced problems lining up text in boundary frames (the frame is quickly shifted or removed). Since there are no longer frames in Word 2000 (at least in the form known in past versions), we will use a text box for this purpose.

Proceed as follows:

1 First insert some empty lines in the document.

This ensures that later you will have paragraphs ready and waiting when you want to create the remaining letter components.

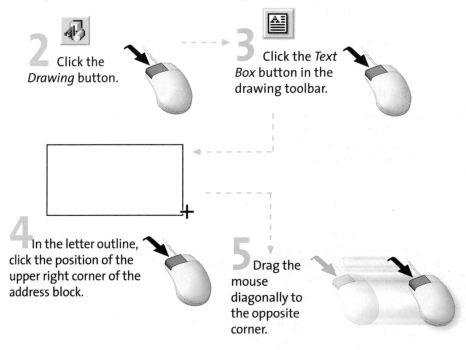

2 Click the *Drawing* button.

3 Click the *Text Box* button in the drawing toolbar.

4 In the letter outline, click the position of the upper right corner of the address block.

5 Drag the mouse diagonally to the opposite corner.

Word now produces a text box, which is framed with a line. You will remove this line.

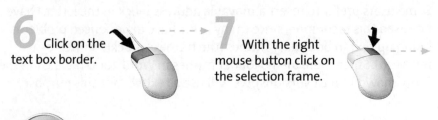

6 Click on the text box border.

7 With the right mouse button click on the selection frame.

8 In the shortcut menu, select the *Format Text Box* command.

9 In the Line section of the *Colors and Lines* tab, set the Colour value to 'No Line'.

10 Change to the *Size* tab.

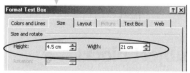

11 Set the height to 4.5 cm and the width to 21 cm.

12 Switch to the *Layout* tab, and click on the *Advanced* button.

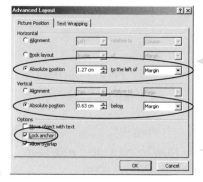

13 Set the position of the text box according to the adjacent illustration.

14 Select the option box *Lock anchor*.

15 Close the open dialog box with the *OK* button.

Finally, you can enter the lines for the sender details in the text box.

Creating reference and subject blocks

As a rule, business letters contain a reference block, in which official correspondence references, telephone numbers, respondents, and so on are specified. To **create** this **reference line**, the following steps must be executed:

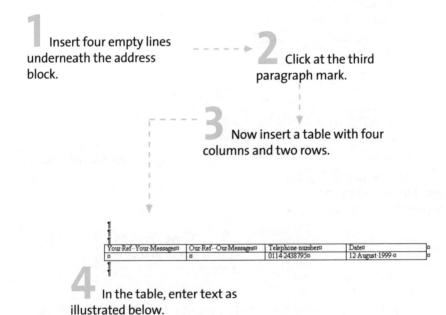

1 Insert four empty lines underneath the address block.

2 Click at the third paragraph mark.

3 Now insert a table with four columns and two rows.

| Your·Ref···Your·Messages¤ | Our·Ref···Our·Messages¤ | Telephone·number¤ | Date¤ | ¤ |
| ¤ | ¤ | 0114·2438795¤ | 12·August·1999·¤ | ¤ |

4 In the table, enter text as illustrated below.

When inserting a table, always be sure to leave an empty paragraph below it. You will find this convenient for entering further text. The technique for working with tables was covered while creating a footer. To make an entry in the table, simply click in the relevant cell. The text in the first row defines the column headings, and should be changed to 8 point size after entry. The lower row, on the other hand, retains the 10 point font size. When creating the table you can pre-enter everything that never or seldom changes (such as telephone number, name).

Use the horizontal ruler to adjust the cell widths to suit. Many users do not use a table for references block, preferring to use tabstops instead. I prefer a table, as it makes text alignment in cells very easy.

The **date** entered on the extreme right illustrates a special feature. It would surely be handy if Word would insert the actual date on which the letter is printed. This can be arranged with a few clicks of the mouse.

1 Click in the table cell in which the date should appear.

2 In the INSERT menu, select the *Field* option.

Word now opens the *Field* dialog box, in which you select fields for insertion.

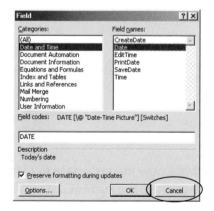

149

3 In the *Categories* list, click 'Date and Time'.

4 In the *Field names* list, click 'Date'.

5 Click on the *Options* button.

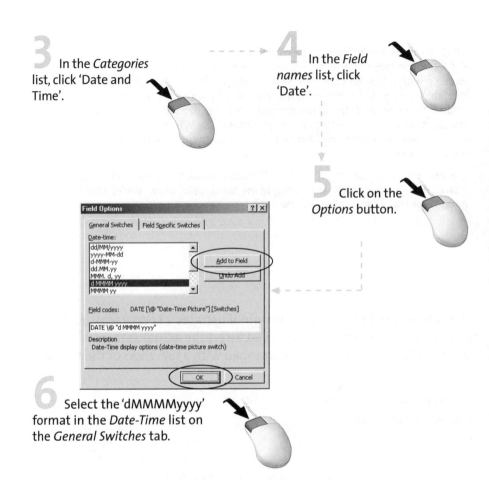

6 Select the 'dMMMMyyyy' format in the *Date-Time* list on the *General Switches* tab.

This format causes the name of the month to be displayed in full. If space is short, select the 'd-MMM-yy' shortform format.

7 Click the *Add to Field* button.

8 Close both dialog boxes using the *OK* buttons.

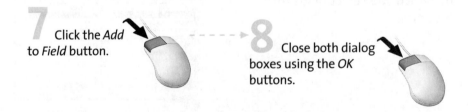

Word now inserts a date field in the table cell. Whenever the document is opened, the current date will be displayed in that cell.

A **field** is a placeholder for data whose value will be determined and inserted by a Word function. In the above case, the field value is the current date, updated automatically each time the letter template is loaded. To update a field manually, select it and press the [F9] function key. Pressing [⇧]+[F9] toggles the display between the field codes and the field value.

Do you want to put together a private letter? Then reference details are not suitable. In this case, omit the table. Instead, add a line with the text 'Place, the...'. Instead of the three stops ..., insert a date field as before. Now you can either right-align the whole line or move the text to the right using the tabulator key.

¶

¶   Thursday,·August·12,·1999 ¶
Object¶
¶

We still need an object block. As a rule, this is located two lines below the reference block and formatted in bold font style.

1 Immediately below the reference block table, insert two empty lines.

2 Enter the word 'Object'.

3 Select the whole line and give it bold formatting.

When the letter is actually being written, a short sentence can be added here, detailing the object of the letter. This step completes the letter heading.

151

Salutation, letter text and closing

To facilitate your writing the actual letter at a later date, I recommend that you add the remaining substitute letter text composed of a form of salutation, a short sentence for the text body, and a form of closing. Further to this, you can still enter the term 'Enclosures:' at the end of the letter.

1 Immediately below the object block, insert two empty lines.

2 On the next line enter the text 'Dear Sir or Madam'.

4 Below this, enter a form of closing, such as 'Yours faithfully'.

3 Now insert a few empty lines, which will later be taken up by the body of the letter.

5 Insert a few empty lines and then enter the term 'Enclosures:' in bold script.

The end of the letter outline now looks like this.

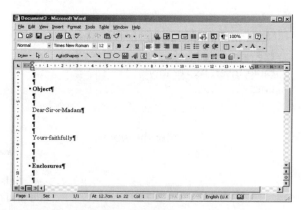

When you come to write a letter, be sure that your closing does not end with a comma, and is separated from the letter body by at least an empty line. The same applies to the Introductory greeting, which, in English, should never be followed by a comma. The first word should always start with an uppercase letter.

Saving the outline as a document template

Have you created a form letter following the above methods? Then it is time to **save** this form letter as a **document template**. This is almost the same as saving a normal document file.

 In the FILE menu, select the command *Save As*.

Word now opens the *Save As* dialog box.

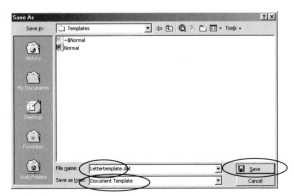

2 Set the *Save as type* list box to 'Document Template'.

When you select the template file type, Word automatically uses the folder in which templates are saved. In the *Save in* box the name 'Templates' appears. The location of this folder can be specified in User templates on the *File Locations* tab of the TOOLS/OPTIONS dialog.

3 Now enter a name (e.g. Lettertemplate.dot) in the *Field name* box.

 4 Click the *Save* button.

5 Close the document window.

Word saves the document as a template.

Composing a letter

When you later want to **write** a **letter** using this **template**, execute the following steps:

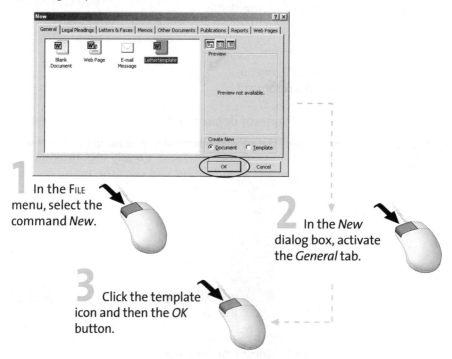

1 In the FILE menu, select the command *New*.

2 In the *New* dialog box, activate the *General* tab.

3 Click the template icon and then the *OK* button.

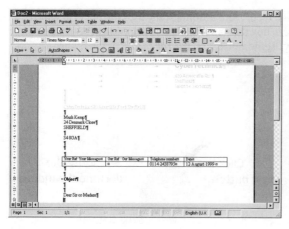

Word loads the template and displays the text as a document. You need now only undertake the completion of the address and write the body of the letter. This corresponds to the procedure for working with a Word template outlined at the start of this chapter.

As you see, it is not particularly difficult to create a document template. You simply compose a sample document. In this, you use the functions Word offers for composing and formatting documents. Finally, you save the result as a *.dot* file in the Templates folder. In this way you can create templates for business letters, invoices, private letters, faxes etc. It couldn't be easier.

Creating invoices

Invoices represent another type of document frequently encountered. Basically it is a letter in which invoice amounts are listed and then added up. Word can be used for this purpose. You have already met most of the necessary functions in the previous chapters and sections. In the following we will see how to write an invoice in Word using the letter template you have just created.

1 Start Word and using the FILE/*New* dialog load the template you have just created.

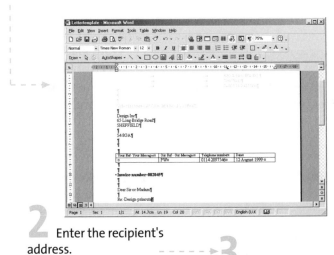

2 Enter the recipient's address.

3 Adapt the data in the reference box as necessary.

4 In the Object line, enter the invoice number. - - - - ▶ **5** Enter a text for the invoice.

After these preliminaries you can list the individual invoice items in the text block, and also put the individual sums and the total sum. To facilitate this procedure, I recommend that you use a simple three-column table.

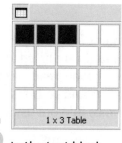

1 x 3 Table

6 In the text block, insert a single-row table with three columns.

7 If necessary, select the table and remove the border lines.

The individual steps were outlined in previous pages while creating the letter template (*see* section 'Completing the footer').

Description·¤	Item·code¤
¤	¤

8 With the mouse, select the vertical dividing lines between the table cells and drag them in the desired direction, left or right.

In this way, adjust the width of the individual table columns as necessary.

9 Enter the column headings in the first row of the table and format them as necessary. - - - - ▶ **10** Next, enter the individual invoice items.

Pressing the ⟨⇥⟩ key moves the insertion point from one table cell to the next. The ⟨⇧⟩+⟨⇥⟩ key combination moves the insertion point to the cell on the left. When you press the ⟨⇥⟩ key in the last cell of a row, Word moves the insertion point to the first cell of the next row down. If you press the tab key in the final cell at the lower right corner, Word adds a new row automatically. Instead of using the tab key to move between cells, you can simply click with the mouse in the relevant cell and then enter the cell content.

When you format the last row in a table or the last paragraph of a document, pressing ⟨⇧⟩ causes the formatting to be adopted for the next line/row. You can forestall this by adding the next line/row before formatting the immediate line/row.

If all has gone to plan, the table structure should appear as illustrated below.

Description·¤	Item·code¤	Amount¤
Digital·Printing·A4¤	DIG·1¤	€6.00¤
Scanning·¤	Sca¤	€12.00¤
Film·Output···A4·cmyk¤	A4·CMYK¤	€32.00¤
Sub·Total¤	¤	€40.00¤
Vat·17.5%¤	¤	€6.80¤
Total·cost¤	¤	€46.80¤

The currency amounts are already provided with a euro sign. Is this sign missing from your keyboard? Then press the ⟨AltGr⟩+⟨E⟩ key combination. The euro sign will be inserted at the insertion point.

A table allows you to list individual invoice items exactly under each other. Invoice amounts are listed in the end column.

Aligning currency amounts

In the illustrated table, the 'Amount' heading is already centred in the table column. If you have a problem with alignment within the table, here is a short tutorial.

157

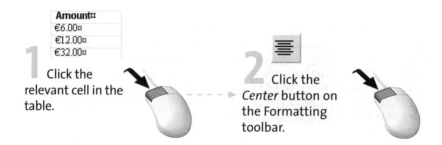

1 Click the relevant cell in the table.

2 Click the *Center* button on the Formatting toolbar.

The cell content will be centred, but there is still a problem with the 'Amount' column. The **currency amounts** are of different widths and consequently not centred cleanly in a vertical line. How do we correct this **alignment**? The aim should be to arrange the currency amounts so that the decimal points are vertically aligned. A left or centred alignment does not help, because the different numbers of digits prevent a columnwise alignment.

The solution is to use tabs. In Word you can set tabs in a table. Working with tab stops was already covered at the start of Chapter 2. Now comes a small additional use.

1 Select the cells that are to hold currency amounts (e.g. by clicking in the first cell and dragging the mouse through the remaining cells).

2 Now keep clicking the tab icon at the left end of the horizontal ruler.

3 When the 'decimal tab stop' icon appears, click on the lower edge of the horizontal ruler at the position where the tab stop should be inserted.

A broken line shows the position of the tab stop.

As soon as a decimal tab stop is set, Word aligns the decimal points of the currency amounts in line with the tab stop. The currency amounts are thus correctly aligned under each other in the column.

4 Click on another part of the table to deselect the cells.

The contents of the table column are now correspondingly aligned.

Table calculations

After these preliminaries, it is now time to **find** the **sum** of the **individual amounts**, calculate the **VAT** and the grand total. Do you already have your pocket calculator ready? Relax: to calculate such values you aren't dependent on your old abacus. Word can handle this task to a certain degree.

1 Click in the table cell in which the calculated results should be displayed. 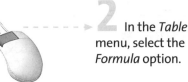 **2** In the *Table* menu, select the *Formula* option.

Word opens the *Formula* dialog box.

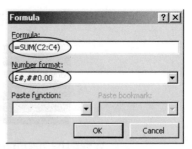

4 In the *Number format* list box, select the desired format.

3 In the *Formula* box, enter the expression for calculation.

5 Close the dialog box with the *OK* button.

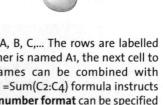

Columns in a table are labelled alphabetically A, B, C,... The rows are labelled numerically 1, 2, ... The cell in the upper left corner is named A1, the next cell to the right is named B1. In formulas, cell names can be combined with mathematical operators (+, -, *, /, sum etc.). The =Sum(C2:C4) formula instructs Word to calculate the sum of cells C2 to C4. The **number format** can be specified in the Number format list box. The euro sign was added manually to the format specification. As you see, even this is no problem. The above diagram shows the formula for the **calculation** of the **subtotal**.

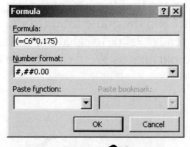

6 Click in the cell for the VAT amount.

7 Access the *Formula* dialog box, and enter the formula =C5*0.175 as in the adjacent illustration.

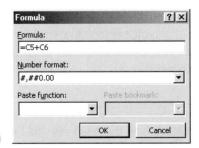

8 In the same manner, insert the illustrated formula (=C5+C6) to calculate the total amount.

Description¤	Item·code¤	Amount¤
Digital·Printing·A4¤	DIG·1¤	€6.00¤
Scanning·¤	Sca¤	€12.00¤
Film·Output···A4·cmyk¤	A4·CMYK¤	€32.00¤
Sub·Total¤	¤	€50.00¤
Vat·17.5%¤	¤	€8.750¤
Total·cost¤	¤	··€58.75¤

9 Select the last two cells in the amount column and add bold, underlined formatting.

After the totals have been calculated, add the remaining text to the invoice. This should then look like the layout illustrated below.

Finally you can spell check the document, save it in a file and print it. The treatment of an invoice is just like that for any other text document. The only difference is the procedure for letting Word perform the calculations in a table.

To add some cells, click on the result cell and then on the *Tables and Borders* button ⊞. In the Tables and Borders toolbar, select the Σ button. Word now automatically inserts the correct addition formula into the current cell, the sum of the adjacent cells is calculated.

Document formatting techniques

The previous pages have already covered several Word functions. These functions enable you to create the more useful types of document, save them and print them. As time passes, you will want to use additional functions. In the following sections I would like to introduce you to some convenience functions, and to some extra options.

Inserting document building blocks with Autotext

When writing letters and other documents, you frequently use the same set form phrases, such as 'Dear Madam', 'Dear Sir', 'Dear Sir or Madam', 'Yours faithfully', and 'With all best wishes'. Typing in a few characters may be no big deal, but busy typists are interested in any labour-saving devices. Wouldn't it be great if such standard phrases could be called up by a mouse click or a key combination?

1 In Microsoft Word, open a new empty document.

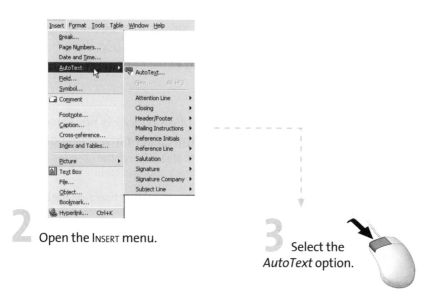

2 Open the INSERT menu.

3 Select the *AutoText* option.

Word now opens a submenu with various predefined building block entries.

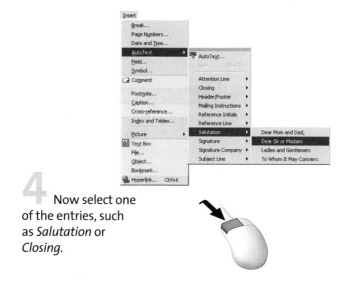

4 Now select one of the entries, such as *Salutation* or *Closing*.

Word displays a further submenu of AutoText entries.

5 Click on the desired text (e.g. Dear Sir or Madam).

¶
Dear·Sir·or·Madam:¶
¶
¶

The matching text building block is now inserted in the document at the current insertion point.

TIP

In Chapter 2 you covered the *AutoComplete* function. This function automatically inserts certain words after the input of a few characters. The *AutoCorrect* function also permits automatic correction while typing (e.g. 'allways' is corrected automatically to 'always'). Which function you use is up to you.

How to define an AutoText entry

Do you need your own document building blocks, which you would like to record as AutoText? Even this is no problem. It only takes a few mouse clicks.

1 Type the desired text in the document.

Greetings·from·Paul

2 Select the text.

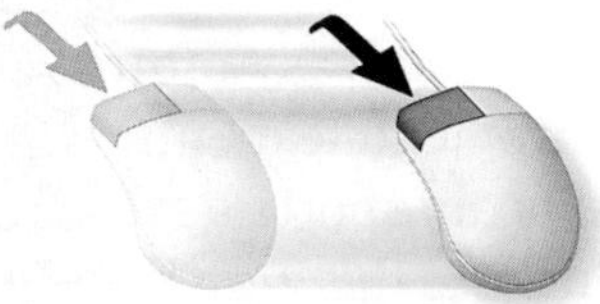

3 In the INSERT menu, select the *AutoText* option, and then the *New* command in the submenu. Alternatively, press the Alt+F3 key combination.

TIP

Unless you want to include the paragraph end marker for formatting purposes, make sure that you select only the text without the marker.

Word opens the *Create AutoText* dialog box.

5 Click *OK.*

4 If necessary, amend the entry in the *Please name your Autotext* text box.

Word records the AutoText entry in the *AutoText/Normal* submenu, from which you can recall it when required.

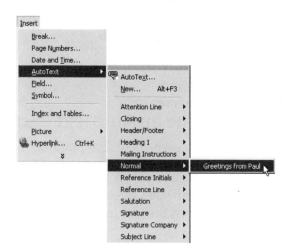

In this way you can build up a collection of frequently used phrases and access them as AutoText entries. But things can be even more convenient. Text entry will only become really efficient when you define keyboard shortcuts to access longer building blocks. I would like to illustrate this with the phrase 'With kind regards'.

1 Type the phrase in the document.

2 Select the phrase.

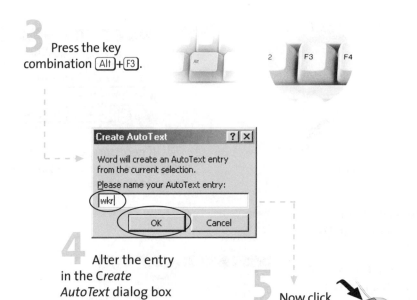

3 Press the key combination [Alt]+[F3].

Create AutoText [?][X]

Word will create an AutoText entry from the current selection.

Please name your AutoText entry:

wkr

OK   Cancel

4 Alter the entry in the *Create AutoText* dialog box to 'wkr'.

5 Now click *OK*.

The document building block is now recorded in AutoText under the name 'wkr'. You can open the INSERT/AUTOTEXT/NORMAL menu to check that the relevant entry is present (*see* page 165).

If an AutoText entry is already defined under the relevant name, Word opens a dialog box and asks whether you want to redefine the AutoText entry. Click the *Yes* button to change the entry; if you wish to keep the old entry click the *No* button and repeat the above steps, giving a new name for the AutoText entry however.

What is the point? Quite simply, accessing such a building block now occurs more quickly.

1 In the document type the letters 'wkr'.

2 Press the [F3] function key.

If all goes to plan, Word replaces the shortcut 'wkr' with the saved AutoText entry 'With kind regards'. How much easier can it get?

Do you often work with documents containing set phrases and boilerplate texts? This is frequently the case with bulk letters, offers, circulars etc. As described above, set up a collection of AutoText entries. When writing the documents, these relevant boilerplate texts and phrases can be accessed via menu or keyboard.

Want a couple more formatting methods?

In Chapter 2 you learnt how selected text could be formatted using the buttons on the formatting toolbar. When you click on one of these buttons, the style of any selected text is correspondingly altered. A second mouse click removes the formatting just applied. If no text is selected, pressing a format button activates the corresponding style of formatting. Subsequently typed text will be formatted accordingly.

Have you entered text with a certain **format** and would like now to **paste** this format to other places in the document? No problem; the solution is only a few mouse clicks away.

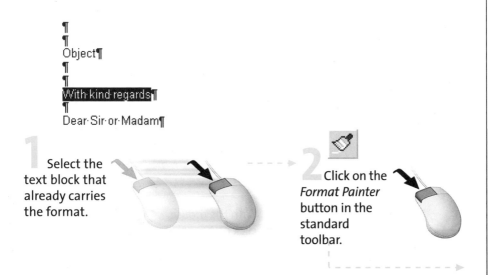

¶
¶
Object¶
¶
¶
With kind regards ¶
¶
Dear Sir or Madam¶

1 Select the text block that already carries the format.

2 Click on the *Format Painter* button in the standard toolbar.

3 Select the new text block with the mouse.

While you select a new block, the mouse cursor takes the form of a stylised paintbrush. The format is transferred when you release the mouse button. The new format becomes visible as soon as the block is deselected.

A single click on the *Format Painter* button lasts for one format transfer only. To format multiple selections, simply select the text whose formatting you want to copy, double-click the *Format Painter* button, and then select the text blocks you want to format. The mouse remains in Format Painter mode until you click on the (still depressed) button again.

A further problem concerns instances of **text** with **unusual formatting**. Sometimes text must be in **superscript** or **subscript** style. Or a number or a word should be **double-underlined**. Even colour enhanced text might be wanted. With a colour printer this could be transferred to the printed page. In Word, this is no problem. Perhaps you would like to try to format some text in *superscript*.

1 Select the text to be formatted.

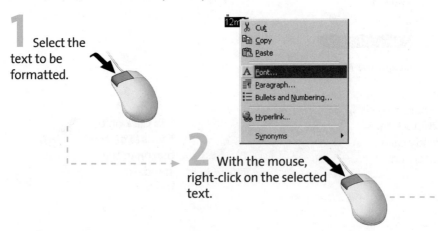

2 With the mouse, right-click on the selected text.

3 In the shortcut menu, select the *Font* option.

Word opens the *Font* tab, on which are to be found all the options for formatting the selected font. Now specify the desired format.

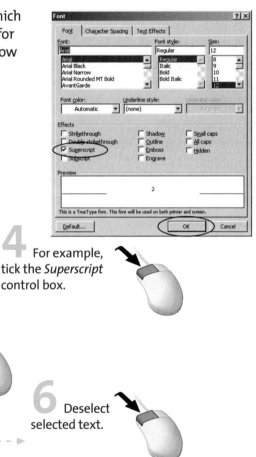

4 For example, tick the *Superscript* control box.

5 Close the dialog box with the *OK* button.

6 Deselect selected text.

$12m^2$ Word now displays the text block in the selected font.

On the *Font* tab, various **underline styles** are available in the *Underline* list box; similarly, different font colours are available in the *Color* list box on the same tab.

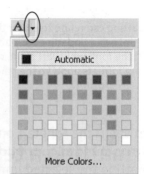

If you write a lot, you might find the above methods for formatting text rather fiddly. In this case, you might find the following table of key combinations more to your liking. If you press one of these key combinations, Word applies the relevant formatting immediately, either to already selected text or to the next text to be typed.

Key combination	Format
Ctrl+[ ]	Clear all formatting.
Ctrl+⇧+B	Toggle bold on/off.
Ctrl+⇧+I	Toggle italic on/off.
Ctrl+⇧+U	Toggle underline on/off.
Ctrl+⇧+D	Toggle double underline on/off.
Ctrl++	Toggle subscript on/off.
Ctrl+#	Toggle superscript on/off.
Ctrl+⇧+G	Toggle uppercase mode on/off.

Formatting can relate to either the paragraph or font.
Bold, italic and underline formatting, for example,
affect the font, while left align, right align and line
spacing formats apply to the paragraph.

Formatting a telephone list

Still on the topic of formatting, I would like to introduce some techniques for
formatting lists. A small telephone number list will serve as an example,
which can be for private or business use. To create this list, it is advisable to
resort to a table. You have already learnt how to create tables.

1 Open a new,
empty document.

2 Create a
table with at least
four columns.

3 Enter the
column headings in
the first row.

The table should now look something like the following illustration:

Name¤	Surname¤	Address¤	☎Telephone·No¤	¤
¤	¤	¤	¤	¤

If necessary, bold format can be used for the headings.

Inserting symbols and special characters

Have you already noticed the stylised symbol of a telephone in the last
table column? Such symbols and special characters appear in many
printed articles. How can they be inserted into a document? You will
discover here how easy it is to do.

1 Click at the point
in the text where the
relevant symbol is to be
inserted.

2 In the INSERT
menu, select the
Symbol option.

3 Word opens the *Symbol* dialog box. Select the *Symbols* tab.

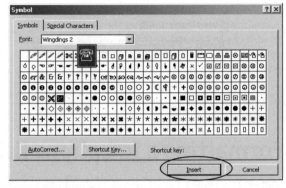

4 In the *Font* list box, select the desired font.

Graphic symbols are especially to be found in the 'Wingdings' font.

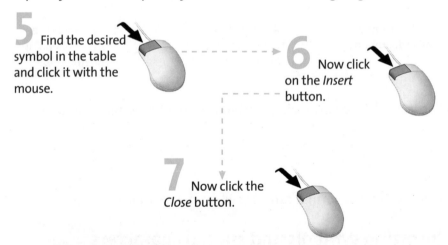

5 Find the desired symbol in the table and click it with the mouse.

6 Now click on the *Insert* button.

7 Now click the *Close* button.

Word has now inserted the selected symbol into the document. Like any other symbol, you can format, copy or delete it.

Working with tables

Have you entered and formatted the table column headings? Then you can now enter the names and telephone numbers. The result might look something like the following illustration.

·Telephone·List¶

Name¤	Surname¤	Address¤	☎Telephone·No¤	¤
Paul¤	Watkinson¤	56·Long·lane-Sheffield¤	0114·2456789¤	¤
Mark·¤	Kemp¤	24·Denmark·Close¤	0114·2789654¤	¤
Peter·¤	Agar¤	189·Whiteways·Rd¤	0114·2896575¤	¤
Ross¤	Keeble¤	2·High·Lane¤	01701·256876¤	¤
Adrian¤	Richards¤	4·Slap·Street¤	0114·2789560¤	¤
John¤	Richardson¤	87·Long·Street¤	0113·2568985¤	¤

¶

Perhaps your list is longer. For the next steps the above example will suffice. When you work with lists, sooner or later you will bump into certain problem areas, which I would now like to address in brief.

Have you taken a lot of trouble to create your list? But, when printing, did you find that there is one entry too many, or something is missing? What is to be done? How can the table be put right? Have no fear, you already know the relevant techniques. Earlier you learnt how to **adjust the width of a table column**. You place the mouse pointer on the dividing line between two cells. You can then move this line left or right by dragging with the mouse while keeping the left button depressed. You must be careful, however, not to select any cells, otherwise the width alteration will apply only to the selected cell(s). Here are a few further tips for working with tables.

To select cells in a table, simply click in the first cell and then draw the mouse over the remaining cells.

1 To select a row, click in the leftmargin beside the first cell in the row.

2 To select a column, click on the topmost line of the column heading.

Selected rows or columns can be cut, copied and pasted using the standard toolbar buttons illustrated on the left.

Cutting, copying and pasting blocks of text was covered in Chapter 2.

Do you need to further divide the cells in a table column? No problem, either.

1 In the standard toolbar, click on the button 🔲.

The mouse pointer takes the form of a pencil.

Surname¤		Address¤	☎
Watkinson¤	¦	56·Long·lane·Sheffield¤	01˙
Kemp¤	¦	24·Denmark·Close¤	01˙
Agar¤	¦	189·Whiteways·Rd¤	01˙
Keeble¤	¦	2·High·Lane¤	01˙
Richards¤	⌀	4·Slap·Street¤	01˙
Richardson¤	¦	87·Long·Street¤	01˙

2 With the pencil, 'draw' the desired dividing line in the table.

The broken line shows the position of the dividing line.

As soon as you release the mouse button, Word divides the relevant cells.

Surname¤	¤	Adi
Watkinson¤	¤	56·l
Kemp¤	¤	24·l
Agar¤	¤	189
Keeble¤	¤	2·H
Richards¤	¤	4·S
Richardson¤	¤	87·l

3 Click on the ⊞ button again to exit the *Tables and Borders* command drawing mode.

Earlier, we saw how to create simple tables using the *Insert Table* button. For more complex tables, however, you are advised to use the ⊞ *Tables and Borders* button. This lets you 'draw' your table with the 'pencil'. In the case of complex tables, this can be a great advantage.

Sorting a table

There is still another technique to be added to what you have learnt already about tables: how to sort a table using sort criteria. Telephone lists are usually arranged alphabetically by name. To **sort** the **table** according to the **content** of a given **column**, proceed as follows:

1 Click in a table cell, or select the relevant table column(s) or cells.

2 In the TABLE menu, select the *Sort* command.

If the command is not showing, click on the last entry at the bottom of the menu in order to display all the commands.

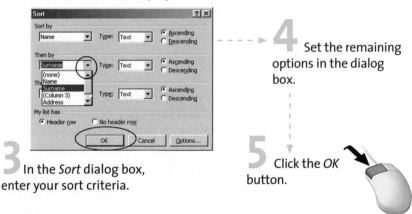

4 Set the remaining options in the dialog box.

3 In the *Sort* dialog box, enter your sort criteria.

5 Click the *OK* button.

Name¤	Surname¤
Adrian✶	Richards✶
John✶	Richardson✶
Mark·✶	Kemp✶
Paul✶	Watkinson✶
Peter·✶	Agar✶
Ross✶	Keeble✶

When the dialog box is closed, Word immediately sorts the table contents according to your specified criteria.

Formatting tables with AutoFormat

Would you like to enhance the table with further effects (such as backgrounds or coloured highlighting)?

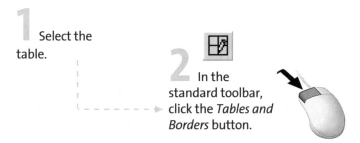

1 Select the table.

2 In the standard toolbar, click the *Tables and Borders* button.

Word now displays the Tables and Borders toolbar. Using the various buttons you can draw lines in the table, rub them out again, sort columns, sum values and much more.

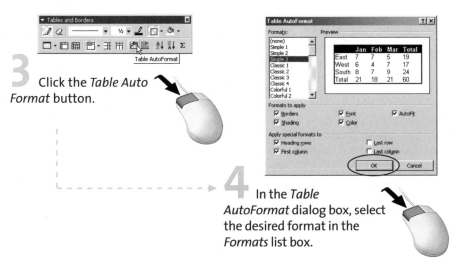

3 Click the *Table Auto Format* button.

4 In the *Table AutoFormat* dialog box, select the desired format in the *Formats* list box.

177

The relevant format style is instantly displayed in the *Preview* display box.

5 Set the *Formats to apply* and other control boxes as required.

6 Click the *OK* button.

The table is now formatted in accordance with your selected criteria.

Inserting page numbers

Finally, I would like to show you, briefly, how page numbers are inserted in Word documents. This is always helpful if you are creating multipage documents for eventual printing.

1 Open a new document.

2 Enter some text.

3 Press the Ctrl + ↵ key combination.

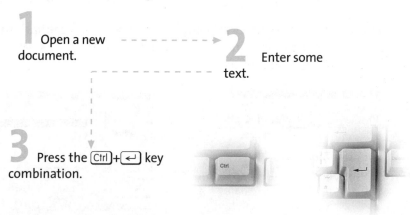

This key combination inserts a **page break**, which is visible as a horizontal dotted line, depending on the status of the hidden characters display toggle.

.............Page Break.............

4 Enter more text on the second page.

5 Move back to the first page.

With the above steps you have created a document to which page numbers can be applied.

1 Now select the *Page Numbers* option in the INSERT menu.

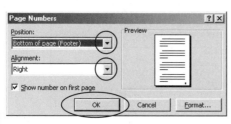

2 In the *Position* list box of the *Page Numbers* dialog box, select the location for the page numbers (Header or Footer).

3 In the *Alignment* list box, select the desired alignment (left, right, centre etc.) for the page numbers.

4 Close the dialog box with the *OK* button.

By this method of page numbering, Word takes the work off your hands. The disadvantage is that the page numbers are located in a header or footer, which is not always desirable for letters or some types of document.

Word now displays page numbers at the specified positions on each page.

Would you like to show page numbers at a predefined page position? This would be helpful, for example, if you are creating a letter template and would like to specify page numbering in the document. This is no great problem; you already know the technique.

179

1 Click at the place in the document where the page number is to be inserted.

2 In the INSERT menu, select the *Field* option.

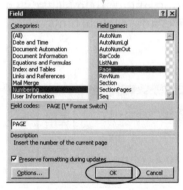

3 Select *Numbering* in the *Categories* list box.

4 Select *Page* in the *Field names* list box.

5 Close the dialog box with the *OK* button.

Page: 1 Word now inserts the field with the current page number at the desired position in the document.

You can now format the field and change its position if necessary (for example, right aligned). In the above example the word 'Page' was set in front of the page number. The page number itself has bold formatting.

Test your knowledge

After working through this chapter, you have met almost everything you need for working in Word. At the very least, you can create the most frequently used documents. Would you like to test your current knowledge once more? Then please work through the following exercises. Relevant practical hints are given on pages 582–3.

1 Create a template for an invoice form.

2 How can you create a letter using your own template?

3 Create a document page with a table.

4 Duplicate a column in the table. Repeat this with a row. Undo these changes.

5 Sort the table by the last column.

6 Create a two-column list using tabs and experiment with the different types of tabstop.

7 Define 'Dear Madam' as an Auto Text entry and store it under 'dm'.

8 Create a table in which only the horizontal dividing lines are shown.

9 Total a table column.

10 Create a document with letters in superscript.

11 Remove the superscript formatting from the document created in Exercise 10.

In the next chapter, you will meet some special Word features, such as creating serial letters.

What's in this chapter?

In the previous two chapters you were introduced to the basic functions of Word. But the program can do substantially more. Obviously, there is not enough space in this book to cover every feature, but you should certainly master features such as serial letters, and inserting graphics in text documents.

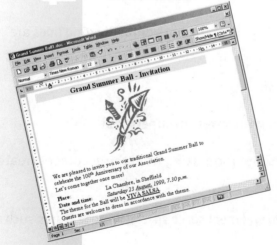

Form letters in Word

Would you like to send the same letter (such as a sales advertising letter) to different addresses? This means composing the letter, personalising the address and salutation, and then printing it. Then doing the same for the next letter. For two letters, that might not be so bad. But when it comes to more than five, you might start thinking that perhaps it would be better to computerise the job.

With the Mail Merge command, Word offers exactly the right tool for this task. The only thing that's missing is the knowledge, how to set things up and get it working.

Form letter basics

To create form letters, you need two things:

⇒ The **main document**, which contains the letter text, sales pitch etc. This document must be set up for the Mail Merge command.

⇒ A **source** file, also called the **data** file, which contains the variable information (such as a list of names and addresses), to be inserted in the form letter.

As a first step, the main document can be created like a normal letter, except that empty spaces are left for the information that is to be inserted later. The control (data) file can be set up equally well in Word, Excel or Access.

Creating the template for the form letter

Before delving into the details of the Mail Merge command, you need a text document, which can serve as a template for the actual letter.

1 Open a new document (e.g. based on an existing letter template) using the *New* command on the File menu.

- - - - - ▶ **2** Write the text of the letter as usual, but leave out details of the recipient as well as the name after the salutation.

The letter might read as follows, for example:

Cybertechnics Digital Studio

Attercliffe Road

Sheffield S9 3QS

Cybertechnics Digital Studio, Attercliffe Road, Sheffield S9 3 QS

...
Street
Town Postcode

Digital Printing

Dear Sir(s),

We are please to be able to inform you that we have recently acquired a digital printer. We are therefore writing to you to offer fast and cost-effective short-run printing for all your company's requirements.

☑ Brochures and small catalogues
☑ Short-run printing

We look forward to helping you.

Sue Muller

---

3 Save this letter outline in a *.doc* file.

Take care to leave empty the recipient data in the letterhead (we have inserted placeholders here for demonstration purposes only). Save the file but do not close it.

Creating the data source file

To create a form letter, you need a data source file, which contains the variable data (listed names and addresses) for the form letter. As a general rule, an address list in Word, Excel or Access format already exists. Do you not have such a file yet? For this example, a corresponding file will be created quickly and saved in Word.

1 Open a new document by clicking the button.

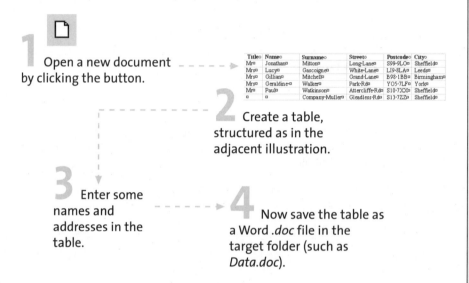

Title	Name	Surname	Street	Postcode	City
Mr	Jonathan	Mitton	Long Lane	S99-9LO	Sheffield
Mrs	Lucy	Gascoigne	White Lane	LI9-8LA	Leeds
Mrs	Gillian	Mitchell	Grand Lane	B98-1BB	Birmingham
Mrs	Geraldine	Walker	Park Rd	YO5-7LF	York
Mr	Paul	Watkinson	Attercliffe Rd	S10-7XX	Sheffield
		Company Muller	Gleadless Rd	S13-7ZZ	Sheffield

2 Create a table, structured as in the adjacent illustration.

3 Enter some names and addresses in the table.

4 Now save the table as a Word *.doc* file in the target folder (such as *Data.doc*).

Afterwards, you can close the *Data.doc* document window.

Now for the form letter

Is the letter outline still loaded, and the data source file available? Then we can start.

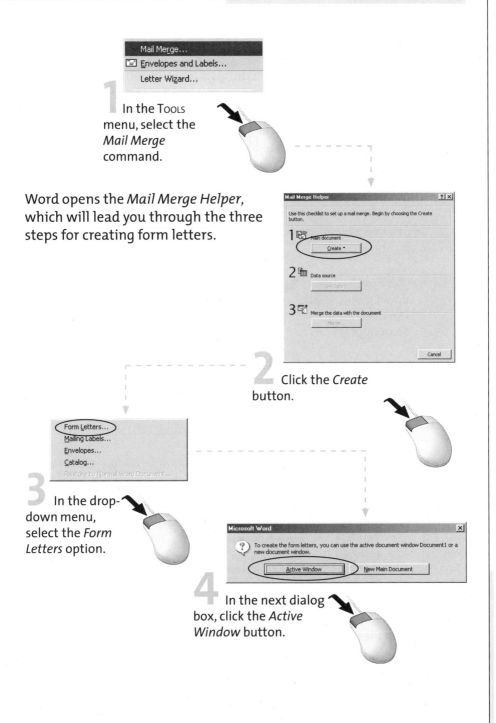

1 In the Tools menu, select the *Mail Merge* command.

Word opens the *Mail Merge Helper*, which will lead you through the three steps for creating form letters.

2 Click the *Create* button.

3 In the drop-down menu, select the *Form Letters* option.

4 In the next dialog box, click the *Active Window* button.

187

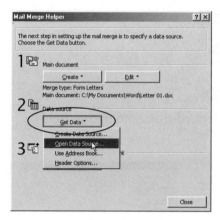

This causes Word to adopt the open form letter as the *Main document*.

5 Click on the *Get Data* button in the *Data source* section.

6 In the drop-down menu, select the *Open Data Source* option.

At this point, the fact that the data source file is already available is an advantage.

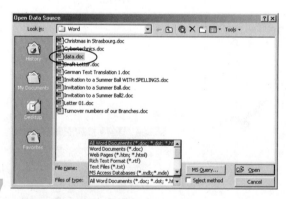

7 In the *Open Data Source* dialog box, select the desired data file *(Data.doc)* with a mouse click.

When the control file is not a Word document, set the actual file type in the *Files of type* list box and then select the data source file, such as an Excel worksheet.

8 Click the *Open* button.

Word reports that the main document contains no **merge fields**.

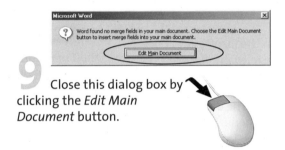

9 Close this dialog box by clicking the *Edit Main Document* button.

Although the main document was prepared in Word as a form letter, and you have also selected the data source file, Word does not yet know how the two files are supposed to merge.

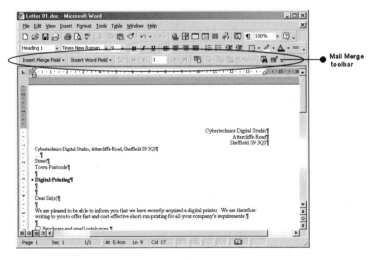

Therefore Word now displays the open document and the mail merge toolbar.

189

For form letters, you need the address data to be taken from the data source file and inserted in each individual form letter. The information as to which data source is to go where is contained in **merge fields**. These are placeholders, which are inserted in the relevant places in the main document. During printing, Word replaces the placeholders with the data from records in the data source file.

1 Position the insertion point at the relevant place in the main document.

2 Activate the *Insert Merge Field* button.

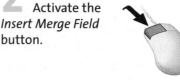

3 Select one of the available field names from the drop-down list box.

Word now inserts the relevant merge field in the document. You can recognise these fields by the 'guillemets'(« »).

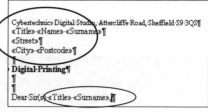

4 Repeat steps 1 to 3 until all the relevant merge fields have been inserted.

The results of the example document can be seen above. Fields have been inserted for the Title, Surname, Name, Street, Postcode and City. The Title and Name fields have also been used again in the salutation.

Have you completed the main document in a similar fashion? Then you can now begin printing the form letters. But before that, you are advised to carry out a small test to preview the merged form letters.

1 In the Mail Merge toolbar, click the *View Merged Data* button.

Pressing this button toggles between displaying the merge field names and displaying the data source file. If the merge fields are correctly inserted, the data for the first record is now displayed in the letter.

Cybertechnics Digital Studio, Attercliffe Road, Sheffield S9 3QS¶
Mr Jonathan Mitton¶
Long Lane¶
Sheffield S99 9LO¶
¶
Digital Printing¶
¶
Dear Sir(s) Mr Mitton,¶

Word has inserted the data from the first data record in place of the merge fields.

You can use the toolbar buttons to **browse through** the **data records in the data source file**. This lets you check the effect of each data record entry on your letter outline.

If desired, the formatting of the individual elements can be changed (to bold, underlined etc.), and their alignment adjusted. This functions just as with normal text. Select the relevant element, and format the merge field to your taste.

How to insert a salutation

The outline above for the form letter shows a minor but clumsy compromise. The salutation in the letter can be 'Dear Sir(s)'. True, the difference between Dear Sir and Dear Sirs is resolved by the bracketed letter (s), but this solution is hardly elegant. The salutation in the letter should really print out selectively as 'Dear Sir' or 'Dear Sirs'. The source data file already contains a field which will determine the salutation (Mr or Messrs). Now you need only inform Word that the **salutation** must be inserted depending on specified **conditions**.

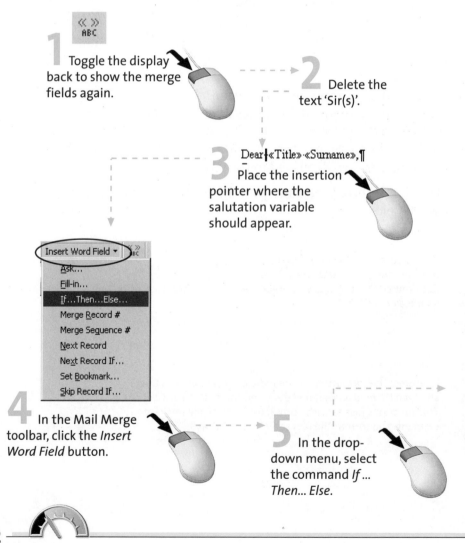

1 Toggle the display back to show the merge fields again.

2 Delete the text 'Sir(s)'.

Dear|«Title»·«Surname»,¶

3 Place the insertion pointer where the salutation variable should appear.

Insert Word Field ▾

- Ask...
- Fill-in...
- If...Then...Else...
- Merge Record #
- Merge Sequence #
- Next Record
- Next Record If...
- Set Bookmark...
- Skip Record If...

4 In the Mail Merge toolbar, click the *Insert Word Field* button.

5 In the drop-down menu, select the command *If... Then... Else.*

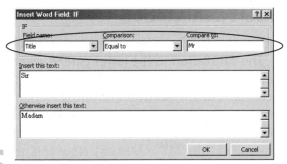

6 In the *Insert Word Field* dialog box, specify the condition as illustrated.

As soon as you close the dialog box, a conditional field is inserted in the document.

In this example, the field name *Title* from the source data file is compared. If the current data record contains the text 'Mr' then Word should replace the conditional field with 'Sir'. The text would then read 'Dear Sir'.

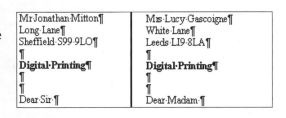

If the Title reads 'Mr', nothing is inserted, that is, in the letter the words 'Dear Sir' appear. You can check this very easily using the *View Merged Data* button.

Starting mail merge printing

When you have entered all the merge fields and conditions in the main document, you can restart the Mail Merge Helper.

1 In the toolbar, click the *Mail Merge Helper* button.

193

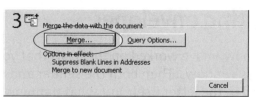

2 In the *Mail Merge Helper* dialog box, click the *Merge* button.

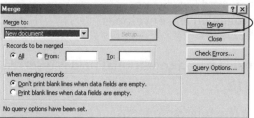

3 In the *Merge to* drop-down list, select an output destination. - - - - - ▶

4 Click the *Merge* button.

Word starts to prepare the form letters. If you selected 'New document', only one letter is produced and displayed in a new window each time. When 'Printer' is selected, Word uses all the specified data records in the data source file.

Printing envelopes

Up to now, I have worked on the basis that you use envelopes with address windows. Then both the sender and recipient data can be printed in the letter itself. But what happens, however, if there are no window envelopes? In this case there are two options:

⇾ You print the envelope using Word. Here the program allows you to print the envelopes at the same time as the documents. Alternatively, you can print the envelopes separately.

⇾ You print labels and stick these on the envelopes.

Printing an envelope

To print the envelope, take the following steps:

1 If the data for the envelope should be saved and printed with the letter, load the document in Word.

If the envelope is to be printed separately, you can bypass this step.

2 In the TOOLS menu, select the *Envelopes and Labels* command.

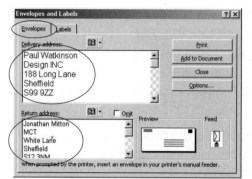

Word opens the *Envelopes and Labels* dialog box.

3 Activate the *Envelopes* tab.

4 Enter the *Delivery* and *Return addresses* in the respective text boxes.

The address can be taken directly from the Address Book of Microsoft Outlook. When you click on the arrow next to the Address Book button, Word displays the name most recently used in the Address box.

On the other hand, clicking on the Address Book button opens a dialog box with a list of contacts defined in Outlook. You can then select a name, which will be adopted complete with address when you close the dialog box.

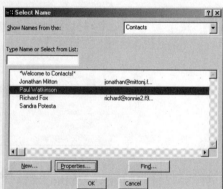

Do you want to print the envelope immediately?

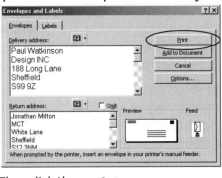

5 Then click the *Print* button.

In this case, Word requests an envelope and prints it. The only difficulty is inserting the envelope in the printer feed so that the address is printed properly.

In the *Preview* box, Word shows the envelope layout, as well as the **correct way to insert it** in the **printer feed tray**.

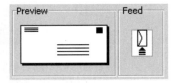

Should the text for the envelope be saved and subsequently printed with the actual document?

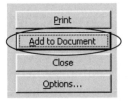

1 On the *Envelopes* tab, click the *Add to Document* button.

197

This button label appears as soon as a document is loaded in Word. Word inserts the envelope data as a separate page at the start of the document. You can subsequently save the document with the envelope data in a file and print it as usual. Word takes note of the envelope and prints it before printing the document.

In principle, the above steps are sufficient to produce envelopes using the *Envelopes and Labels* dialog. In everyday use, however, there are many special cases that must be taken into account. Envelope formats differ considerably, therefore the envelope text should be saved direct with the document.

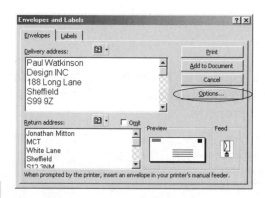

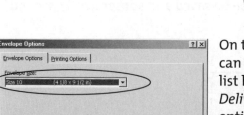

On the *Envelopes* tab, click the *Options* button.

On the *Envelope Options* tab you can **select** the **Envelope size** in a list box of the same name. In the *Delivery address* section there are options where you can adjust the font and the position for the addresses.

The *Printing Options* tab shows the options for inserting the envelope into the printer. By clicking one of the boxes in the *Feed method* group, you determine which variation Word will use. Also on this tab, you can define the **sheet feeder** for the envelope.

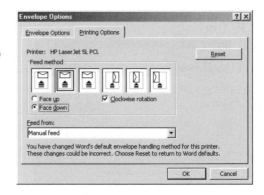

Not all printers support the options displayed. For example, envelope printing from top or bottom can be selected; however, if the printer can only print one way, then only the one option is available. You can experiment to find the correct set-up or do what the author usually does: use window envelopes wherever possible.

Making envelope labels

Larger envelopes suggest the use of labels, to be stuck on the envelope before posting. Word also supports the printing of labels.

1 In the TOOLS menu, select the *Envelopes and Labels* command.

Word opens the *Envelopes and Labels* dialog.

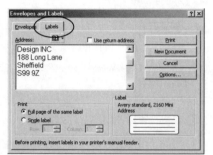

2 Activate the
Labels tab.

3 Enter the delivery and,
if necessary, the Return
address in the *Address* box.

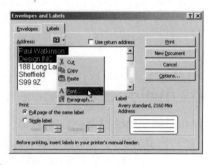

4 In that case, select
the *Return* button.

5 Right-click the
selected block.

6 In the
shortcut menu,
select the *Font*
command.

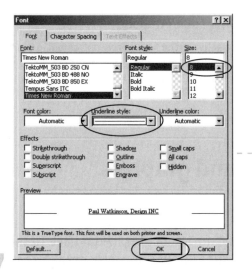

8 Select *Underline style.*

7 Set the font size to 8 points.

9 Close the *Font* dialog with the *OK* button.

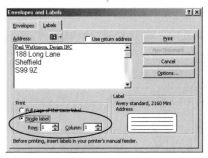

10 In the *Print* section, select the options for the number of labels and their layout.

11 Click the *Print* button.

Word then prints the data on the labels.

Processing text and graphics

Documents often include a logo or picture. For this purpose, Word
offers various functions. You can insert graphics as well as use the
Word drawing tools. In this tutorial section, I would like to show you
the most important techniques for working with graphics in Word.

An invitation with integrated graphic

Do you still have the invitation to the summer ball, which you
created as an exercise in Chapter 2? How would it be if you jazzed
this invitation up a little? The example illustrated below contains a
graphic and also sports a **shading effect** in the **title line**.

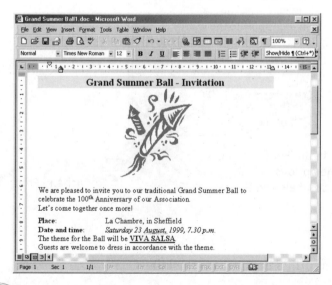

Also the graphic bullets used here differ from those used in the Chapter 2 example. Dressing-up the invitation is not a big job. In the process shown below you will become acquainted with some very useful Word functions.

Open the invitation document which you saved in Chapter 2.

If you don't have the file any more, start a new document and type in the text. Afterwards, follow the instructions in the the next sections.

Adding shading to a line of text

As a first step, the title line should be given a grey background. In Word this can be achieved using the Shading function.

Grand·Summer·Ball·--·Invitation¶

1 Select the first line.

When selecting the line, take care to include the paragraph marker. The subsequent formatting will then apply to the whole paragraph. If you only select the text, the grey background will only apply to the text.

2 Click the *Tables and Borders* button.

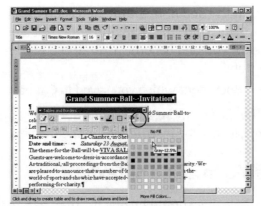

3 In the Tables and Borders toolbar, click the arrow next to the *Shading Color* button.

Word opens a *palette* of available *shading colours*.

4 Click one of the colour boxes.

Word then displays the text with a shaded background in the selected colour.

Inserting a graphic in the document

A graphic can contribute to the pleasing appearance of the document. Word allows you to insert picture files, as well as drawing elements and ClipArt items.

To insert a picture in the document, execute the following steps:

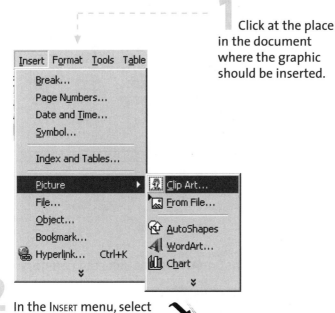

1 Click at the place in the document where the graphic should be inserted.

2 In the INSERT menu, select the *Picture* option.

Word opens a submenu of available options.

3 Click the *ClipArt* option.

Word now opens a
dialog box for selecting
ClipArt graphics from
the 'Clip Gallery'. The
ClipArts delivered with
Word are arranged in
categories.

4 Click on
a category.

Word now opens the page with ClipArts in the selected category.

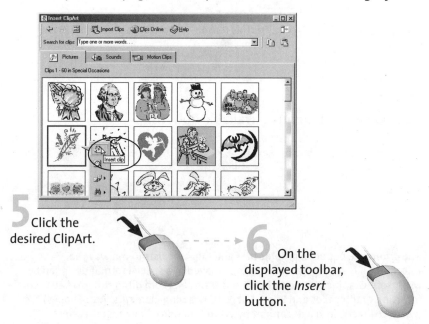

5 Click the
desired ClipArt.

6 On the
displayed toolbar,
click the *Insert*
button.

Word inserts the ClipArt picture
into the document.

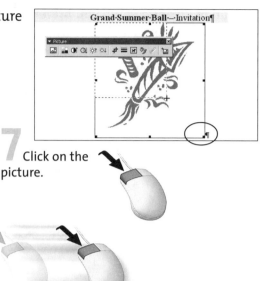

7 Click on the
picture.

8 Now you can adjust
the size of the picture by
pulling the sizing handles.

In Word, a graphic usually represents a paragraph. Text is therefore arranged
above and below the graphic. For this reason, it is recommended that in the
invitation you use centre alignment for the relevant paragraph.

If, on the other hand, you
would like to locate **text** and
graphics alongside each
other, I recommend that you
work with a table. Then you
can insert the graphic in one
cell, while locating the text in
the other cell.

Alternatively, if you click on the picture
the *Picture* toolbar is displayed. This
toolbar contains a *Text Wrapping*
button. If you select this button, Word
opens a menu with various options for
flowing text around pictures. The
Behind Text command offers a simple
way of inserting a **watermark** into a
document. It is up to you to decide
which methods you wish to use.

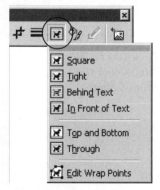

207

Instead of ClipArt, would you prefer to insert a picture from a file into the document? This is also no problem.

1 Execute steps 1 to 3.

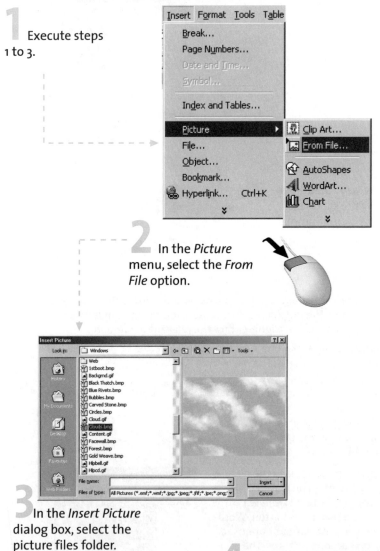

2 In the *Picture* menu, select the *From File* option.

3 In the *Insert Picture* dialog box, select the picture files folder.

4 Click on a file to display it in the preview box.

TIP If the **picture preview** box is not visible, click on the button illustrated in the adjacent diagram and select the *Preview* option in the submenu.

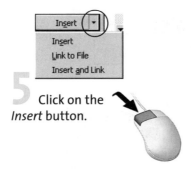

5 Click on the *Insert* button.

Alternatively, you can click the arrow next to the button and select one of the menu options.

TIP As a rule, it will be enough for your purposes if you just click the *Insert* button. The two other commands get Word to link the picture file to the document in a particular way. For example, the *Link to File* command causes Word to save only a 'pointer' to the picture file with the document. When you open the document, Word automatically opens and displays the picture file as well. The advantage of this method is that the size of the document file is reduced, and any changes to the picture file are automatically taken care of when loading. The disadvantage is that if the picture file is deleted or moved to another folder, it cannot be displayed when the document is loaded.

Just as with ClipArt, you can change the size of the inserted picture and also locate it using the *Text Wrapping* button.

Drawing in Word

Word has other functions which allow you to draw directly in the document window. You can call up these functions very easily using the drawing toolbar.

1 In the *Standard* toolbar, click on the *Drawing* button.

Word displays the drawing toolbar, normally at the bottom of the window.

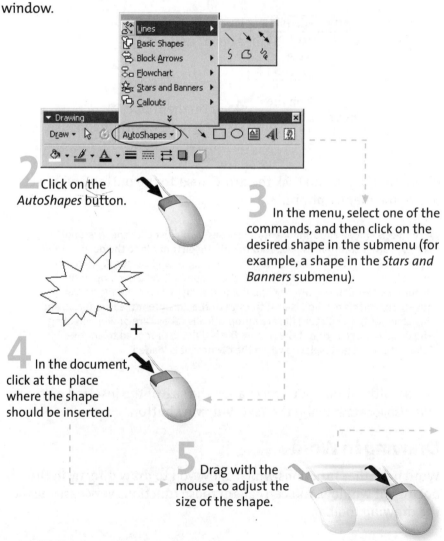

2 Click on the *AutoShapes* button.

3 In the menu, select one of the commands, and then click on the desired shape in the submenu (for example, a shape in the *Stars and Banners* submenu).

4 In the document, click at the place where the shape should be inserted.

5 Drag with the mouse to adjust the size of the shape.

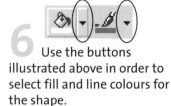

6 Use the buttons illustrated above in order to select fill and line colours for the shape.

The paintpot icon determines the **Fill colour,** and the paintbrush the **Line colour** for the shape. The result might appear as illustrated.

With the *Text Box* button, you can overlay and inscribe drawing objects with text.

If you click on the shape, Word outlines it with sizing handles. With the mouse, you can then move it, change its size, or erase it using the _ key.

Special effects with WordArt

Perhaps you have noticed the *WordArt* option in the *Insert/Picture* menu. The drawing toolbar also has an *Insert WordArt* button with which to call this function. WordArt allows you to display text in characters with special effects. I would like to show you how this works, using a title.

1 In the standard toolbar, click on this button.

2 In the drawing toolbar, click this button.

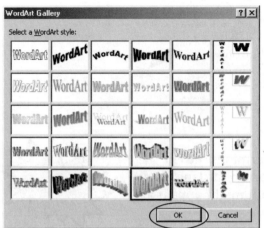

3 In the *WordArt Gallery* dialog, click one of the various formats on offer.

4 Click the *OK* button.

5 In the *Edit WordArt Text* dialog, enter the text for a title.

6 If necessary, select a font style and size.

7 Close the dialog box with the *OK* button.

Word now displays the entered text with the selected script characters in the document. You can select this ornamented script, move it to any desired location, and change its size. By pressing the _ button, the selected WordArt script can be removed.

Using bullets and numbering

As a final step, the invitation to the summer ball is to be given some fancy bullets. In contrast to the version used in Chapter 2, these bullets will be selected individually.

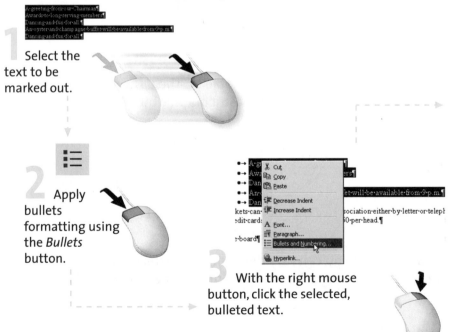

1 Select the text to be marked out.

2 Apply bullets formatting using the *Bullets* button.

3 With the right mouse button, click the selected, bulleted text.

4 In the shortcut menu, select the *Bullets and Numbering* command.

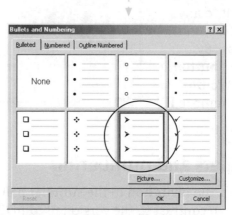

5 In the *Bullets* tab, click the box with the desired symbol.

Further bullet characters are available via the *Customize* button. The *Picture* button allows you to choose a graphic bullet from a collection of pictures.

❖ → Geri·Halliwell·will·be·presenting·her·latest·hit·Mi·Chico·Latino.·¶
❖ → Gazza·will·read·some·of·the·most·beautiful·Shakespeare·love·sonnets.·¶
❖ → Pavarotti·will·dance·the·final·scene·from·the·Swan·Lake·with·Barbra·
Streisand.·¶
The·raffle·price·will·be·a·bois·de·rose·suit·with·a·wrap·skirt·from·this·
season's·YSL·haute·couture·collection·The·second·price·will·be·a·weekend·
for·two·in·Positano,·on·the·Amalfi·coast.¶
Remember·our·motto:·"Parva·sed·apta·mihi"¶
Program·¶
➤→A·greeting·from·our·Chairman¶
➤→Awards·to·long·serving·members¶
➤→Dancing·and·fun·for·all.¶
➤→An·oyster·and·champagne·buffet·will·be·available·from·9·p.m.¶
➤→Dancing·and·fun·for·all.¶

When you close the tab with the *OK* button, Word formats the selected section with the chosen bullet characters. Here, two different characters have been used as examples.

In this manner, you can vary the bullet characters almost at will, and consequently change the tone of your document substantially.

Test your knowledge

After working through this chapter, you are now the master of most of the basic Word functions, and can already take on quite a variety of tasks. For further progress, you should use the program Help files or consult further publications. To check your knowledge, you can attempt the following questions. The answers are on page 583.

1   Which files are needed to create a form letter?

2   In a form letter, how can the salutation be changed in conformity with singular and plural?

3   In Word, how can a graphic be inserted into a document?

4   In Word, how are Drawing commands accessed?

5   How can you change the graphic used for an ornamented bullet?

6   Create a table, and sort it in numerical order.

In the next chapter, you will be introduced to the Microsoft Excel application, which is also part of the Microsoft Office package.

What's in this chapter?

Excel 2000 is the spreadsheet application of the Microsoft Office 2000 suite. Excel allows you to use the recurring calculations and analysis you need in all tasks. In this chapter, you will learn what a spreadsheet actually is, and get to know the most important Excel functions. Then you can start the program, create spreadsheets, print and save.

217

Spreadsheets: what are they?

If you have never worked with Excel or another spreadsheet program, you may be asking yourself, what exactly is a spreadsheet? Have you perhaps already worked through Chapter 1 and read the section 'What is Office?'? The gist of it is that such a program puts worksheets for receiving data at your disposal. With this data you are able to carry out calculations. All well and good, but still somewhat abstract, isn't it?

Let us take a concrete **example**: at the end of the month, you wonder where your money has gone. To do this, in future, write down your **expenditure** in a **list** and calculate either daily or weekly your total expenditure.

Normally you would note the individual figures in the form of a table on a piece of paper. The total would then appear in the bottom line.

This table shows not only the amount of expenditure but also what the money has been spent on.

Every time you enter new figures (also known as data), the calculator is turned on and the sum of the column is worked out. In a monthly evaluation, this allows you to handle everything reasonably. However, what would

Expenses	
Rent	1800.00
Additional Expenses	300.00
Insurances	500.00
Telephone	300.00
Phone	200.00
Spending Money	1500.00
School Material	100.00
Clothing	90.00
Other	1500.00
Total	3300.00

happen if, instead, you wanted to do your evaluation on a daily or weekly basis? Then you or your calculator would have to be in top form.

The silly thing is to keep on going through the same calculations. You will no doubt find numerous similar examples in your daily life (cashbook, lists for controlling costs, budget control, statements for travel costs etc.). Wouldn't it be nice if your computer could take these calculations off your hands? You simply have to enter the numbers into a table (here the example is concerned with expenditure) then your computer calculates the desired results and shows them in a table.

It is at this point that Excel comes into its own, because this is exactly the type of work it can do for you. Look at the following picture. It shows the

Excel window, in which a housekeeping book is represented as a table. Even the incomings and outgoings are shown in separate sections.

The user need only enter the incomings and outgoings in the corresponding column. **Excel** then **automatically calculates** the resulting cumulative totals and shows these as well as the difference between the two.

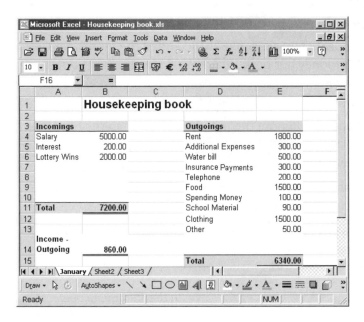

How to start Excel

After this lengthy introduction, we can now get going. For the next explanation, you will need the Excel Window. Do you know how to start Excel 2000? Calling up the program is exactly the same as Microsoft Word or any other Office programs.

What is demonstrated here with a simple example can be used for larger problems. The great thing is that once Excel has the calculations formula, it takes over all the operations. The results are shown in a table and can be saved, printed or analysed graphically with a few mouse clicks. You will see how these work in the following pages.

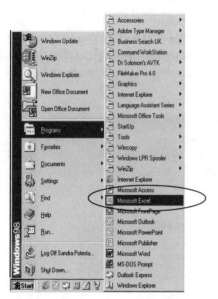

1 In the taskbar, click on the *Start* button.

2 In the *Start* menu open the PROGRAM menu and choose the *Microsoft Excel* option from the submenu.

Microsoft Excel then opens a window with a blank worksheet – similar to other Windows programs. You should already know the most important **Windows elements** from Chapter 1.

You can start Excel by choosing the *New Office Document* command from the *Start* menu. Then, from the general dialog box, choose *Blank Workbook*. These steps are explained in detail in Chapter 1. Double-clicking on an Excel-XLS-Document file starts it.

Your workplace in the Excel window

After calling up Excel the program provides a new document, and shows this in the application window. Just like in Word or any other Windows programs, the window consists of a document area, a menu list and several bars with a number of icons.

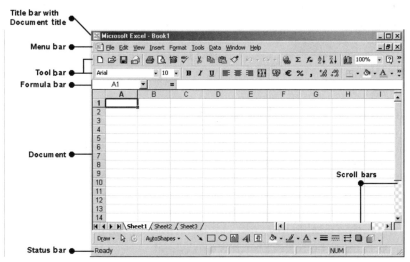

In the Excel **menu bar** you can call up individual commands concerning the creation of the document just like in Word. The names of the menus and the menu commands are, on the whole, the same as in Word. In addition the **standard bar**, which contains the buttons and elements which allow you to save and print the document and also perform markings, is similar to Word. You will already know some of the buttons from previous chapters but others might be new to you.

The **document area** (inner part of the window) is used for performing of calculations. The scroll bars for controlling vertical and horizontal screen scrolling are incorporated into this document area.

221

In the status bar Excel gives you tips as to what exactly is happening. Usually 'Ready' is displayed in the bottom left-hand corner of the window; this means that Excel is waiting for a further entry from you. When Excel is working out results for the table the word 'Point' will appear briefly. When 'Enter' appears, this means that a cell is being worked on. In addition the bar also shows other information.

You can see that applications within the Office 2000 suite are very similar to each other. Therefore, in Excel you will find some things that you learnt in the Word chapter.

And you should also know...

Before we get down to business, you should learn some basic concepts of Excel. Without knowing these basic concepts, you will find it difficult to understand the relevant handling instructions. When you open Excel, you will see a document window with a blank spreadsheet. The spreadsheet is recognisable by the grey gridlines (they can also be seen when creating a table in Word). However, in Excel we do not refer to them as tables; the correct term is **worksheet.**

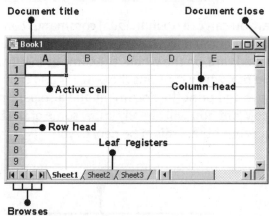

If you look closely at the document window, you will see that Excel has loaded three blank Worksheets.

These can be seen at the bottom of the document window, where there are three tabs named 'Sheet 1' to 'Sheet 3'.

In Excel, these index tabs will be described as **sheet tabs**. By clicking on these sheet tabs, you can switch between individual worksheets. 'Sheet 1' is therefore the name of your first worksheet.

In an Excel document, individual worksheets are arranged with tabs in the same way as when filing hanging files in an office. The technical term for an Excel document is **workbook**. This workbook binds all the worksheets into one document, and, if required, saves them in a file with the XLS extension.

An Excel document can hold up to 255 worksheets. The four buttons in the bottom left-hand corner allow you to move between worksheets. The worksheets could be tables, charts or have other contents. A standard Excel document has three worksheets.

A worksheet is divided by columns and rows to create a table. The individual areas of the table are called **cells.**

In the worksheet one of these cells is emphasised by a black border. This is the **active cell** which means that you can enter items in this cell.

In order to choose a cell and carry out entries, it is sufficient to click on the desired cell and type something. Alternatively, you can use the cursor keys to move between the cells.

Key	Direction

One cell above.

One cell below.

One cell to the left.

One cell to the right.

One cell to the right.

 +

One cell back on the row.

By pressing the ⏎ key, the active cell jumps by either one row or one column.

In the table area you will see that the mouse pointer takes the form of a small white cross.

Whenever you see this shape, it means that Excel is prepared to carry out an action on the worksheet (such as highlighting a cell or entering a value). However, if you move outside the table on to a menu, you will notice that the mouse pointer returns to its normal arrow shape.

> You already know about the change of shape from Word, where the pointer takes on the shape of a text cursor when it is in the document window.

> Use the scrollbars to move about in the worksheet. When you click on the vertical arrow and move it, Excel shows the present row number as a ScreenTip. Move the horizontal arrow to see the column number appear.

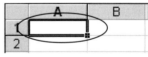

When you work in Excel, the **cell address** within the Worksheet is also important. In calculations, you must define the cells involved in the operation. One glance at the document window shows that the **columns** are identified with letters A, B, C etc. The **rows** are **numbered** from 1 to n. In order to state where a cell is situated within the worksheet you need to use the row and the column. This type of addressing will be encountered quite often.

The cell in the top left-hand corner of the worksheet therefore has the address A1 (which means column A and row 1).

If you would like to give a cell range as a single address, then separate individual cell addresses with a colon. The range of the four cells A1, A2, B1 and B2 can then be specified by the address A1:B2. A1 refers to the cell in the top left-hand corner of the area whereas B2 is the cell in the bottom right-hand corner.

225

Make a few entries

For the first exercise, you can enter something into the worksheet.

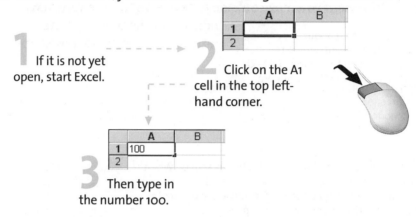

1 If it is not yet open, start Excel.

2 Click on the A1 cell in the top left-hand corner.

3 Then type in the number 100.

The entered number will appear on the left-hand side of the active cell.

4 Press the ⏎ key.

Two things now happen: firstly, the entered number will now be on the right-hand side of the cell. And secondly, A2 is now the active cell.

By pressing the ⏎ key, your entry will be inserted into the table cell.

5 Now type 'Hello' into the cell numbered A2.

Excel now shows the entry on the left-hand side of the cell.

	A	B
1	100	
2	Hello	
3		
4		

Numbers are always on the right-hand side whereas text is always on the left-hand side of the cell. These settings can be set by formatting (discussed later).

After every entry, the active cell always moves one place further. In order to change the direction it moves in, you need to choose the Tools/Option command. In the *Edit* tab, choose the direction with the direction option (*see* Chapter 11).

The keyboard behaves exactly the same as in Word when entering things in Excel. You can use uppercase or lowercase letters.

Dealing with the formula bar

Have you succeeded in creating the above entries? Then perhaps you have noticed the row just above the document window. This is the **formula bar**. In this bar Excel displays the information about the active cell. If you click on a cell, its address as well as its contents will immediately appear.

In this case, cell A2 with the message 'Hello' is displayed. The formula bar contains this information. The content of the formula bar will change as soon as you enter something new.

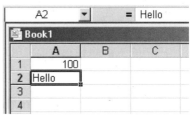

This is what the bar looks like when something is entered into a cell.

The *Cancel* button with the red cross ends your entry and deletes the typed data (text, numbers). The previous cell content will become visible again. Pressing the Esc key has the same effect.

⇥ The green tick represents the 'Enter' option. By clicking on the corresponding icon or pressing the ⏎ key, Excel moves the entry from the formula bar into the active cell. The equals sign button, which is

known as Edit Formula, allows you to call up functions. We will return to this topic in the next chapter.

Correcting entries

When typing in values you are bound to make mistakes, or the values that you enter will change at a later point and you will have to re-enter the new values. If you notice the mistake while you are entering it, you can press the Esc key to stop it. If you have already confirmed the entry by pressing the ⏎ key then press the Ctrl+Z key combination to delete the alteration.

To delete the contents of a cell, it is sufficient to highlight the cell and then press the Del key. Type anything in and the cell will overwrite with the new text.

Would you like to change a specific content of a highlighted cell? Then the formula bar can help you further still.

1 Click on the desired cell.

Excel shows you the value in the formula bar.

2 In the formula bar, highlight the part of the value that you want to correct.

X ✓ = Hello

3 Type in something new then press the ⏎ key.

X ✓ = Shirt

Excel transfers the changes to the cell. But it is only the highlighted part that is overwritten.

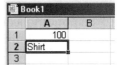

As in Word, you can highlight either the whole cell content or just a part of it. Press the [Del] key to remove the highlighted part. If you only click on one character, Excel places a vertical bar as the **insertion point**. If you press the [Del] key, the character to the right of the insertion point is deleted, while the [⇐] key deletes the character to the left of the insertion point.

When you press the [Ins] key, Excel toggles between the insert and overwrite mode. If the status bar shows the OVR symbol, the overwrite mode is active. If you now enter text, the characters in the formula bar to the right of the insertion point are overwritten. This action has already been seen in Word and other Windows programs. The correction you choose (inputting a new value or overwriting part of an existing one), is entirely up to you. With numbers, you would usually enter a totally new value, while with longer text you might prefer to amend the cell content by editing it in the formula bar.

Closing a document or ending Excel

Before we continue with a concrete example you should also know how to close a document (a worksheet) and how to exit Excel. This is not a difficult task and you have already learned the procedures in Word and other Windows programs.

1 Open the FILE menu.

2 To close a document, choose the *Close* command.

3 However, if you click on the *Exit* button, then the document will close and Excel will be exited simultaneously.

In a dialog box, Excel asks if you would like to save the document. By pressing *Yes* you save the document.

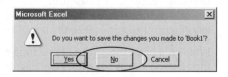

 Click on *No* to delete the last modifications to the document.

Housekeeping with Excel

Now we can make it more realistic, by using an example. At the end of the month, do you sometimes ask yourself where all your money has gone? To be able to answer this question, some people keep a housekeeping book, in which they enter the monthly (or weekly) incomings and outgoings. Then, at the end of the month, it is easy to check one's finances and see where all the money has gone.

Adding up various sums of money can be very tiresome. If you want to calculate different expenditures and compare them, this means even more operations. At the start of this chapter we said that Excel is suited to all tasks, especially when you need recurring calculations. So how about using Excel to work out our housekeeping money?

The housekeeping book could be structured in the following way: the first column contains incoming funds, and the second contains outgoing funds. The balance is shown in a separate row.

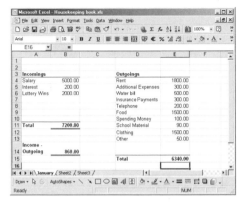

Naturally it is up to you how to design your own housekeeping book and you can do it differently if you wish. But, for practice, the design shown here is suitable. While you are doing it you will learn a lot about Excel too.

1 If the program is not open, start Excel.

2 Open a new workbook by clicking on the *New* button.

Renaming worksheets

You are now ready for the next steps. But before you start entering your incomings and outgoings, I would like to show you how the sheet tab describes the individual worksheets. When opening a new workbook, Excel shows three default worksheets, named 'Sheet 1' etc. It would be better if the worksheets were described with names like 'incomings' or 'January' or 'February', as this gives you a direct clue to the content of the sheet.

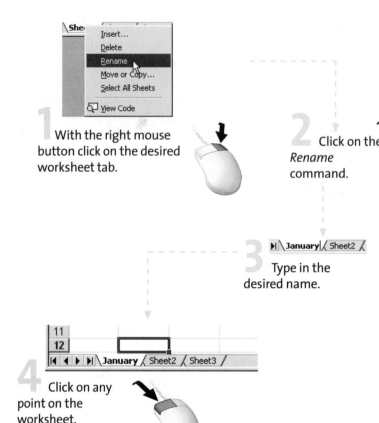

1 With the right mouse button click on the desired worksheet tab.

2 Click on the *Rename* command.

3 Type in the desired name.

4 Click on any point on the worksheet.

Excel now applies the new name to the worksheet.

Creating the incoming funds column

Now we can start with the entries for the 'incomings' section.

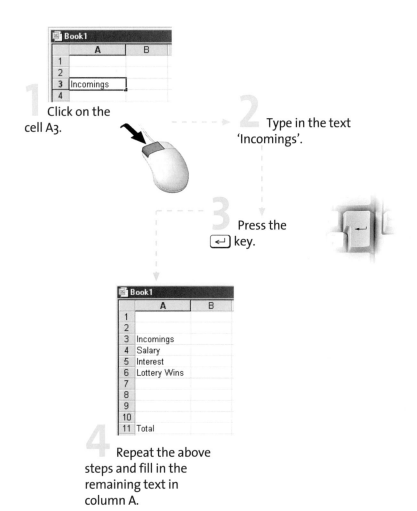

1 Click on the cell A3.

2 Type in the text 'Incomings'.

3 Press the ⏎ key.

4 Repeat the above steps and fill in the remaining text in column A.

By pressing the ⏎ key, Excel moves the active cell to the next line. Therefore, you only need to type the text and then press the ⏎ key.

TIP

If you make a mistake, simply press the Ctrl+Z key combination. Excel undoes the last command. If you have already confirmed the entry and want to correct it, refer to the section on 'Correcting entries'.

Inserting the 'Outgoings' section

Now enter the Outgoings column.

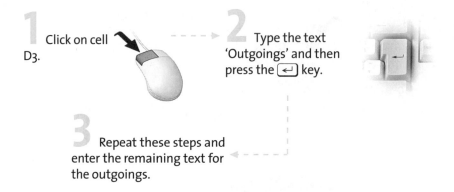

1 Click on cell D3.

2 Type the text 'Outgoings' and then press the ⏎ key.

3 Repeat these steps and enter the remaining text for the outgoings.

The tables should then look like the following.

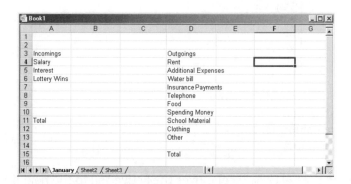

Creating the text for a housekeeping book is easy, isn't it?

Correcting the column width

A quick look at the table above and you can see an obvious problem. No, I don't mean the formatting of the text – I will discuss that later. Take a look at column D. Some of the text is too long and it stretches to column E. You will soon see why this is a problem. As soon as you type something in column E, the text in column D is cut short.

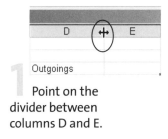

An example here is the 'Insurance Payments' entry, which is shortened.

In this case, this is not too bad, because you can still understand 'Insurance P'. But sooner or later there will be an occasion when Excel cuts off part of an entry that is essential.

The solution is quite simple: simply make the column width the desired size. Perhaps you already know how this is done. You performed the same exercise when creating tables in Word.

1 Point on the divider between columns D and E.

If you have done everything correctly, the mouse pointer will take on this form ⊕.

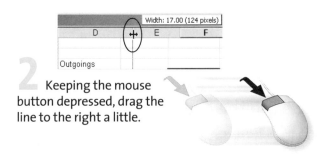

2 Keeping the mouse button depressed, drag the line to the right a little.

The width of the column will be shown as ScreenTips.

D	E	F
Outgoings		
Rent		
Additional Expenses		
Water bill		
Insurance Payments	23	
Telephone		
Food		

As soon as you let go of the left mouse button, Excel applies the new column width. Provided there is enough space, the entire entry will now be shown.

You can change row height In the same way. Simply point on the left edge on the top of the row and drag the row divider up or down.

Now we can enter values

As soon as you have entered all the text for the 'Incomings' and 'Outgoings', we can begin entering the numbers.

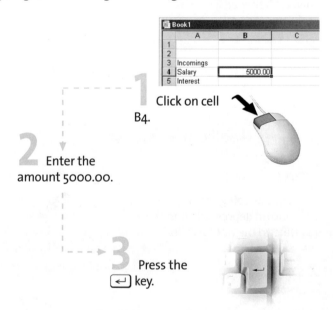

1 Click on cell B4.

2 Enter the amount 5000.00.

3 Press the ⏎ key.

The worksheet now looks like this. But hold on a minute! What's happened now? We typed in the value 5000.00.

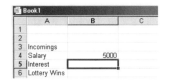

So why is it that Excel only shows the amount 5000? Perhaps it was a mistake in the entry.

4 Repeat steps 1 to 3 above.

The same thing has happened again? This is silly. Now we want to know what's going on!

5 Click once again on cell B4.

6 Enter the amount 5000.01.

Now when you press the ↵ key Excel shows the correct value.

Every cell in Excel is not only allocated a value, but also a **cell format** for representation of cell content. In a new worksheet Excel uses the default 'General' cell format. This format allows you to enter different types of entries in cells (text, numbers and so on). Excel then 'optimises' information for the cell content. If you enter a number that has only zeroes after the decimal point, these decimal points will be cut off. You need to select a cell format suitable for your values. We will see how this is done below (then we can set the same cell format for the entire column).

The **cell format** determines how Excel should show text, numbers or other cell content. Bold type and left sided text can be set in the cell format just as the decimal points are.

237

The cell format is also responsible for some mysterious effects in Excel, that have caught me out. Look at this table extract. In column A are the incomings.

	A	B
1	Input	
2	'13.5	12:00
3	'100.00	100
4	'20.00	2.00E+01

Book2

The figures in column A are preceded by an apostrophe (such as '13.5). This signals that the numbers are to be treated as text. Column B shows the representation in Excel. You already know the effect on row 3. But how do you explain the 13.5 or the 12:00? The cell format plays the deciding role. I typed a value into cell B2, then clicked on it and pressed the Del key. I then wrote 13.5 over it. The cell still retains the cell format after deletion and the new entry takes this on. We will see how to remove the cell format in the next chapter.

7 Now enter the remaining values.

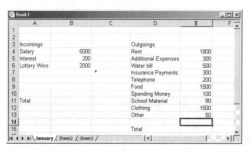

The result should look similar to what is shown here.

Formatting values

We now return to the problem of the missing places after the decimal point. We could not understand why Excel should cut off the digits after the decimal point. In order to change the format of the number representation, we must first **highlight the cells** (otherwise you have to go through all the steps for each individual cell).

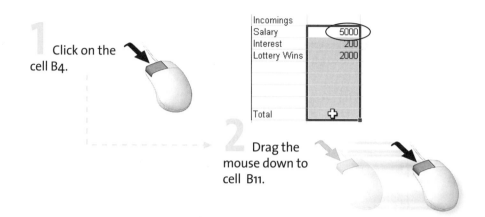

1 Click on the cell B4.

2 Drag the mouse down to cell B11.

Excel then highlights the cell area that lies in between these cells.

In the formatting bar Excel displays the two *Increase Decimal* and *Decrease Decimal* buttons, which are next to each other.

3 Click twice on the *Increase Decimal* button.

Excel adds a place after the decimal point for each click of the mouse. The result looks like what is shown here. As you have highlighted the cell area right up to the 'Total' field, the cell format will be set even for the blank cells. Enter a value here later, and this will automatically appear in the relevant representation.

3	Incomings	
4	Salary	5000.00
5	Interest	200.00
6	Lottery Wins	2000.00
7		
8		
9		
10		
11	Total	
12		

4 Repeat the above steps for the 'Outgoings' section.

239

The table should now show the number representation as follows.

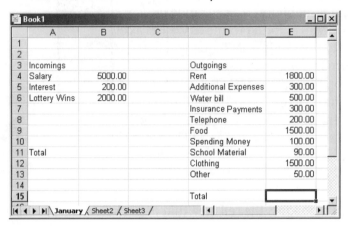

	A	B	C	D	E
1					
2					
3	Incomings			Outgoings	
4	Salary	5000.00		Rent	1800.00
5	Interest	200.00		Additional Expenses	300.00
6	Lottery Wins	2000.00		Water bill	500.00
7				Insurance Payments	300.00
8				Telephone	200.00
9				Food	1500.00
10				Spending Money	100.00
11	Total			School Material	90.00
12				Clothing	1500.00
13				Other	50.00
14					
15				Total	

If you want to reduce the number of decimal places, click on this button.

In the next chapter you will learn further possibilities for formatting cell content.

Calculations

The table so far looks quite good, but you are presumably interested in the totals of the incomings and outgoings and perhaps even the balance of these two figures. This is no problem in Excel.

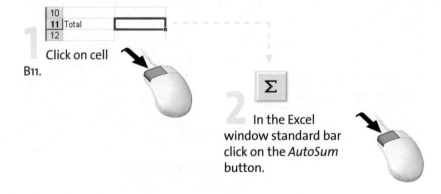

10	
11	Total
12	

1 Click on cell B11.

2 In the Excel window standard bar click on the *AutoSum* button.

Excel recognises your intention and in the worksheet it highlights a a cell range by framing it with a dotted frame as well as a cell adjacent to the range. This shows you that these numbers are to be used for the calculation. The formula '=SUM(..)' is now entered into cell B11. The entry B4:B10 in the bracket represents the highlighted cell range.

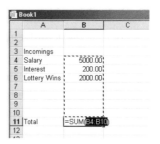

 Press the ⏎ key, to confirm the formula.

Excel then shows the results in cell B11. As we have already set the cell format in the previous steps, the result will automatically have places after the decimal point.

When you choose the *AutoSum* button, Excel analyses the surrounding area. If it finds values in the rows or columns, it highlights the corresponding cells. But you can highlight a range at any time by dragging the mouse over it. Excel then surrounds the area with a flashing dotted line. As soon as you confirm this by pressing the ⏎ key, Excel calculates the total and shows it in the target cell. In this way, you can total other cells, not just adjacent ones.

When you use the procedure above, the entire total is calculated, even though some of the cells are blank. This means that you can enter values into rows 7, 8, 9, and 10 and Excel will calculate the new total, without you having to change the formula. This is the strength of Excel: it simply does the calculation again and immediately shows the results.

1 Repeat the above steps, in which you click on cell E15 and then turn on the 'AutoSum' function.

If you have done everything correctly, Excel should then enter the total of the outgoings in the relevant cell.

In the next step we only have to calculate the difference between the incomings and outgoings. When you see the result, you will know whether to cry or to celebrate. But at least you then know where your money has gone and how much you have left.

1 Click on cell E14.

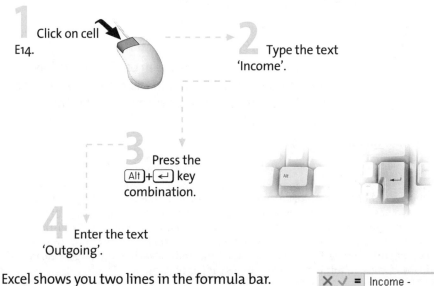

2 Type the text 'Income'.

3 Press the Alt + ↵ key combination.

4 Enter the text 'Outgoing'.

Excel shows you two lines in the formula bar.

X ✓ = | Income - Outgoing|

5 Press the ↵ key.

Income -
14 Outgoing
15

Excel now shows the result in cell E14. The input is shared between two lines.

The only job left now is to ascertain the difference between incomings and outgoings. To do this, you have to calculate the difference between the contents of cells B11 and E15 and enter it in cell B14. This is possible with only a few clicks of the mouse.

Within a cell the text can be spread over several lines by pressing the [Alt]+[↵] key combination .

1 Click on cell B14.

Now click on the formula bar and type in the formula '= B11 – E14'. But Excel knows a more elegant variety.

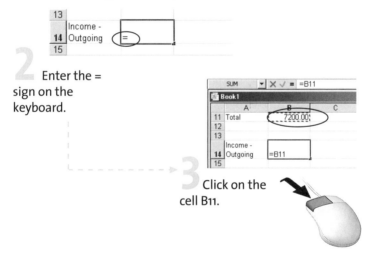

2 Enter the = sign on the keyboard.

3 Click on the cell B11.

Excel highlights the cell clicked on by surrounding it with a flashing dotted line. This shows that the value is in the calculation. At the same time the cell address B11 is put into the target cell as well as being displayed in the formula bar.

4 Now type in a minus sign on the keyboard.

243

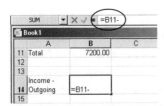

Excel recognises that you want to add further expressions to the formula. The cell now contains the calculation part as a formula.

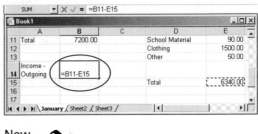

Now click on the cell E14.

Press the ↵ key to conclude the formula.

Excel shows the results of the calculation in the target cell.

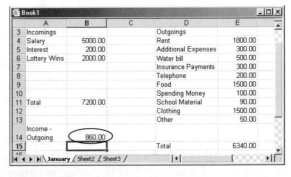

If you want to see the formula again, just click on the cell. Excel then shows the formula in the cell and in the formula bar; you can then click on the formula bar and correct the formula if it is needed.

After these steps, you will see the result of your incomings/outgoings balance calculation. Obviously that lottery win has saved the balance: it stands at 860.00 in your favour. You can now try to change the data in the 'incomings' and 'outgoings' columns. As soon as you have typed in a value and pressed the ⏎ key, Excel will show the updated results straight away. Could you have it any easier? And this is exactly the strength of Excel. As soon as you have entered the calculation formula into a worksheet, Excel takes over all the calculations for you.

Formatting the worksheet contents

The calculations created in the example above offer the desired functions, but it doesn't look very good. Therefore you should format the contents of your calculation range.

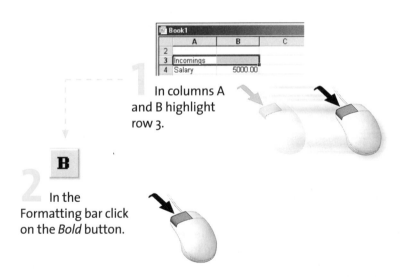

1 In columns A and B highlight row 3.

2 In the Formatting bar click on the *Bold* button.

As soon as you click on the button, Excel shows the relevant cells in bold print.

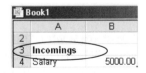

In this way you can make a highlighted cell underlined or italic. You only have to click on the appropriate button in the formatting bar.

4 Highlight the A3:B3 cell range again.

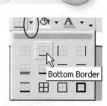

5 Click on the arrow next to the *Borders* button, and then in the palette click on the *Bottom Border* button.

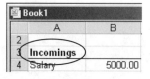

Now when you remove the highlight, Excel shows the corresponding range both bold and underlined.

The Borders button underlines the entire cell, whereas if you choose the *Cell/Border* command from the FORMAT menu, this will only underline the content. You should decide between these two options when formatting a table.

Incomings

There are several things you can do with cells concerning format. Next you will learn how to **copy a cell format**. You will perhaps know the techniques from Word.

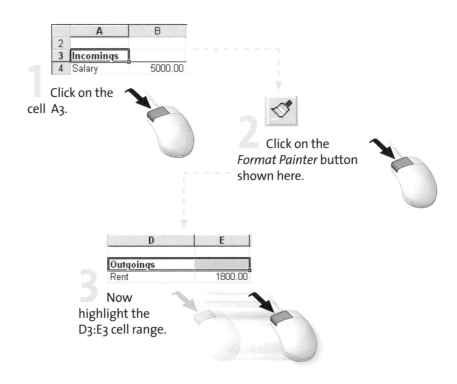

1 Click on the cell A3.

2 Click on the *Format Painter* button shown here.

3 Now highlight the D3:E3 cell range.

Excel will now copy the cell format of A3 and transfer it onto D3 and E3. Consequently, the heading of the 'outgoings' column will also be formatted bold and underlined. You can see this more clearly when you remove the highlighting.

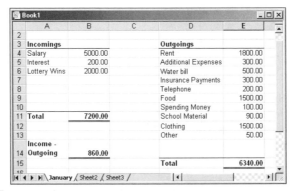

4 Use the techniques described above to format the remainder of the cells.

247

The double border of the totals cells can be found under the *Borders* button.

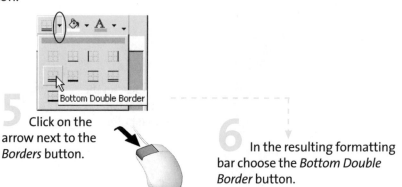

5 Click on the arrow next to the *Borders* button.

6 In the resulting formatting bar choose the *Bottom Double Border* button.

Do you see the two buttons directly next to the *Borders* button? Would you like to colour in the **cell background** or the **cell content**?

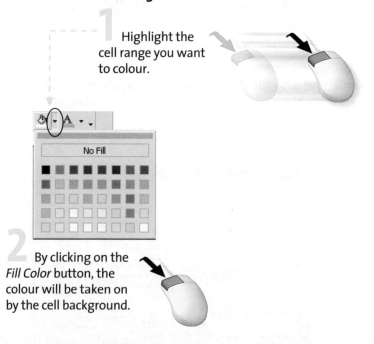

1 Highlight the cell range you want to colour.

2 By clicking on the *Fill Color* button, the colour will be taken on by the cell background.

If you choose the arrow next to this button, Excel will open a palette so you can choose the fill colour. One click on a colour area will close the palette and result in that colour being applied.

Here you can see a cell area with the column 'incomings' whose background for the title row is grey. The area for the entries, however, would be yellow.

3	**Incomings**	
4	Salary	5000.00
5	Interest	200.00
6	Lottery Wins	2000.00
7		
8		
9		
10		
11	**Total**	**7200.00**
12		

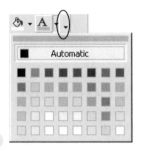

3 By clicking on the *Font Color* button the colour will be transferred on to the cell background.

By choosing the arrow next to this button, Excel will open a palette so that you can choose the font colour.

Take care when entering colours that there is a contrast between the background and the content. A combination of white letters on a yellow background is not very visible.

You can use these functions to make the cells in the worksheet appealing by providing them with background colour, colouring the cell contents, or giving the cells borders.

Altering the font size for headings

Do you want to include a heading in your worksheet? This heading can be done in bold type and with a different font size. You must know how to do these actions already, from Word and previous sections.

1 Click on cell B1.

2 Type in the text 'Housekeeping book' and then press the ⏎ key to insert the word into the cell.

3 Highlight the cell content again by clicking on it.

4 Click on the *Bold* button in order to make the font bold.

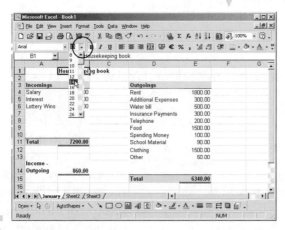

5 In the formatting bar, click on the arrow next to the *Font size* button; this will then give a list of various font sizes.

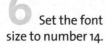

6 Set the font size to number 14.

Now the font of the heading is in bold type and also somewhat bigger than the headings in the table.

You should already know the steps for formatting a cell. When working with Word or other Windows programs, you use almost exactly the same techniques. You can also see here that many actions are the same in all Windows programs and soon you will be able to use all programs intuitively.

Saving the workbook

Have you created the housekeeping book as detailed in the steps above? Save the workbook as a file for later use; such a file can then be reloaded, updated and printed. You will now learn the relevant steps for doing this.

1 Click on the *Save* button in the standard bar.

Alternatively you could do this by clicking on the *Save* or *Save As* commands in the FILE menu. For a new document the dialog box *Save as* appears in all cases.

The *Save As* dialog box contains a list on the left-hand side for you to choose the folder where you want to save this file.

251

2 If relevant, click on the desired folder (such as *My Documents*).

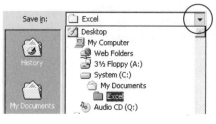

In the *Save As* dialog box you can choose the drive and the folder that you wish to save the file in. You can open the list by clicking on the arrow in the *Save in* box. You can open a folder by double-clicking on the relevant symbol.

For our purposes, we should save the document in the *My documents/ Tables* folder. This submenu will already appear in the picture shown here. If this folder does not exist, you can insert it directly into the dialog box by clicking on the *Create New Folder* button. The relevant steps have already been explained for Word. If needed, look back to Chapter 2.

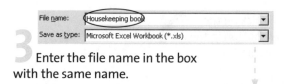

3 Enter the file name in the box with the same name.

TIP
If needed, you can choose the save format in the *Save as type box*. For our purposes, the 'Microsoft Excel Workbook(*.xls)' is fine.

4 Click on the *Save* button.

TIP
The extension *.xls* does not need to be typed in with the file name. As long as the *Microsoft Excel Workbook* (*.xls) type is chosen in the *Save as type box*, Excel will automatically use the *.xls* extension.

Excel closes the dialog box and saves the workbook in a file in the desired folder with the *.xls* extension.

If you wish to save a workbook under a new name, choose the *Save as* command from the FILE menu. Then the *Save As* dialog box shown above will open and you can enter the new name.

If you want to save a previously saved file that you have now edited, then all you have to do is click on the *Save* button. Excel then saves the changes into the

corresponding file without asking any more questions.

Reloading a workbook

Have you exited Excel and now want to reload a workbook that has already been saved? This is accomplished with only a few mouse clicks, and you have already learnt the techniques in Word.

1 Start Microsoft Excel.

2 In the standard bar click on the *Open* button.

The *Open* dialog box will open and here you can choose the drive, the folder and the file.

3 In the left-hand list, click on the symbol of the folder where you had saved the file (in this case *My Documents*) in order to select it.

If needed, choose the submenu (in this case *Tables*) by double-clicking on its symbol.

4 Highlight the desired file by clicking on it (e.g. *Housekeeping book.xls*).

5 Click on the *Open* button.

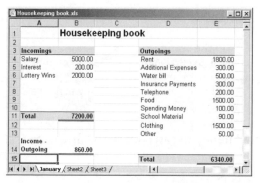

Excel then loads the workbook and shows it in the document window.

Printing a worksheet

Perhaps you would like to print out the results of your housekeeping book (or any other worksheet)?

In the standard bar, click on the *Print* button.

Excel now prepares the printout. During this time you will see this dialog box.

Have you pressed the *Print* button by mistake? If so, click on the *Cancel* button. Excel then stops the printout.

In a document with several pages you can also see how many pages you are printing.

Excel only prints the cell area that has content. Since a worksheet has 255 columns (with the names A, B, ... , AA , AB, etc.) and has rows numbered from 1 to 65 ,536, the rest of the blank cells to the right and at the bottom of the Worksheet will not be printed.

The printing of a worksheet takes place in the background. Therefore while Windows is printing, you can continue to work on Excel or any other program. If there is a problem with the printing, then look at the Appendix where you will find tips on solving printing problems.

Printing options and landscape for large worksheets

Some tables are wide, so they will not fit on to a standard format sheet when printed. If the cell area with the values is wider than one sheet, Excel will print the information on several sheets. You can then stick the sheets together in order to create the table.

255

In most cases, though, it is simpler to print the table crossways on to the sheet. One more question: can I just highlight one section of a table and print it out? Or is it necessary to print the whole worksheet? These choices can be carried out with a few mouse clicks.

If the table is only slightly wider than a sheet, you could try to reduce the column width, then the table may be able to fit on to a single sheet when printed.

1 In the FILE menu choose the *Print* command, or press the Ctrl+P key combination.

Excel then opens the *Print* dialog box. Here you can choose the desired print options.

♦ The *Copies* pane allows you to set the **Number of copies**.

♦ In the *Print range* pane you can decide whether to **print** all the worksheet or only individual **pages**.

♦ In the *Print what* pane you can choose options for **Printing a Selection**, the **Entire workbook** or the **Active sheet(s)**.

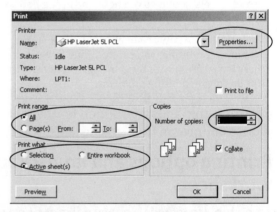

2 In order to choose print settings then click on the *Properties* button.

Excel now shows a dialog box with the print properties.

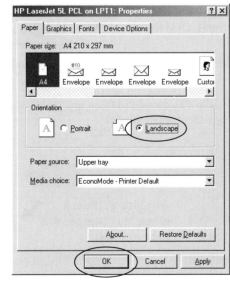

The structure of the *Paper* tab is dependent on your printer.

Click on the *Landscape* option in the *Orientation* box in the *Paper tab*.

Close the dialog box by clicking on the *OK* button.

As soon as the *Print* dialog box is closed, by clicking on the *OK* button, Excel uses the landscape option for the table. In the landscape option more columns can fit on to one page. This setting stays until you finish using Excel. The next time you start Excel the default print settings (Portrait) will be applied.

Inserting and removing page breaks

Have you created a table with a particular structure? Then, in these circumstances, the page breaks that Excel automatically uses when printing may not be suitable for your table. Do you want Excel to print table contents that logically go together, on separate pages? If so, insert the appropriate page breaks into the table yourself.

1 Click on the cell where the page break is to be inserted.

TIP

Have you noticed the dotted vertical line to the right of column I? This is the column where Excel uses a page break when printing. Then column J, if it needs printing, will appear on a new page.

TIP

If the *Page Break* command is not visible, click on the chevron at the bottom of the menu. Excel will then insert all the missing commands.

Insert	Format	Tools	Data
Cells...			
Rows			
Columns			
Worksheet			
Chart...			
Page Break			
Function...			
Name			
Comment			
Picture			
Object...			
Hyperlink... Ctrl+K			

2 In the INSERT menu choose the *Page Break* command.

Excel now places both a horizontal and a vertical page break immediately above and to the left of the marked one. You will recognise this page break by its dotted vertical and horizontal lines.

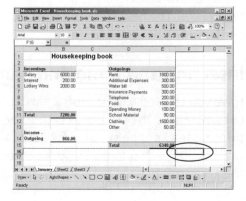

Would you like to **remove** this **page break** now?

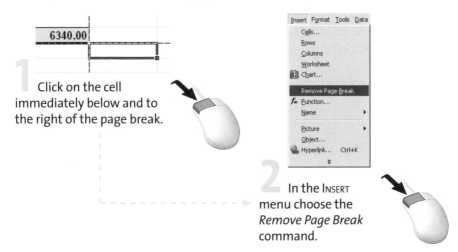

1 Click on the cell immediately below and to the right of the page break.

2 In the INSERT menu choose the *Remove Page Break* command.

Excel removes the dotted lines and so the page break has been removed.

Calling up Print Preview

Print Preview is often useful for assessing the table. It is exactly for things such as page breaks that the print preview is useful in order to see if the table will fit on to an A4 sheet.

1 In the standard bar click on the *Print Preview* button.

Excel opens a preview window showing a scaled down view of the document page. Using the buttons on the top bar you can even zoom in or out.

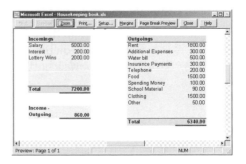

2 To close the preview, simply click on the *Close* button in the top bar.

259

Excel then returns to the
standard display of the
worksheet.

Would you like to see a preview of the page set up?

1 In the print preview menu click on the
Page Break Preview button in the top bar.

Excel then changes to
this preview. It shows a
scaled down
representation of the
table.

The page numbers are
displayed on to the
corresponding pages in
grey. The pages are
surrounded by a blue
border.

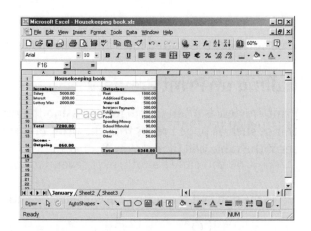

To remove this preview follow the following steps:

1 In the standard bar
click on the *Print
Preview* button.

Excel now shows the table in the preview again. The top bar contains the *Normal View* button.

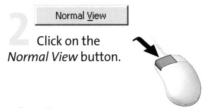

Normal View

2 Click on the
   Normal View button.

Test your knowledge

Now you have learnt the most important Excel functions for saving a table. You can print, save, format and reload documents. As a test of your knowledge, answer the following questions. The answers are on page 584.

1 How do you save a worksheet under a new name?

2 Create a table where the cell contents are centred.

3 How do you enter larger font text in a cell?

4 How do you create a total over several rows?

5 Create a cell with a calculations formula that multiplies the contents of the two above cells together, then adds 10 and finally divides the outcome by 10.

6 How do you highlight an area in a cell?

7 In Excel how do you set the number of decimal places for a figure?

In the next chapter, you will learn further functions for working with Excel.

Further Excel functions and diagrams

What's in this chapter?

In the previous chapter, you got to know the basics of Microsoft Excel. You can now create and operate a simple table. In this chapter, I would like to introduce you to further functions of this program. In the first example we will produce tables and then we will process the data graphically as a chart. Along the way, you will learn further important and helpful Excel functions. Additionally, you will experience how an Excel document presentation can be used for calculations. This knowlege provides you with the basis for becoming an Excel Expert.

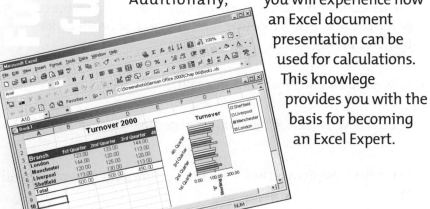

Creating a turnover report

Have you gone through the Excel exercises in the previous chapter? If so, we can get going with the next exercise. As an example, let's take a small firm that has four branches in different towns. The owners of the firm would like to have a report showing the quarterly turnover figures for the branches, as well as the total turnover.

Branch	1st Quarter	2nd Quarter	3rd Quarter	4th Quarter	Total
London	123.00	133.00	0.00	0.00	256.00
Manchester	144.00	120.00	0.00	0.00	264.00
Liverpool	120.00	125.00	0.00	0.00	245.00
Sheffield	113.00	130.00	0.00	0.00	243.00
Total	500.00	508.00	0.00	0.00	1008.00

The corresponding table could look something like this.

After what we have learnt in the previous chapter, it should be clear to you that this table can be made to look more elegant.

Here I have completed an example of the finished table in question. The worksheet also contains another graphic representation of the turnover, next to the table.

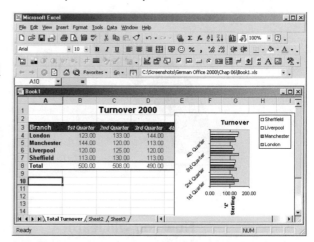

In the learning steps of this chapter, we will see how to create such a table.

1 Start Excel and make sure that a new workbook is loaded.

- - - - ▶

2 **Sheet1** Click on the 'Sheet 1' button to open the relevant spreadsheet.

You are now ready to create the turnover report.

Entering row legends

The previous table contains the names of the corresponding branches in the left-hand column, which are included in the turnover statistics. This column with the names should now be entered in the table. As a reminder, here are the steps:

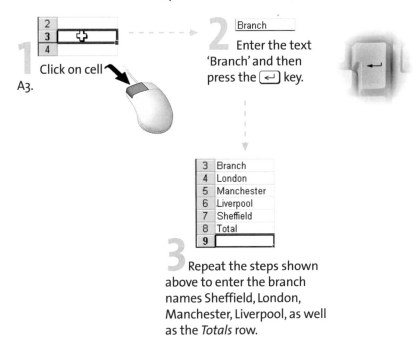

1 Click on cell A3.

2 Enter the text 'Branch' and then press the ⏎ key.

3 Repeat the steps shown above to enter the branch names Sheffield, London, Manchester, Liverpool, as well as the *Totals* row.

Every time you press the ⏎ key, Excel enters the typed character in the cell and then moves the 'active cell' one row down.

If you do not want to enter anything into a cell, then simply press the ⏎ key again. Excel then highlights the cell that lies below this cell as the new 'active cell'.

If you make a mistake while entering something, press the [Ctrl]+[Z] key combination to undo the last command. If you only notice the mistake later on, correct the corresponding cell content. You can find details on this in Chapter 5.

Entering column headings

Now you can also enter column headings for the table on to the worksheet. You already know how to do this.

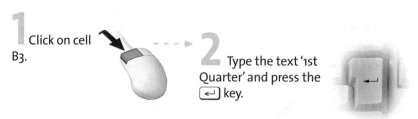

1 Click on cell B3.

2 Type the text '1st Quarter' and press the ⏎ key.

	A	B	C
1			
2			
3	Branch	1st Quarter	
4	London		
5	Manchester		

Unfortunately, Excel now expects an entry in this column, i.e. after pressing the ⏎ key the active cell is moved to cell B4 directly below.

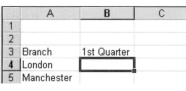

3 Click on cell C3.

4 Type in the text '2nd Quarter' and now press the ⇧ key.

Excel enters the value into cell C3 and then positions the highlighted active cell onto D3.

	A	B	C	D
1				
2				
3	Branch	1st Quarter	2nd Quarter	
4	London			
5	Manchester			

In order to **carry out** a **sideways entry**, press the ⇧ key instead of the ⏎ key. However, you should notice that you can also change the direction that the highlighted active cell shifts to when you press the ⏎ key (TOOLS/OPTIONS menu, *Edit* tab, *Direction* list).

Using the AutoFill function

When filling in a few cells, the AutoFill function is really helpful. It is often the case that neighbouring cells contain a series of values that follow on from each other e.g. 1, 2, 3, ... or January, February. This is similar in the column headings, where the sequence 1st Quarter, 2nd Quarter, 3rd Quarter and 4th Quarter is necessary. Excel offers you the 'Auto Fill' function, with which you are able to fill a entry area with the same value or a series.

I would like to show you how this works, using the column headings and also a further example.

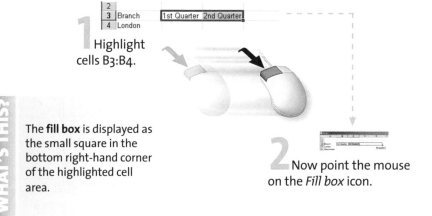

1 Highlight cells B3:B4.

The **fill box** is displayed as the small square in the bottom right-hand corner of the highlighted cell area.

2 Now point the mouse on the *Fill box* icon.

The mouse pointer will now take on the form of a black cross.

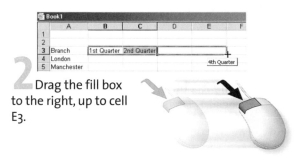

2 Drag the fill box to the right, up to cell E3.

Excel shows the information to be supplied.

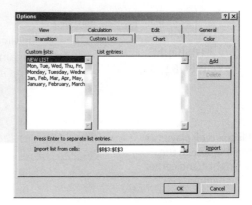

As soon as you release the left mouse button, Excel will apply the data to the highlighted cells.

This AutoFill function is extremely useful when entering series. Excel uses the information in the highlighted cells in order to decide what should be entered in the cells that are to be filled in. If a series is recognised (such as the 1, 2, 3, ... sequence), the series will be continued when filled in. The above heading row contains the numbers 1, 2, 3, ... along with the text. This means that Excel can recognise the series even with the text.

As well as numbers series and texts that contain numbers, Excel also has several text series. You can call up these options from the TOOLS/OPTIONS command and the *Custom Lists* tab. You can also define some series on this tab (*see* Chapter 11).

When using the AutoFill function, it is not compulsory to fill the highlighted cells with a series. You can also use the function to transfer the same value to a cell area.

Have you created the heading row? If so, we can now fill in the data area with zeroes before any further work is done, and to prepare it for displaying values. This is by no means urgently required, but the following steps simplify it a bit.

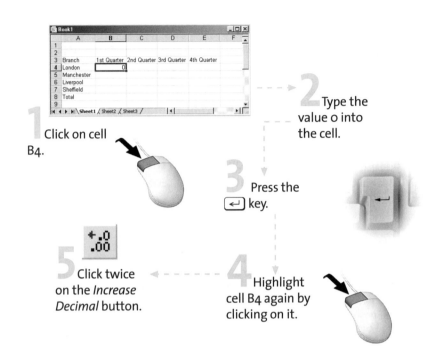

Type the
value 0 into
the cell.

Click on cell
B4.

Press the
↵ key.

Click twice
on the *Increase
Decimal* button.

Highlight
cell B4 again by
clicking on it.

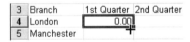

Excel then enters two decimal
places there.

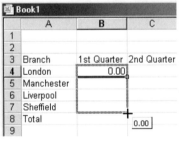

Click on the *Fill
in* button there.

Drag the *Fill in*
box over the cells
of the column that
are to be filled in.

269

As soon as you let go of the left mouse button, Excel will fill in the highlighted area with the value 0.00 from the highlighted cell.

3	Branch	1st Quarter	2nd Quarter
4	London	0.00	
5	Manchester	0.00	
6	Liverpool	0.00	
7	Sheffield	0.00	
8	Total	0.00	
9			

Because only one cell was highlighted, Excel cannot recognise any series, therefore it only transfers the entered value of the highlighted cell. It is also interesting to note that the cell format is also transferred.

You can use the *Fill in* box of an area to delete cells too. In the above example the value 0.00 is also transferred to cell B8 where the total is to be entered. Drag the *Fill in* box of the (still) highlighted area back to cell B7, then Excel will make the content of cell B8 go grey. If you now let go of the mouse, the cell content (but not the cell format) will disappear.

	A	B
2		
3	Branch	1st Quarter
4	London	0.00
5	Manchester	0.00
6	Liverpool	0.00
7	Sheffield	0.00
8	Total	

1 As a test, enter the value 1.0 into cell B5.

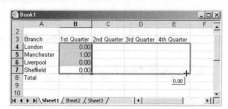

2 Now highlight the first column.

3 Drag the *Fill in* box of the highlighted area to the right, over the cells of the table that are to be filled in.

As soon as you let go of the left mouse button, Excel will fill in the highlighted area with the values from the first column. Notice that row 5 is filled in with the value 1.00, which means that Excel uses the individual values for every row.

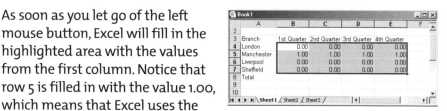

4 Put the value in row 5 back to 0.00.

If the function cannot recognise a series (for example, because only one cell was highlighted), the value of the first highlighted cell will be transferred to the target area.

By holding the ⌈Ctrl⌋ key while you drag, a series will be produced (with numbers).

Excel shows this in the ScreenTip. Let go of the mouse button and Excel will fill in the area with a series of numbers.

Calculating totals

Now the totals of the individual rows and columns should be calculated. You already know how this is done from the previous chapter. I would now like to show a few of the finer points. In order to **determine** the **quarterly totals** of the individual **branches**, go through the following steps.

1 In the 'Total' row, click on cell B8.

This row should receive the column totals.

2 Click on the *AutoSum* button.

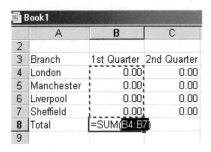

Excel now shows the cell area above the active cell surrounded by a border.

	A	B	C
2			
3	Branch	1st Quarter	2nd Quarter
4	London	0.00	0.00
5	Manchester	0.00	0.00
6	Liverpool	0.00	0.00
7	Sheffield	0.00	0.00
8	Total	=SUM(B4:B7)	
9			

3 Confirm the choice by pressing the ⏎ key.

Excel now shows the first total.

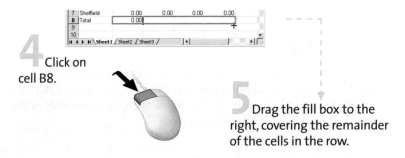

4 Click on cell B8.

5 Drag the fill box to the right, covering the remainder of the cells in the row.

As soon as you let go of the mouse button, Excel transfers the formula to the rest of the cells. Excel then automatically calculates the column totals.

In a similar way you can now **determine** the **row totals** for the individual branches.

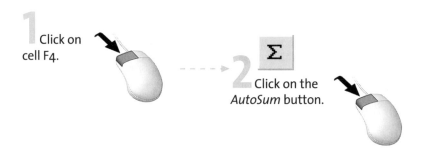

1 Click on cell F4.

2 Click on the *AutoSum* button.

Excel then highlights the cells to the left of this with a dotted line.

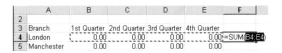

	A	B	C	D	E	F
2						
3	Branch	1st Quarter	2nd Quarter	3rd Quarter	4th Quarter	
4	London	0.00	0.00	0.00	0.00	=SUM(B4:E4)
5	Manchester	0.00	0.00	0.00	0.00	

3 Confirm this choice by pressing the ⏎ key.

Excel then inserts the sum formula into the cell, shows the corresponding result and then highlights the cell underneath as the active cell.

4 Highlight cell F4 again.

5 Drag the cell fill box down to cell F7.

0.00
0.00
0.00
0.00

As soon as you let go of the mouse button, Excel transfers the formula to the other highlighted cells and shows the calculated totals. You can now check the formulae by clicking on the cell again. Excel seems to follow your train of thought, and adapts the cell area when copying a formula.

Generally, when copying a cell content with a formula by dragging the mouse, Excel adapts this cell reference to the changed cell address. This may not, however, always be correct. If you copy a formula between places the formula will not be corrected, therefore you should click on the copied cell with the mouse and check the formula in the formula bar.

Now, the only thing to determine is the total sum of the year's turnover.

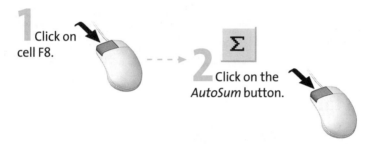

1 Click on cell F8.

2 Click on the *AutoSum* button.

Excel then highlights the above cells, which contain the part totals, by surrounding them with a dotted border.

3 Confirm this by pressing the ⏎ key.

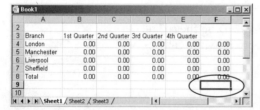

Excel inserts the formula for the total sum into the cell and then shows the calculated result. Then it highlights the cell below as the new active cell.

If you do not want to show the value with two decimal places, you can format it appropriately. You have already learnt these steps in previous sections.

Now we just have to fill the table with values.

1 Enter the values of the turnover figures into the table.

The result looks like this. Now you can also check the results of the totals.

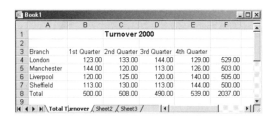

	A	B	C	D	E	F	
1			Turnover 2000				
2							
3	Branch	1st Quarter	2nd Quarter	3rd Quarter	4th Quarter		
4	London	123.00	133.00	144.00	129.00	529.00	
5	Manchester	144.00	120.00	113.00	126.00	503.00	
6	Liverpool	120.00	125.00	120.00	140.00	505.00	
7	Sheffield	113.00	130.00	113.00	144.00	500.00	
8	Total	500.00	508.00	490.00	539.00	2037.00	
9							

Creating a table with AutoFormat

Finally, the table should be made to look more appealing.

1 In cell C1 fill in the table title, which is already shown in the above step.

2 Rename the 'Sheet 1' tab 'Total turnover'.

If you have any problems in changing the name, look back to the 'Renaming spreadsheets' section in Chapter 5.

How would you like to format the table? In the previous chapter, we saw how to format the cells manually with background colour and lines. If necessary, you can delegate this task to Excel. The program has an AutoFormat function, which supports some interesting effects.

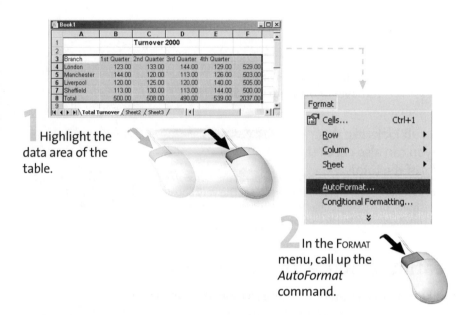

1 Highlight the data area of the table.

2 In the FORMAT menu, call up the *AutoFormat* command.

The corresponding function opens a dialog box, in which different formatting suggestions for tables are presented to you.

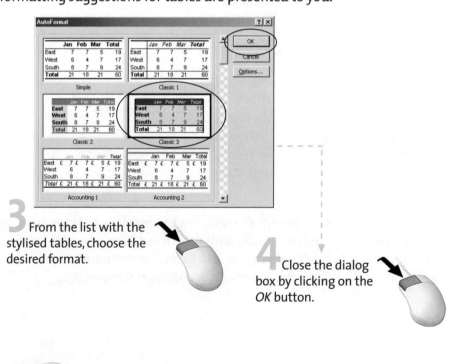

3 From the list with the stylised tables, choose the desired format.

4 Close the dialog box by clicking on the *OK* button.

Excel then transfers the format to the highlighted area of the worksheet. The result looks something like this.

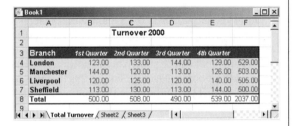

To remove this format, follow these steps. In the *AutoFormat* dialog box, choose the *None* option. You will find this option at the very bottom of the format suggestions. Use the scrollbar to leaf through the format list. As soon as you close the dialog box by clicking on the *OK* button, the new format will be inserted.

If you like the finished table, you should save the results in a file called *Turnover2000.xls* for further practice. The relevant steps are described in the previous chapter. By the way, the table will be needed again in a later chapter.

Processing data as charts

As well as working through calculations, another strength of Excel is the representation of values as charts. With a few mouse clicks, you can convert the contents of a table into a bar chart, a line chart or a pie chart, among others. I would like to show you how this works, by using the turnover table as an example. Have you still got the workbook with the turnover data that was created in the previous exercise?

1 In Excel, load the file with the workbook. - - - - - - ▸

2 Click on the *'Total turnover'* sheet tab.

\Total Turnover ⁄

277

Are you ready for the next exercise? We will now display the turnover table data as a **column chart**.

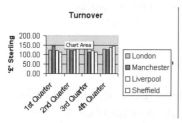

The results will look something like this. For the branches, the quarterly turnover will be represented as columns. Alternatively, you could put the bars horizontally and produce a **bar chart**.

1 In the worksheet, highlight the data in the A3:E7 cell range.

1 In the standard toolbar click on the *Chart Wizard*.

A **wizard** is a program that leads you through a specific course of actions. By means of dialog boxes, the wizard asks for information, and prepares the chart in the background. You have already met one type of wizard: the Office Wizard.

The conversion of table data into a chart is carried out in several steps. A **wizard** leads you through these steps, and from time to time asks for the necessary information.

After choosing the *Chart Wizard* button, Excel starts the corresponding function. The wizard announces its presence in the first step with a dialog box, in which you must select the chart type and the chart subtype.

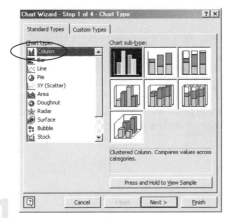

In the *Standard type* tab, in the *Chart type* area click on the *Column* entry.

Normally this type is already entered.

Choose a chart subtype from the corresponding category.

279

As an experiment you can choose different chart types. In a sort of preview, you are shown a representation of what the chart would look like. If you want to know what it would look like exactly, click on the *Press and Hold to View Sample* button. Excel then inserts a **sample** of the chart on to the tab, based on the highlighted table data.

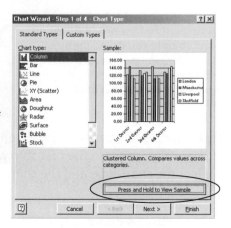

On the bottom row, the wizard has several buttons. By clicking on the *Next* and *Back* buttons, you are able to toggle between the individual steps. By clicking on *Cancel* the Wizard will be exited, without setting a chart. The button in the left-hand corner calls up the Help. At any point you can click on the *Finish* button. The wizard then uses the standard settings for the production of the chart.

3 Click on the *Next button*.

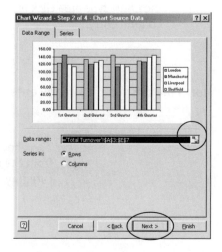

In the next step, the wizard opens a dialog box for choosing the data range of the chart.

4 As this was highlighted before you called up the wizard, you can click on the *Next* button.

Otherwise, in the *Data Range* box click on this button and highlight the data range on the worksheet. When you press the key or click on the button again, the tab will come back on screen.

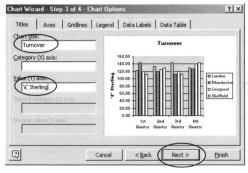

5 If you want, on the *Title* tab, you can enter a chart title as well as text for the axes legends.

6 Click again on the *Next* button.

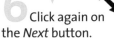

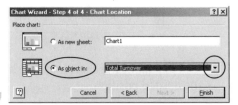

7 In this last step, decide where the chart is going to be inserted by clicking on one of the options fields.

281

The *As new sheet* option creates a *Chart* worksheet. You should then enter the sheet name into the corresponding box. Normally, however, the *As object in* option is highlighted and the current worksheet is chosen as the target. But you can choose the worksheet by clicking on the list.

8 Click on the *Finish* button.

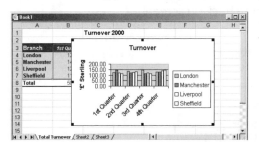

The wizard then takes your design and creates a chart from the table data. The chart will be entered on to the '*Total turnover*' worksheet.

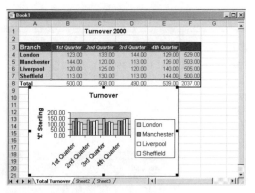

9 Highlight the chart and drag it to the desired position.

You can change the chart size using the drag handles (the small boxes on the edge) shown on the border of the highlighted chart.

Changing the chart type

Do you want to work on the chart later (for example, change the type of chart)?

1 Highlight the chart by clicking on it.

2 In the standard toolbar click on *Chart Wizard*.

The wizard appears in a dialog box again and leads you through the steps outlined above.

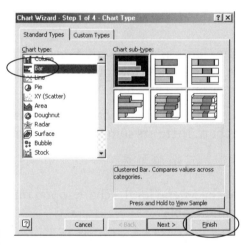

3 In the *Chart Type* box, click on the *Bar* entry.

4 Choose a chart subtype from the corresponding category.

5 Click on the *Finish* button.

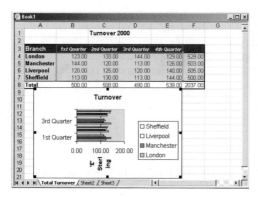

The wizard then produces a bar chart like the one in this diagram. Naturally you can click on the *Next* button and go through the other steps to set the chart options.

Creating a pie chart

In many evaluations, you see pie charts as a representation of different data. As a very simple example, we will show the total sums for the year turnover of the branches in the form of a pie chart.

This is very simple: you only need to highlight the data, call up the Chart Wizard and then choose a pie chart. There are some details to take into account:

⇥ The branch names will serve as the legend for the chart, so you must include the first column of the data table.

⇥ The results are in the last column of the table and are the basis for the chart.

In Excel, this task can also be solved with a few mouse clicks.

Branch	1st Quarter	2nd Quarter	3rd Quarter	4th Quarter	
London	123.00	133.00	144.00	129.00	529.00
Manchester	144.00	120.00	113.00	126.00	503.00
Liverpool	120.00	125.00	120.00	140.00	505.00
Sheffield	113.00	130.00	113.00	144.00	500.00
Total	500.00	508.00	490.00	539.00	2037.00

1 Highlight the two cell areas A4:A7 and F4:F7.

You probably have problems highlighting these two areas without involving the cells in between. First, highlight the A4:A7 cell range. Then hold down the ⎗Ctrl⎘ key and highlight the F4:F7 cell range. You should note that, by pressing and holding down the ⎗Ctrl⎘ key, you are able to **highlight independent cell areas**.

2 In the standard toolbar click on the *Chart Wizard* button.

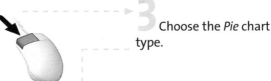

3 Choose the *Pie* chart type.

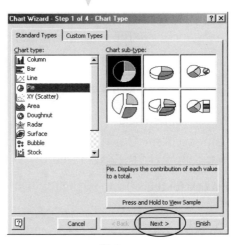

4 Click on the *Next* button.

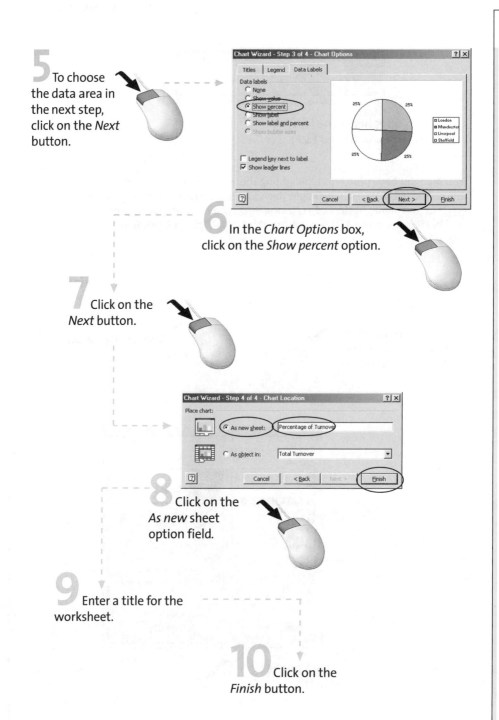

5 To choose the data area in the next step, click on the *Next* button.

6 In the *Chart Options* box, click on the *Show percent* option.

7 Click on the *Next* button.

8 Click on the *As new* sheet option field.

9 Enter a title for the worksheet.

10 Click on the *Finish* button.

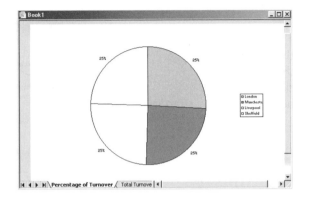

Excel now shows a new
chart sheet with a pie
chart on it.

You can see that creating a chart with Excel is no problem. The wizard
offers many other options for the creation of a chart, that will not be
discussed in this book. If you need to, consult the Help program or
additional literature (e.g. *Excel 2000 In No Time*, Prentice Hall).

Further Excel work techniques

You have already learnt much about Excel in the previous pages. A great
deal will also be known to you because of its similarities with other
Office and Windows programs. Now we will look at some specialised
work techniques, which you may need quite often.

Highlighting cell ranges

You have used the highlighting of cell ranges, in an Excel calculations
table, many times on the previous pages. To reinforce the relevant
techniques I would like to go over them once again and show
a few tricks.

1 Open a new workbook.

	A	B	C	D
1	COSTS			
2				
3	**Expenses**	**Year**	**Month**	
4	Credit Card	1400.00		
5	Leasing Rates	2800.00		
6	Insurances	1300.00		
7	Taxes	435.00		
8	Sum	5935.00		
9				
10	Petrol		300.00	
11	Repairs		500.00	
12				

Book2 — Sheet1 / Sheet2 / Sheet3

2 Enter the table shown here into the worksheet.

We will go through some exercises with this example.

1 Click on cell A5 as the top left corner of a cell range.

2 By holding down the left mouse button, diagonally drag the pointer to cell B8.

	A	B	C	D
1	COSTS			
2				
3	**Expenses**	**Year**	**Month**	
4	Credit Card	1400.00		
5	Leasing Rates	2800.00		
6	Insurances	1300.00		
7	Taxes	435.00		
8	Sum	5935.00		
9				
10	Petrol		300.00	
11	Repairs		500.00	
12				

Book2 — Sheet1 / Sheet2 / Sheet3

Excel colours in the relevant cells of this rectangular area. The area is highlighted.

Would you like to highlight another area that is not adjacent to this one? You have used this technique before.

3 During the following steps, hold down the Ctrl key.

4 Click on cell A10.

5 Click on cell C10 ...

6 ... now drag the mouse to cell C11.

The result looks like this. Excel highlights several non-adjacent areas.

	A	B	C	D
	Book2			
1	COSTS			
2				
3	Expenses	Year	Month	
4	Credit Card	1400.00		
5	Leasing Rates	2800.00		
6	Insurances	1300.00		
7	Taxes	435.00		
8	Sum	5935.00		
9				
10	Petrol		300.00	
11	Repairs		500.00	
12				

Sheet1 / Sheet2 / Sheet3 /

TIP

To remove a highlight, it is sufficient to click on a non-highlighted cell.

	A	B	C	D
	Book2			
1	COSTS			
2				
3	Expenses	Year	Month	
4	Credit Card	1400.00		
5	Leasing Rates	2800.00		
6	Insurances	1300.00		
7	Taxes	435.00		
8	Sum	5935.00		
9				
10	Petrol		300.00	
11	Repairs		500.00	
12				

Sheet1 / Sheet2 / Sheet3 /

1 Now click on the column head of a worksheet.

Excel highlights the entire column.

TIP

If you hold down the mouse button and drag the pointer over several row or column heads, these will also become highlighted.

2 Click on the start of a row on the worksheet.

Excel highlights the entire row.

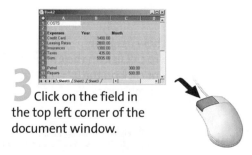

3 Click on the field in the top left corner of the document window.

Excel highlights the whole worksheet. Here are some techniques for highlighting with the keyboard:

Key	Effect
Ctrl + A	Highlights the whole worksheet.
Ctrl + ⇧ + →	Highlights the cell to the right of the current cell.
Ctrl + ⇧ + ←	Highlights the cell to the left of the current cell.
Ctrl + ⇧ + ↑	Highlights the cell above the current cell.
Ctrl + ⇧ + ↓	Highlights the cell below the current cell.

There are more key codes for highlighting in a table. Personally I prefer using the mouse so that I don't have to learn the key combinations above.

Cutting and pasting

As in Word and other Windows programs, in Excel you can cut out cell ranges and paste them into other places.

1 Highlight the cell range that you want to move. - - - - - ▶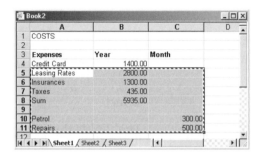

2 Click on the *Cut* button or click on the Ctrl+X key combination.

In contrast to Word, the cut out area does not disappear! Excel simply highlights the relevant cell range by surrounding it with a dotted row.

By pressing the Esc key, Excel clears the *Cut* option.

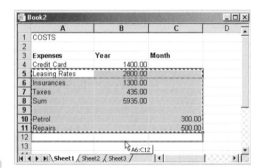

3 Using the mouse, you can now drag the dotted border line to another cell.

Excel displays the new position of the range with a grey row.

As soon as you let go of the mouse button, Excel pastes the highlighted and cut area to its new position. Is the dragging too difficult for you or for some other reason not possible?

1 Then follow steps 1 and 2 above.

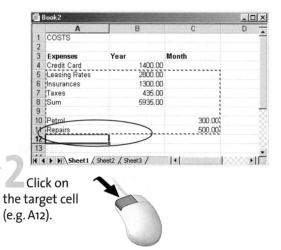

2 Click on the target cell (e.g. A12).

This can be a cell in the highlighted range, in another book or in another worksheet. Excel removes the highlight, but the dotted line stays.

3 Click on the *Paste* button, or press the Ctrl+V key combination.

Excel pastes the previously highlighted and cut area to the new position.

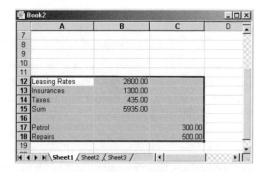

You can undo the paste straight away by pressing the Ctrl+Z key combination.

Sometimes when pasting, the clipboard toolbar appears. Microsoft Office 2000 can hold several cut out document areas (from Word, Excel etc.). The list shows you, in stylised symbols, what and how many cut outs are saved. Click on the symbol of the desired cutout in order to paste it into the document.

Copying

Alternatively, you could highlight a cell area and place it in another area as a copy.

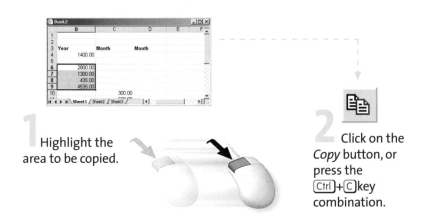

1 Highlight the area to be copied.

2 Click on the *Copy* button, or press the [Ctrl]+[C] key combination.

Excel highlights the area with a dotted line.

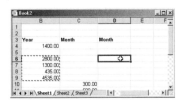

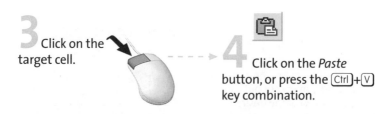

3 Click on the target cell.

4 Click on the *Paste* button, or press the `Ctrl`+`V` key combination.

Excel makes a copy of the highlighted area in the new position.

In this way you can transfer data from one worksheet to another document at any time.

Would you like to insert or remove entire rows or columns from the worksheet? Highlight the column/row, open the context menu and call up the corresponding command. You can manipulate cells in a similar way.

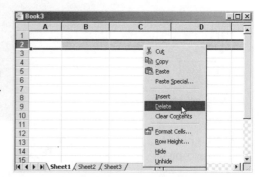

Using the thousand decimal point

For the representation of large numbers, the thousand figure is often interrupted by a decimal point.

You can do this in Excel with a simple mouse click. Here is a somewhat modified worksheet for identifying motor vehicle costs.

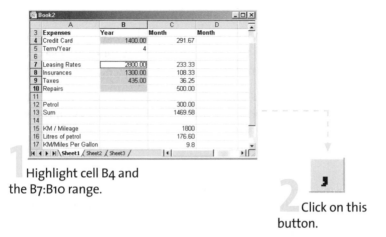

1 Highlight cell B4 and the B7:B10 range.

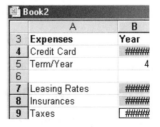

2 Click on this button.

Excel now shows the values with a point after the thousand figure.

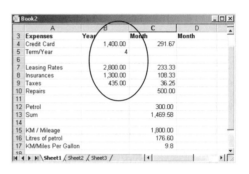

Notice that the button for the thousand decimal point indicator moves the numbers to the middle of the column. This does not always look that good in a table column with different number formats.

Help, the numbers have disappeared !

Sometimes there is a surprise when working in Excel. Perhaps it has already happened to you in the previous example when inserting the thousand decimal point.

You change something on a table, all the numbers disappear and, in their place, the # symbol appears in the cells, as shown in the picture here.

	A	B
	Book2	
3	**Expenses**	**Year**
4	Credit Card	#####
5	Term/Year	4
6		
7	Leasing Rates	#####
8	Insurances	#####
9	Taxes	#####

When this happened to me for the first time, I was somewhat stunned. But the solution is simple: with the # sign Excel is saying that there is not enough room in the cell to show the whole number. To avoid mistakes being made by numbers being cut off, Excel uses the # symbol.

How do we get the numbers back? You just have to make the column wider. As soon as enough room is available, the numbers will return.

You can practise this by making a column narrower so that the numbers do not fit. Then increase the width of the column to see the numbers again. Still having problems with changing the column width? In Chapter 5 you will find a description of the relevant steps.

As well as the # sign, there are other signs that Excel uses to inform you of mistakes in the worksheet. The following table contains an overview of these error indicators.

Indicator	Meaning
#DIV/0	Division by 0 in a formula.
#NV	Necessary value not available.
#NAME?	A given name of an Excel area is not available.
#ZERO!	A given intersection is improper.
#NUMBER!	The number is being used incorrectly.
#REFERENCE!	Illegal reference to a cell.
#VALUE!	False number or operator used.

You will find more details on these mistakes in the Excel Online Help.

Showing currency amounts

One point that I have not yet mentioned is currency amounts. Until now the values would have simply been entered and provided with decimal points. It is important, however, to have the currency signs within the table. You could certainly enter £ or euro into a column title. But for some currencies this is not possible.

The solution in Excel comes in the form of the currency symbol and the euro symbol buttons.

Try to carry out the following steps. Then the effect of the two buttons will become clear quickly.

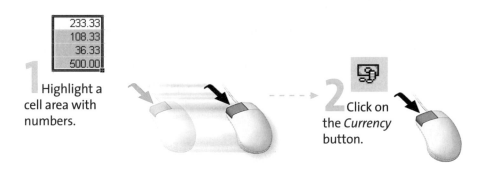

1 Highlight a cell area with numbers.

2 Click on the *Currency* button.

As soon as you remove the highlight, the currency symbol is entered in the cell. In the English Excel version, this is '£'.

£	233.33
£	108.33
£	36.33
£	500.00

3 Highlight the cell area again.

4 Click on the *euro* button.

€	233.33
€	108.33
€	36.33
€	500.00

Excel now adds the euro symbol to the corresponding numbers.

With these two buttons you can see that Excel can apply the currency signs directly to the values.

297

Applying specific cell formats

You have already received some information concerning the formatting of cells in Excel. In Excel the format of a cell influences considerably the display of the cell contents. I have briefly pointed out the relevant problems in another section. For the purposes of clarification, we will try another little experiment here.

1 In an empty cell, enter the value 12:00.

Excel shows the value as the time.

| Time | 12:00 |

2 Delete the cell content. ┈┈┈➤ **3**

| Time | 13.5 |

Now enter the value 13.5 in the cell.

| Time | 12:00 |

As soon as you press the ⏎ key, Excel will show the value 12:00 once again in the cell.

The explanation for Excel's behaviour is quite simple: after the first entry the corresponding cell is provided with the 'Date/Time' format, and before it is shown, Excel changes the entry so that it has the right presentation. However, when deleting the cell content, the cell format remains. Type another value into the cell; Excel takes this in, but once again shows the old cell content with the old format. Sometimes this leads to baffling results.

So, how can we set the cell format back to the default form? And how can we set specific cell formats?

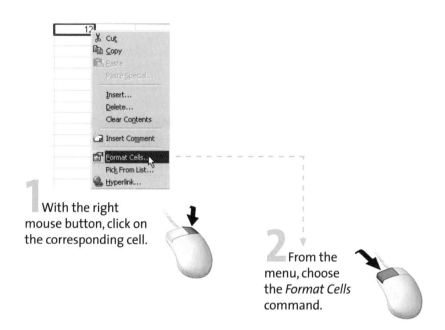

1 With the right mouse button, click on the corresponding cell.

2 From the menu, choose the *Format Cells* command.

Excel now opens the *Format Cells* dialog box, which contains several tabs for setting cell formats. On the *Number* tab find the entry for the relevant cell format. The *Category* list shows the cell formats that are available for the cells. Here is where a user-defined format for the time is used.

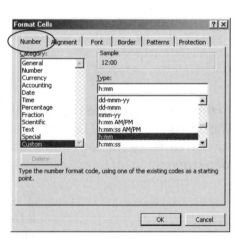

1 To return the cell to the normal format, click on the *General* entry.

Excel shows a preview of the cell in the *Sample* area.

2 Close the tab by clicking on the *OK* button.

The entry 13.5 now appears in the display.

In the *Format Cells* dialog box, you also had the opportunity to influence the cell content display. Let's suppose that you would like to enter some foreign currency amounts into a table (and convert the amount, if necessary).

1 On a new worksheet, enter the currency value.

- - - - - - - - - - ▶

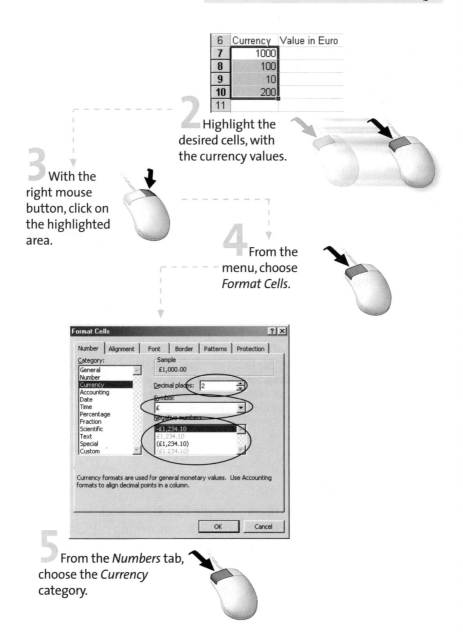

6	Currency	Value in Euro
7	1000	
8	100	
9	10	
10	200	
11		

2 Highlight the desired cells, with the currency values.

3 With the right mouse button, click on the highlighted area.

4 From the menu, choose *Format Cells*.

5 From the *Numbers* tab, choose the *Currency* category.

In the tab, Excel now shows the setting of two decimal places, the currency symbol and also the display of negative numbers. If you would like to have a particular presentation of negative numbers, choose the *Negative numbers* option.

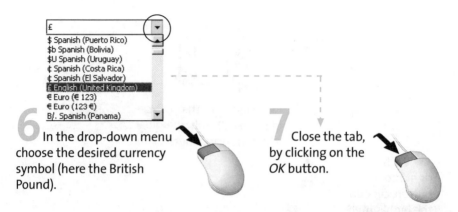

6 In the drop-down menu choose the desired currency symbol (here the British Pound).

7 Close the tab, by clicking on the *OK* button.

Excel now shows the cells with the chosen format and the currency values.

In this way you can format cells just as you like.

	A	B
	Book4	
4	Time	12:00
5		
6	Currency	Value in Euro
7	£1,000.00	
8	£100.00	
9	£10.00	
10	£200.00	
11		

> In the *Custom* category, you are able to set your own format (the explanation of which is unfortunately not in this book). In the other tabs you can also influence the appearance of the cell as well as the arrangement of the cell content. Perhaps you could experiment a little with these options.

Using functions

Up until now, you have learnt only simple **functions**, such as AutoSum. The program can offer much more though, concerning calculations. On the previous pages, you have learnt the options on currency values. How would you show these values in pounds or euros?

Here you can see an expanded table with columns for the currency values in pounds as well as euros.

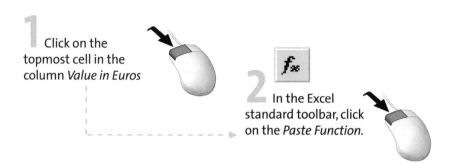

1 Click on the topmost cell in the column *Value in Euros*

2 In the Excel standard toolbar, click on the *Paste Function.*

Functions are calculation instructions that are preset in Excel. A function has a name and is called up with parameters. The value of these parameters are evaluated and the function enters the results in the active cell. The sum function will be given as =SUM(A1:A3), for example. The A1:A3 cell range is the parameter here. The calculation instructions state only that the cell contents are to be calculated.

Excel now opens the *Paste Function* dialog box. In the *Function category* column, Excel lists all the available categories. The right hand column *Function name* lists the names of the corresponding functions. When you highlight a function, the function definition is entered into the dialog box.

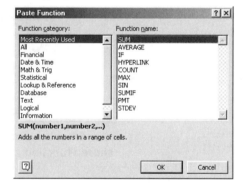

For the next step, the function for the conversion of currency values will be used.

3 Choose the *All* option from the *Function category*.

4 Choose the EUROCONVERT entry as the *Function name.*

303

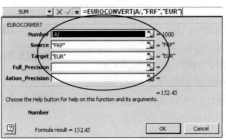

5 Close the dialog box by clicking on the *OK* button.

Excel opens the formula palette, where the parameters for the function are called up.

6 Enter the parameters for the chosen function.

> **TIP**
>
> In order to enter a cell reference into a table, click on this button 🔢 in the corresponding field. The formula palette will disappear and you can now highlight on the worksheet. As soon as you press the ⏎ key, the formula palette will return. You can see the formula expression in the formula bar.

7 After entering the necessary parameters, click on the *OK* button.

Excel transfers the formula to the active cell and shows the results.

For the EUROCONVERT function, you must have at least three parameters. The first parameter, *Number,* is displayed in the cell that has the value to be converted. The *Source* and *Target* parameters serve for the application of a character string, that sets the source currency and the target currency. With FRF the French franc will be chosen as the source currency, while EUR sets the euro as the target currency. The Pound is shown in instead of the pound sterling. A list of the currency symbols can be seen in the Excel Help.

For the result, you will see the calculated euro value in the target cell.

Currency	Value in Euro	Value in Pounds
£1,000.00	152.45	
£100.00		
£10.00		
£200.00		

If you want to correct the formula after entry, click on the cell or highlight the formula in the formula bar and just click on the *Paste Function*. The formula palette will be called up again, and you can change the parameters.

Now the other cells need to be worked on.

1 Copy the conversion formula for currency values into the row below.

2 Click on the top row of the *Value in Pounds* column.

3 Put the conversion formula for euro values in pounds in the next column.

4 Copy the formula into the rest of the cells in that column.

Here you can see the finished table, where the currency value has been converted from French francs to euros and then to pounds.

Currency	Value in Euro	Value in Pounds
£1,000.00	152.45	=EUROCONVERT(B7,"EUR","£")
£100.00		
£10.00		
£200.00		

305

You can see the conversion formula for euros to pounds in the table. You have only changed the parameters for the currency sign.

With this simple practice, you have not only learnt how to apply a formula. As a by-product you have also produced a conversion formula between two currencies. It should now be easy, with your knowledge, to create a table with a conversion formula between euros and pounds, pounds and euros or other currencies.

AutoCorrect and spell check

When entering text into a worksheet, you can avoid typing and spelling errors. We have already covered this in the first chapter with Word. This Autocorrect function works exactly the same in Excel as it does in Word, e.g. 'teh' is spotted as a mistake and changed automatically to 'the'.

1 Click on the *Spelling* button.

Excel opens the *Spelling* dialog box.

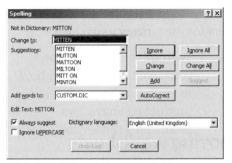

Carry out the corrections in this dialog box. The buttons have the same function as in Word.
If necessary, read the end of Chapter 2 to see what you need to do here.

Opening a new worksheet

Normally, Excel opens a new workbook with three worksheets. Sooner or later, you may need an extra worksheet in your workbook. A new blank worksheet can be entered with a few mouse clicks.

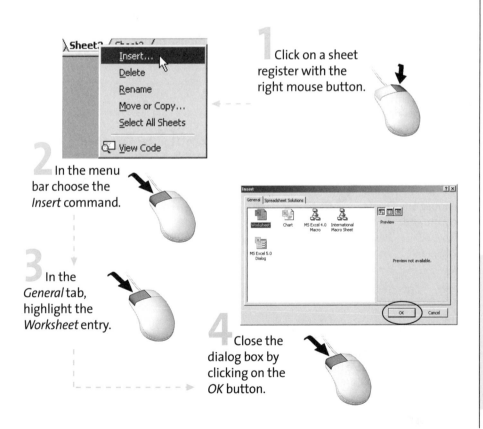

1 Click on a sheet register with the right mouse button.

2 In the menu bar choose the *Insert* command.

3 In the *General* tab, highlight the *Worksheet* entry.

4 Close the dialog box by clicking on the *OK* button.

In this tab, you do not only have to insert blank worksheets as the form of a table. The symbols on this tab allow you to insert worksheets for charts, presentations and so on.

Excel then enters a new blank worksheet into the workbook.

Choosing, deleting and moving worksheets

Does the workbook contain several worksheets? Would you like to move these to another workbook and work on them?

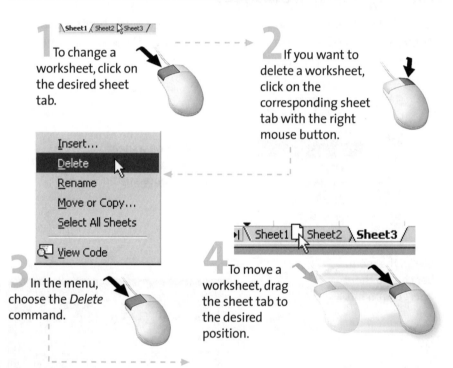

1 To change a worksheet, click on the desired sheet tab.

2 If you want to delete a worksheet, click on the corresponding sheet tab with the right mouse button.

Insert...
Delete
Rename
Move or Copy...
Select All Sheets
View Code

3 In the menu, choose the *Delete* command.

4 To move a worksheet, drag the sheet tab to the desired position.

By clicking on the buttons in the bottom left of the document window, you are able to scroll through the visible area of the sheet tab.

5 To increase the size of the sheet tab, drag the partition row between the sheet tab and the picture scroll bar to the right.

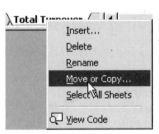

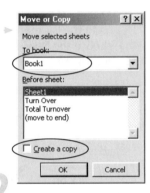

1 To copy or move a worksheet, click on the sheet tab with the right mouse button and choose the *Move or Copy* command.

2 In the *Move or Copy* dialog box, choose the target workbook.

3 Choose the worksheet that contains the highlighted worksheet, in the *Before sheet* list.

4 To copy a sheet, highlight the *Create a copy* button.

5 Close the dialog box by clicking on the *OK* button.

With this technique, you can move or copy worksheets between workbooks too.

Creating calculations in Excel

We will now use what we have learnt in the previous sections to create calculations in Excel. The program already contains a template in the form of a Spreadsheet Solutions that takes much of the work from you.

1 In the FILE menu choose the *New* command.

2 In the *New* dialog box activate the *Spreadsheet Solutions* tab.

3 Click on the *Expense Statement* icon.

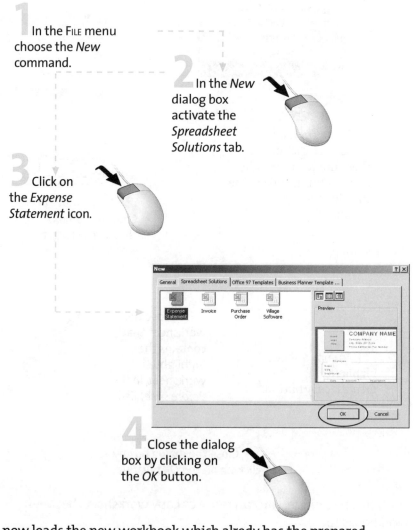

4 Close the dialog box by clicking on the *OK* button.

Excel now loads the new workbook which alredy has the prepared calculations formula.

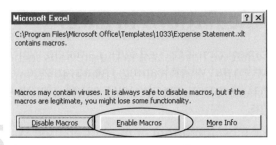

5 The query mentions macros; confirm by clicking on the *Enable Macros* button.

Macros are collections of program instructions that let them be automatically carried out. The advantage of macros is that these commands can be repeated quite often. The risk is that macros may contain destructive instructions, such as deleting hard disks. Therefore, Excel offers you, when loading a new document, the choice of whether to include the macros or not by asking this query. You can enable or disenable the macros by clicking on the appropriate button.

Now the calculations formula will be loaded. Supply the formula with an address and enter the calculation position. By clicking on the *Adapt* button you can supply master data such as the VAT rate. The *Calculation* toolbar allows you to call up additional functions.

You can then print the calculation formula, save it as a workbook and reload it later on. The formula is organised as a workbook structured as a spreadsheet. The execution is carried out by a macro, which is automatically carried out when loading. The advantage of this spreadsheet is that Microsoft has already created a formula, which helps you in calculations.

You now know the most important or most often used Excel functions. Certainly, there is still a lot to know about this program. You can always find out more in publications that deal with Excel on a more in-depth basis.

Test Your knowledge

To test your knowledge, you should answer the following questions. The answers are on page 585.

1 Create a worksheet with the cell values taken from another worksheet.

2 Create a table with some values in a column. In two other cells, give the minimum and maximum values of the column.

3 Convert amounts of euros to another currency.

4 Create a table showing the market share of three products. Show the market share in a pie chart.

5 Create a table with address data and then sort the table according to address or post code.

What's in this chapter?

Do you have to give presentations frequently? If so Microsoft PowerPoint is just the right tool for you. With PowerPoint, the presentations program in the Microsoft Office 2000 family, you can produce overheads, Web sites and slides, or you can design and reproduce your presentations directly on your computer. This chapter will give you a short introduction to PowerPoint's various functions. You will see how to create an entire presentation and you will get to know the most important functions. At the end, you will be able to start up the program, create a presentation, and give a slideshow. Later on you will know how to print and save your presentations.

You can already:

Now you will learn:

PowerPoint – the first steps

Do you frequently create or give presentations? Have you been wasting time putting together the slides in Word or other design programs, and worrying about the time lapse between your original idea and the production of it? If so, perhaps you should look more closely at PowerPoint. The program is *the* presentations work tool. With just a few clicks of the mouse you can produce material of a professional standard for various presentation media. A presentation is already shown as a PowerPoint document and its reproduction is no problem. With PowerPoint even the creation of leaflets and advertising brochures is possible.

In PowerPoint, some details are treated differently to those in Word or in Excel, so the structure of this chapter will be a little different to the previous ones.

Now let us start PowerPoint

Before we go into details, we should start Microsoft PowerPoint.

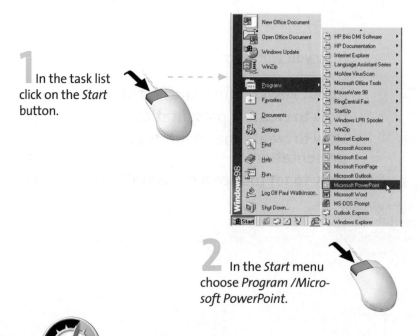

1 In the task list click on the *Start* button.

2 In the *Start* menu choose *Program /Micro-soft PowerPoint*.

When you open a document in Word or Excel, you simply open a blank document. In PowerPoint, however, you will see a dialog box which asks you exactly what you want to do.

TIP

The question in the *PowerPoint* dialog box allows you to load an existing presentation as well as set up a new one. When setting up a new presentation it is recommended that you either use the wizard or set it up on a pre-prepared document template. You can choose these options directly from the option field. You will find an explanation about how to create a presentation later on.

CAUTION

You can highlight the control button *Don't show this dialog box again* in the *PowerPoint* dialog box. The text in this dialog box will then disappear. In this case click on the *New* command in the FILE menu to create a new presentation (*see below*). You will find tips on recalling the dialog in the index.

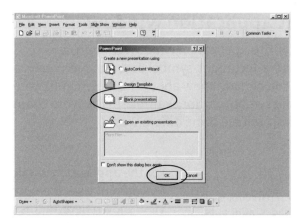

1 In the *PowerPoint* dialog box click on *Blank presentation* in the option choices.

2 Confirm this by clicking on the *OK* button.

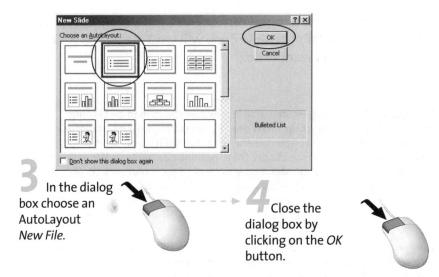

3 In the dialog box choose an AutoLayout *New File*.

4 Close the dialog box by clicking on the *OK* button.

PowerPoint now produces a new document on the basis of the AutoLayout. This AutoLayout lets you decide which elements (headings, lists, graphics etc.) to insert into the page. You then see the application Window with the chosen layout.

The PowerPoint application window

Similar to Word or Excel, this application window contains a representation of the new document, symbol bars and menu bars as well as the status bar. You already know about these elements; you will find tips for the drawing symbol bar, for example, in the Word chapter. In PowerPoint, however, you will see some differences.

The presentation can be prepared for **various media** (screen, overhead slides, print outs, 35mm slides). For the listener, leaflets can be produced, and for the speaker there are additional notes.

For the application window, PowerPoint uses the normal view shown here. In this view you immediately see an overview of your presentation with the document page as well as various windows containing help information.

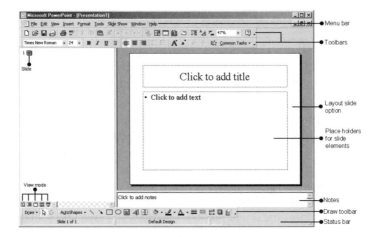

A presentation is made up of one or more pages. In PowerPoint these pages will be described as slides. The layout view of the slide appears in the right-hand part of the document area.

On the left, PowerPoint displays the stylised pages of all the slides of a presentation as a structure (only one slide is available here).

Notes are given for every slide (e.g. with regards to the content or tips concerning presentation). These notes are entered in the window below the document window.

In the status bar, PowerPoint informs you of the number of the slide as well as of the presentation template being used.

With the above steps, a blank document with the normal design will be produced (i.e. a white background). This can then be filled with text. PowerPoint, however, also lets you use more colourful designs with corresponding backgrounds, colour and font combinations. These designs can be called up from the prepared **design templates.**

Getting to know PowerPoint

Microsoft PowerPoint is a program with extremely powerful functions. For reasons of space, the introduction to PowerPoint in this book must be condensed into one chapter. However, on the following pages you will learn the basis of how to quickly create your own presentation. Further information is supplied by the Help program. In order for you to quickly acquire a first impression of the possibilities of PowerPoint, call up the prepared Microsoft PowerPoint – Online Presentation.

A requirement for the following steps is that the wizard is switched off. Furthermore, the Office 2000 CD-ROM must be inserted in the installation drive. PowerPoint then loads the Online Presentation from the CD-ROM and shows it on the screen.

Have you still got PowerPoint loaded? If not, start the program.

Are you ready? Then the presentation can start on screen.

1 Call up the *PowerPoint* Help program from the help menu.

Alternatively, you can also press the F1 key or click on the *Microsoft PowerPoint Help* icon in the symbol bar.

2 Choose the symbol *First Step* from the *Content* register card, and then double-click - - - - - - ▸ on the heading 'Start of the Online learning program to the introduction of PowerPoint'.

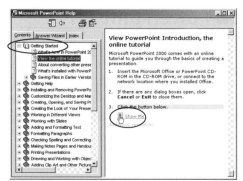

3 In the *Help* window click on
Show me, next to the pointer.

Are the wizard's speech bubbles
appearing instead of the *Help*
window? If so, click on the speech box
in the first speech bubble and type in
'getting to know PowerPoint'.
Confirm the entry by clicking on the
Search button. In the next speech
bubble, click on the point 'Start the
Online Program for the introduction
to PowerPoint'. Then follow step 3.

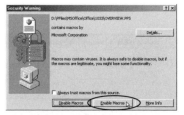

4 Confirm the dialog box
with the macro warning by
clicking on the *Enable Macros*
button.

PowerPoint now starts the presentation. The slides take up the whole screen. By clicking on the buttons shown you can leaf through the slides.

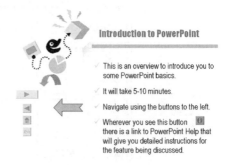

You can exit the presentation by either clicking on the exit button or pressing the [Esc] button. As the presentation was created in PowerPoint it then shows the slides in the applications window. You can then have a look at the construction of these slides.

Ending PowerPoint

Ending PowerPoint is really simple as you have carried out the process many times.

1 In the FILE menu choose the command *Exit*.

If you simply want to close the document, in the FILE menu choose the *Close* command.

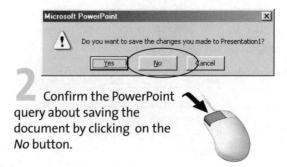

2 Confirm the PowerPoint query about saving the document by clicking on the *No* button.

In this case the document would not be saved. When closing down the Online program you should always decline to save any changes you have made. Saving a presentation will be explained later.

A few more hints

Before you read the following section and start creating your own presentation, there are a few things to think about. Most importantly, your presentation first. Settle the following points before the conversion to PowerPoint.

⇉ **Who is the target group?** Visualise the target group for your message. Is the presentation going to take place in an auditorium before a mixed public group, a specialist group, laymen, or a mixed professional group? Match the content and the message to the target group.

⇉ **What do I want to say?** This question stands in the foreground of every presentation. Make it clear what message you want to get across to your listeners (or readers in the case of Web sites and leaflets). Plan highlights, so that your listeners don't forget everything you've said.

⇉ **How do I want to visualise it?** With PowerPoint, many visual media are available to you, from overhead projections on slides to on-screen presentations. The influence of the media corresponds to the visual preparation of the presentation.

Once you have thought about these questions, it is a good idea to sketch your ideas for each slide on paper first. This allows you a quick overview of the material so that you can recognise the essential part without getting bogged down in the details.

When the sketches are ready, let the conversion into PowerPoint begin. Before designing the slides, put some thought into the layout of the slides. In a professional situation, most drawbacks that exist relate to corporate identity or corporate design. If this is the case for you, you must think about how these drawbacks will transfer to PowerPoint.

Remembering the motto 'less is more', you should not include more than three or four points per slide. The listener can take in these points quickly. In order to fill up the space you should use a large font (at least size 36); this means that the people in the back rows can still read it without having to use opera glasses.

Also, most speeches are limited by time, so plan beforehand the time you will allow for each point. A good idea is one or two minutes per slide. The time allowed for the speech therefore affects the number of slides.

To avoid problems with corporate design, create a slide in a standard layout. Be sparing with the use of different writing styles and sizes. Use the largest possible font size. Be brave enough to leave white spaces on the slide. Work with bullet points, paragraphs and indentations. Include pictures on the slide only if they really bring something essential to the text!

Decide the colours for the background and the contents of the slide. As well as any corporate design problems, there may be restrictions on the presentation media to take into account (paper print-outs have a different effect to overhead projections or slides).

The corporate identity (CI) defines the picture of an undertaking to the outside (public) and to the inside (colleagues). A part of the undertaking identity is the corporate design. This rules the co-ordination of letterheads, prospectuses, forms etc. with regard to slogans and logos.

Pay attention to colour co-ordination, in order to have sufficient contrast between the background and the contents. Complementary colours give a good contrast and generate attention. Related colours or different shades have a balancing/calming effect, but be critical with regard to their contrast.

Only when the above questions are answered should you start to convert the presentation.

Do the above explanations seem a little complicated to you? With reference to the presentation content, you yourself must have a clear understanding. When creating a presentation, PowerPoint helps you out by providing design templates with prepared presentation designs, where the background and colour ranges are already fixed.

Creating a presentation

At the start I stated that a presentation in PowerPoint is made up of one or more slides. Therefore, the first step in creating a PowerPoint presentation is generating the requested slides. These slides can either be provided blank or with a set design. The program offers you many possibilities in this respect.

When first starting PowerPoint it is a good idea to rely on the help of the AutoContent Wizard. This leads you through the steps of creating a presentation, calls up the necessary information and then draws up a slide setting for the prepared presentation. All you need to do then is provide the content of the slides.

The alternative is to use one of these prepared presentations as a basis for your own. PowerPoint offers various designs with corresponding prepared slide settings. Or you can choose the blank presentation option from the PowerPoint dialog box at the start of the program and then insert the slides into the presentation yourself. In the following sections I would like to introduce these possibilities to you.

Go with the AutoContent Wizard

There are many ways of calling up the wizard in PowerPoint.

If you have just started PowerPoint, register the program with the *PowerPoint* dialog box.

1 Click on the *AutoContent Wizard* options box.

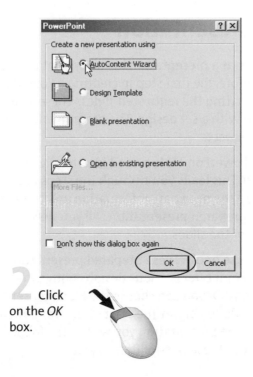

Click on the *OK* box.

If PowerPoint is already loaded, you could also call up the wizard using the following steps.

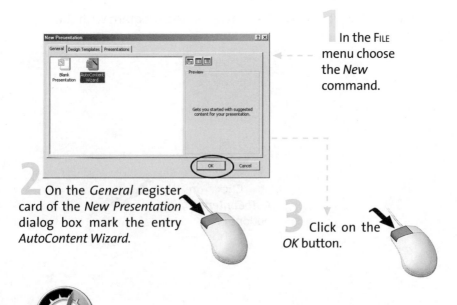

In the FILE menu choose the *New* command.

On the *General* register card of the *New Presentation* dialog box mark the entry *AutoContent Wizard*.

Click on the *OK* button.

In both ways the wizard announces itself with the opening of a dialog.
By clicking on the *Next* and *Back* panels in the wizard's footer bar you are
able to change between the individual stages.

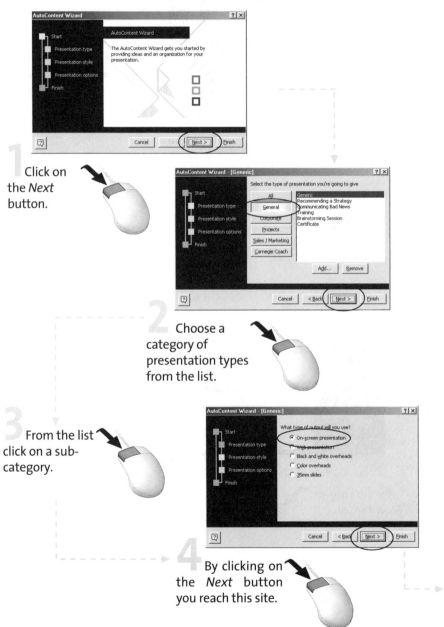

Click on
the *Next*
button.

Choose a
category of
presentation types
from the list.

From the list
click on a sub-
category.

By clicking on
the *Next* button
you reach this site.

5 Click on one of the option fields for a choice of output types.

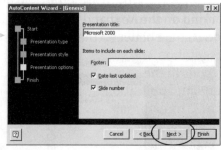

6 By clicking on the *Next* button you reach this site.

7 Complete the presentation title and, if necessary, the text and footer.

8 Set the options for the date and slide number.

9 By clicking on the *Next* button you reach the last site.

10 Click on the *Finish* button.

The wizard evaluates your input and from that it produces the slides for a presentation. You see the results in the PowerPoint application window. The external frame of this slide, as well as the structure, are already established.

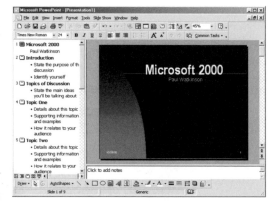

The presentation content for every slide can now be completed. To do this, just click on the free definable parameter contained in the slide and the text or content will be entered. How this works exactly will be explained later on.

The advantage of the AutoContent Wizard is that all the slides are provided with the same design. As well as that, the wizard leads you through the steps for creating the printout format etc. The disadvantage is that you only get to see the results when you press the *Ready* button. Also, the choice of presentation types seems a little unclear to me.

Presentation models

Do the disadvantages of the AutoContent Wizard that have been described bother you? Do you already know of something better with PowerPoint, or would you like to make use of the power of the program? Would you expect to see a preview of the slide design at the selection of presentation types? Before you manually design an individual slide for a presentation, I would like to show you an alternative. PowerPoint has ready-made models for presentations. These models use a design and particular background for every slide. To use a presentation model, carry out the following steps:

1 In the FILE menu choose the command *New*.

PowerPoint opens the *New Presentation* dialog box.

2 From the *Presentations* tab choose the desired model.

The preview in the right half of the window provides you with a first impression of the slide layout.

3 Click on the *OK* button to close the dialog box.

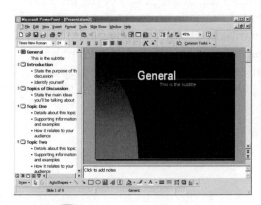

PowerPoint then creates the presentation on the basis of this model. The example shown here differs from those calculated by the AutoContent Wizard simply through the standard heading as well as the missing footer.

You can now decide which medium to use.

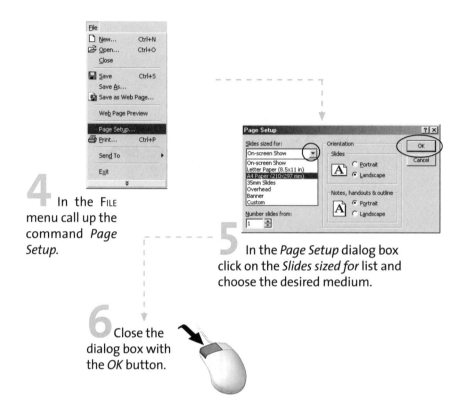

4 In the FILE menu call up the command *Page Setup*.

5 In the *Page Setup* dialog box click on the *Slides sized for* list and choose the desired medium.

6 Close the dialog box with the *OK* button.

Creating a new presentation yourself

You can also design a completely new presentation and create all the slides yourself.

1 In the symbol bar click on the *New* button.

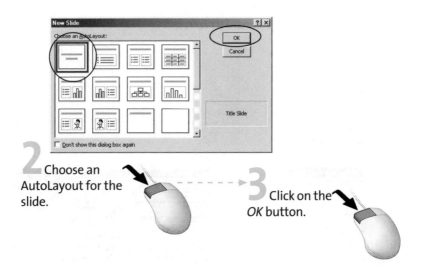

2 Choose an AutoLayout for the slide.

3 Click on the *OK* button.

Excel now shows you the new presentation which, in contrast to the other two approaches, consists only of a slide. The advantage is that you can insert a new slide into the presentation at any time, so that you have complete control over the slide layout.

The page layout and the choice of media can be determined when required by clicking on the command *Page Setup* in the FILE menu – as described in the previous section.

Saving the presentation

After designing the presentation you can then save the layout. This guarantees that, before the contents are entered, the framework is available in a file and can be reloaded again.

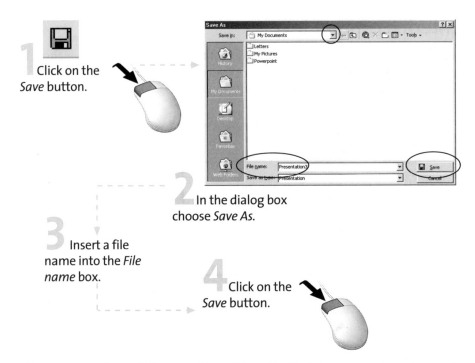

1 Click on the *Save* button.

2 In the dialog box choose *Save As*.

3 Insert a file name into the *File name* box.

4 Click on the *Save* button.

The presentation will be saved in a file with the file name extension *.ppt*. You can load this file again later on in PowerPoint and work on it.

If you would like to save your presentation under a new name and in a different file, choose the option *Save As* instead of *Save* in the FILE menu. The *Save As* dialog box will appear again and you can change the target folder as well as the file name.

If you have changed anything in the presentation, click once again on the *Save* button to store the changes in the file.

Creating the contents of a presentation

In the previous section you have learned how to lay out a presentation in PowerPoint. As soon as the program shows you the slides in formation, you are ready for the next step. It is worth forming your ideas first and then providing each slide with its own contents in turn.

Entering content text

Adding contents to the slides is really simple. As soon as you have chosen an AutoLayout, PowerPoint fits the corresponding free definable parameter into the structure of the slide.

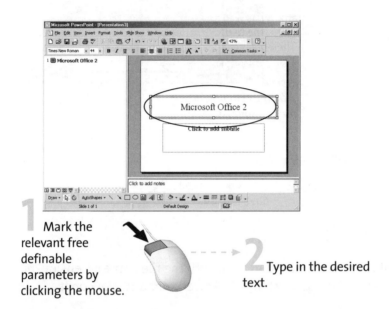

1 Mark the relevant free definable parameters by clicking the mouse.

2 Type in the desired text.

The text will appear in the free definable parameters of the slide window as well as in the structure.

If you would like to add notes to the slide just click on the relevant window and enter these notes.

Correcting entries

In typing the text there is always the chance that you will make a mistake or perhaps you would like to correct the text later on.

⇥ If you notice the mistake as you enter it, press the keys Ctrl + Z to undo the entry.

⇥ Otherwise click on the relevant text and type over it. You can, therefore, highlight pieces of text and, by pressing the Del key, erase it completely or type over it with new text.

In this respect PowerPoint behaves similarly to Word. There is also a grammar check which can be obtained by clicking on the corresponding button in the symbol bar. If necessary re-read the details of text correction in Chapter 2.

If you want to delete the parameter as well as the text, highlight the whole area (the text and the border can be seen). Then press the (Esc) button to delete it.

Click to add a subtitle

Formatting pieces of text

To format a piece of text in a slide, carry out the following steps:

1 Highlight the text to be formatted.

Microsoft Office 2

2 Click on one of the *Format* buttons either to allocate the format or to cancel it again.

To a large degree, PowerPoint uses the same buttons as Word or Excel in the mark-up of texts.

B *I* <u>U</u>   Use one of these buttons to make the font bold, italic, underlined or shaded.

In order to make the font size larger or smaller use these two buttons.

Think of the minimum font size as 36 point.

You can also choose the font and the size by using these two list fields.

The alignment of the paragraphs is controlled by the keys opposite.

You can convert paragraphs in the free definable parameter into lists or numbered points by using these two buttons.

If these formatting features are not sufficient, take the following steps:

1 With the right mouse button click on the passage.

2 In the FORMAT menu choose the command *Font*.

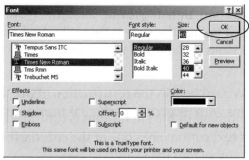

3 In the *Font* dialog box choose the desired format option.

As well as the font, size and style, in this dialog box you can also choose the colour.

4 Close the dialog box by clicking on the *OK* button.

PowerPoint then utilises the format options that have been set on the relevant piece of text.

Tips on formatting

PowerPoint offers you a whole series of formatting options. However, there is always the danger that manually formatting the text will make it worse rather than better. For example, a bad colour combination can reduce the contrast in the report.

A mixture of different font styles and sizes does not especially improve the presentation. Under the keyword Typography there is sufficient literature to be found on the correct arrangement of texts.

Be sparing with highlighting. Formatting long pieces of text in italics considerably reduces its legibility. The same goes for bold type and underlining.

Above all, when formatting manually you should bear in mind that the AutoLayouts in PowerPoint already provide the correct font size for the corresponding slide elements. The slide is then allocated another outline model, where colours and background will be correspondingly fitted (*see below*).

If you let the Office Wizard help in the construction of the slide, it will supervise your actions with respect to particular framework criteria.

If the format of your text contravenes one of the criteria, the wizard inserts a light bulb symbol into the layout.

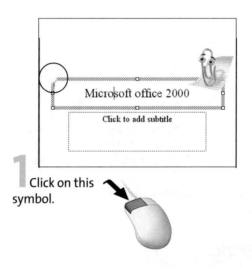

1 Click on this symbol.

In a speech bubble the wizard now gives you hints and tips about correcting the layout or the text.

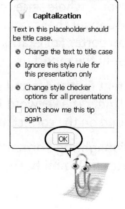

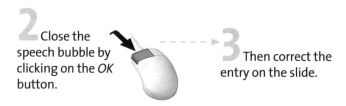

2 Close the speech bubble by clicking on the *OK* button.

3 Then correct the entry on the slide.

Adding or removing slides

Do you need more slides than are available in the presentation? With a few mouse clicks you can insert an additional slide into the presentation.

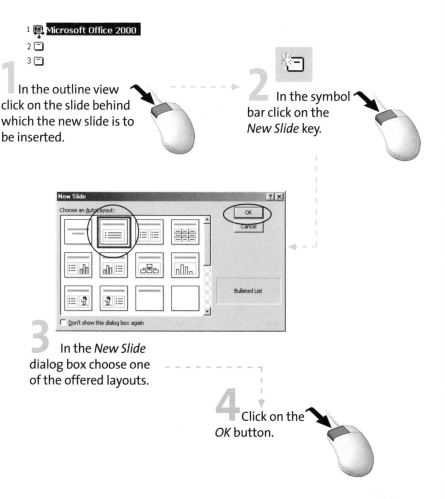

1 In the outline view click on the slide behind which the new slide is to be inserted.

2 In the symbol bar click on the *New Slide* key.

3 In the *New Slide* dialog box choose one of the offered layouts.

4 Click on the *OK* button.

339

If you have clicked on the control button *Don't show this dialog box again*, this dialog box will not appear in future. You can call it up in the FORMAT menu; by clicking on the *General* tab you will find the command *Slide layout*.

Always choose the AutoLayout that you will come to next. By doing this you will not delete any important information.

The above steps will let PowerPoint insert a new slide. The slide already possesses the free definable parameters in accordance with the chosen layout.

Do you want to remove a slide from the presentation? Then carry out the following measures:

You can highlight more than one slide by holding down the Ctrl button.

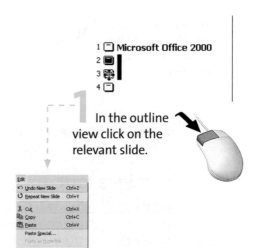

In the outline view click on the relevant slide.

Have you deleted a slide by mistake? Press the key combination Ctrl+Z straight away, and PowerPoint will undo the last command.

In the EDIT menu choose the command *Delete Slide*.

Rearranging slides

Should the sequence of slides be changed?
This can be carried out directly with the mouse.

1 In the outline view highlight the symbol of the desired slide.

1 ☐ Microsoft Office 2000
2 ☐
3 ☐
4 ☐

2 Drag the symbol of the slide to its new position in the outline view.

As soon as you release the left mouse button PowerPoint files the relevant slide.

PowerPoint also has a slide sorter view (*see below*). This enables you to move the slides about by clicking on the mouse.

Adapting slide layout

Have you structured a slide on the basis of an AutoLayout, but are not convinced that this layout is suitable for your requirements? Would you like to allocate a background to the slide, or fit the layout on to a model? This can also be done later on with a few clicks of the mouse.

1 Highlight the slide in the outline view.

2 With the right mouse button click on an empty place on the slide.

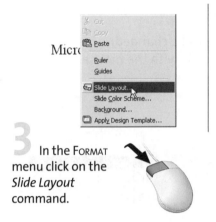

Micro

3 In the FORMAT menu click on the *Slide Layout* command.

PowerPoint will now open the *Slide Layout* dialog box.

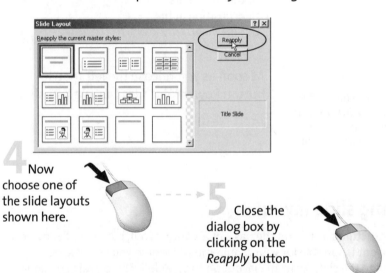

4 Now choose one of the slide layouts shown here.

5 Close the dialog box by clicking on the *Reapply* button.

Making use of Apply Design

When you lay out a presentation with the wizard, it provides each individual slide with a background style as well as all the slides having the same font style and colour composition. You can also allocate these layout characteristics to manual presentation slides. For this you need the provided PowerPoint Apply Design.

Using the right mouse button, click on an empty place on the slide.

In the context menu choose the command *Apply Design*.

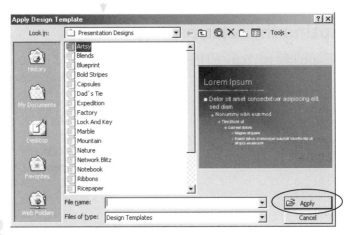

In the *Presentations Design* dialog box choose one of the designs offered.

By clicking on a design it will be shown on the right-hand side.

Close the dialog box by clicking on the *Apply* button.

343

PowerPoint applies this design to the relevant slide. Not only will the background pattern be changed, but PowerPoint also adapts the colour co-ordination etc. to fit the design.

Microsoft Office 2000

- ■Microsoft Word 2000
- ■Microsoft Excel 2000
- ■Microsoft Access 2000
- ■Microsoft PowerPoint 2000
- ■Microsoft PhotoDraw 2000
- ■Microsoft Outlook 2000

The colour co-ordinator sets the colours to be used for the background, the text etc.

Adapting the colour range

Would you like to change the design's colour co-ordination?

1 In the outline view highlight the slide.

2 Using the right mouse button, click on an empty space on the slide.

> ✂ Cut
> 📋 Copy
> 📋 Paste
>
> Ruler
> Guides
>
> 🖾 Slide Layout...
> Slide Color Scheme...
> Background...
> 🖳 Apply Design Template...

3 In the context menu call up the command *Slide Color Scheme*.

PowerPoint will now open the dialog box colour scheme.

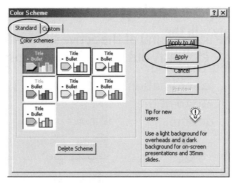

4 On the *Standard* tab choose one of the pre-defined colour ranges.

Would you like to determine the colour range?

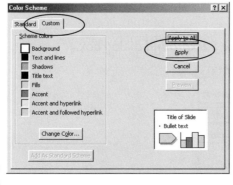

5 Change the colours on the *Custom* tab.

6 Determine the colours for the individual categories.

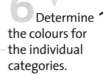

7 As soon as you close the dialog box by clicking on the *Apply* or *Apply to All* buttons, PowerPoint will transfer the new colour range to the chosen slide or all the slides.

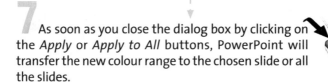

Arranging the slide background

In order to furnish the background of the active slide with a colour, a colour range, a graphic etc., carry out the following steps:

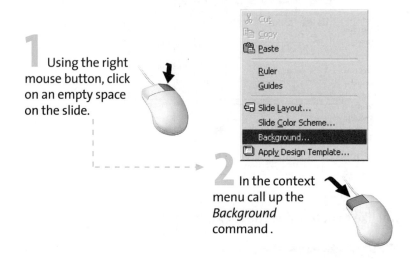

1 Using the right mouse button, click on an empty space on the slide.

2 In the context menu call up the *Background* command.

PowerPoint will now open the *Background* dialog box.

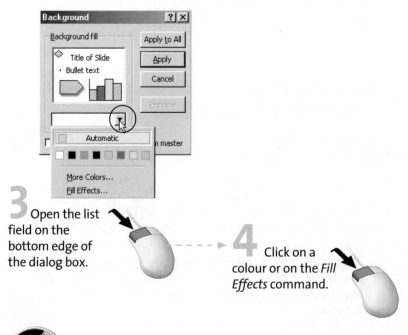

3 Open the list field on the bottom edge of the dialog box.

4 Click on a colour or on the *Fill Effects* command.

Would you like to use a fill effect to define the slide's background?

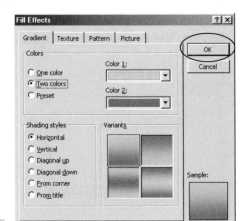

5 On the *Gradient* tab choose the colours and the shading style. - - - - - - - - ▶ **6** Close the dialog box by clicking on the *OK* button.

As soon as you close the dialog box by clicking on the *OK* button the background of the active slide will be given the colour range. With the remaining tabs you can give the slide background a structure, a model or a graphic. At this point you should carry out your own experiments with the functions in question.

Reproducing a presentation

As soon as you have created a presentation and have saved it in a file, the question of how to reproduce the slides arises. First, you have to load the presentation, then you can print out the slides from a printer or some other output device. Furthermore, PowerPoint supports the presentation on screen. The relevant steps are shown here.

Loading a presentation

Have you saved the presentation and exited PowerPoint? If so, next time you start you can load it directly from the PowerPoint dialog box.

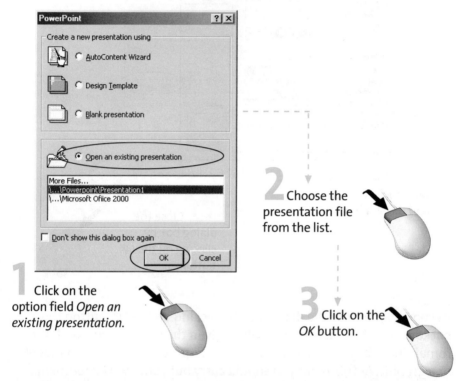

2 Choose the presentation file from the list.

1 Click on the option field *Open an existing presentation*.

3 Click on the *OK* button.

PowerPoint loads the presentation and shows this in the applications window.

If the program is already open, or you would like to choose the presentation file from a dialog box, do the following steps:

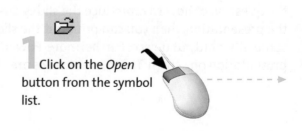

1 Click on the *Open* button from the symbol list.

2 In the *Open* dialog box select the file and then the presentation file.

3 Close the dialog box by clicking on the *Open* button.

By clicking on the arrow next to the *Open* button a menu is shown containing additional options on opening a workbook. You can, for example, open the presentation and write-protect it. This prevents saving unwanted changes to the presentation.

PowerPoint then loads the presentation and shows it in the applications window.

In many cases, to load a saved document, you don't have to use the *Open* dialog box. We have already seen that for Word and Excel, opening the FILE menu in an application will show the last four files used. Clicking on the corresponding file will load it.

Changing the display mode

In creating the slides shown on the previous pages, you will presumably have used the 'Slide view' mode in the applications window. This is the standard drawback of PowerPoint. However, the program supports further representations of the presentation that we will look at briefly.

In the bottom left-hand corner of the application window, you will see five buttons: these allow the display mode to be changed.

The far left button is usually active and this is the 'Normal view' that PowerPoint has been using on the previous pages. The button second from the left represents the 'Outline view'. Choose this view to enlarge the outline; the remainder of the window therefore is reduced in size. Using the third button, the 'Slide view', the program enlarges the window with the slides in favour of the rest of the window.

Click once on the *Slide Sorter View* button.

PowerPoint now shows you a miniature view of the slide in a window. This allows you to have a quick overview of the presentation.

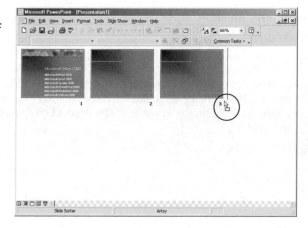

You can highlight a slide by clicking on it, and then move it to the desired position in the presentation. Or in the EDIT menu, choose the command *Delete File* to delete it. You can make a copy of a file by either using the *Duplicate* command in the edit menu or by pressing the key combination of Ctrl+D.

The last button on the very right allows you to view the set of slides in sequence on the screen (*see below*). Perhaps you should try choosing the various display modes once. You will then get an immediate overall view of how they work.

Calling up the slide show

One of the strongest features of PowerPoint lies in the possibility of being able to see your presentation run through on the screen, and to practise your presentation before you do it for real with overhead projections and slides. Presentations are being carried out more and more often directly from the screen using PowerPoint. The screen content is transferred by a projector ('video beamer') on to a screen. To call up the presentation take the following steps:

By clicking the mouse, highlight the first displayed slide of the presentation.

Alternatively you could press the F5 button, or choose the command *Run Slide Show Presentation* from the slideshow presentation menu.

Click on the *Slide Show* button.

351

PowerPoint then switches to a full picture presentation and shows the current slide.

Microsoft Office 2000
- Microsoft Word 2000
- Microsoft Excel 2000
- Microsoft Access 2000
- Microsoft PowerPoint 2000
- Microsoft PhotoDraw 2000
- Microsoft Outlook 2000

3 By clicking the mouse you can then leaf through to the next slide.

During a presentation you are able to leaf through all the slides by clicking the mouse. By pressing the Esc key you can exit the presentation.

Remember that the program can still support further functions during the slide show. Do you know how these functions are called up?

You can set up your PowerPoint presentation so that stylised keys appear on every slide. By clicking on these keys you can call up a menu.

Next
Previous
Go ▶

Meeting Minder...
Speaker Notes

Pointer Options ▶
Screen ▶

Help
End Show

1 Click on this key.

If you haven't got the buttons, click on any point of the slide with the right mouse button to call up the menu.

PowerPoint opens a menu with commands on the control of a presentation. The meaning of the commands *Next* and *End Show* should be quite clear.

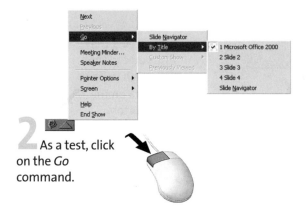

2 As a test, click on the *Go* command.

The menu is now expanded to include a submenu.

3 Click on the *By Title* command.

If necessary, you can now call up individual slides directly by their accompanying slide title in the presentation.

4 Click on the command *Slide Navigator*.

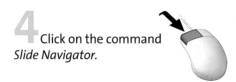

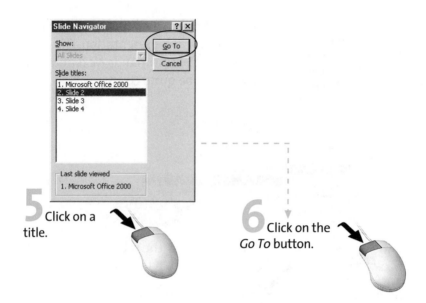

5 Click on a title.

6 Click on the *Go To* button.

The dialog box closes and the slide is shown.

7 In the menu click on the *Speaker Notes* command.

PowerPoint inserts your notes about the relevant slide into the dialog box.

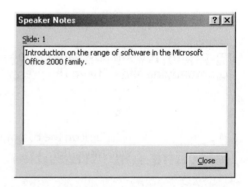

During the presentation, would you like to highlight something on the slide?

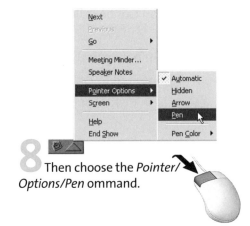

8 Then choose the *Pointer/ Options/Pen* ommand.

PowerPoint will now use a picture of a pen as the mouse pointer. With the *Pen Color* menu command you are also able to choose the pointer colour.

- Microsoft Outlook 2000
- Microsoft PhotoDraw 2000

Then, by holding down the left mouse button, you can draw on the slide with the pen.

To change the pointer back from a pen, click on the slide with the right mouse button, then Pointer Options on the menu back to *Automatic*.

Using the command *Screen/Delete pen* you can delete your highlights on the current slide. These highlights will also be removed as soon as you move on to another slide.

Would you like to briefly break up the presentation? If so, in the *Screen* menu choose the command *Black Screen*.

Selecting slide transition options

During the slide show presentation you can make use of some of PowerPoint's special effects (e.g. automatic picture change, fading effects). You have to set these options before starting the presentation.

All the options for the slide show presentation can be called up from the SLIDE SHOW menu.

Do you want to carry out a particular effect in between the slide changes, e.g. fading?

Then choose the *Slide Transition* command.

PowerPoint opens the *Slide Transition* dialog box.

In the *Advance* box determine how the transition to the next slide should occur.

3 In the *Effect* box choose the type of transition between the slides.

4 If necessary, you can set the option for the speed of transition by choosing either *Slow*, *Medium* or *Fast*.

5 Click on the *Apply* button.

The options for the slide transition will now be applied to the current slide and the one following it. By clicking on the *Apply to All* key the options are assigned to all of the slides.

Using animation

A nice touch is to use animations during a slide presentation. You may want only the headline to appear when you call up a slide, and to call up individual points on the slide by clicking the mouse. This can be achieved with a few clicks of the mouse.

1 Select the slide that you would like to animate.

2 On the slide, highlight the parameter of the elements that you want to animate.

The animation always refers to the placeholder. If you would like to show the text on a slide straight away, you must do this on a separate placeholder.

Then, in the sub-menu click on the desired animation effect.

In the *Slide Show* menu choose the *Preset Animation* command.

You can switch off the animations effect by repeating the above steps and then clicking on the button *Off* in the corresponding menu. If the menu commands are grey and faded out, you either haven't highlighted a placeholder or have highlighted a wrong placeholder.

Now when you call up the on-screen slide presentation, the animation effect will already be in place.

Placing buttons on to slides

On some slides you find stylised buttons which allow you to navigate through the slide show presentation. To put these switch areas on to a slide, follow these steps:

Select the slide you wish to work on.

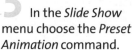

In the SLIDE SHOW menu call up the *Action Buttons* command.

3 In the *Slide Show* menu choose the *Preset Animation* command.

4 On the slide, click on a point where you would like the top left corner of the button to appear.

5 By holding down the left mouse button, drag the pointer diagonally until the button is the desired size.

As soon as you release the mouse button, the program inserts the button into the slide.

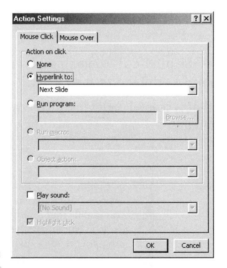

6 In the *Action Settings* dialog box, allocate the desired options to both register cards.

As a rule, the *Hyperlink to* option will be highlighted and the displayed slide will be established. You can also connect a program or a macro with the button.

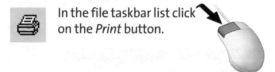 **7** Close the dialog box by clicking on the *OK* button.

By clicking on the *Slide Show* button, when the presentation is played back, PowerPoint applies the chosen option.

Printing the presentation

Do you want to print the presentation on a printer (or an output device)?

 In the file taskbar list click on the *Print* button.

PowerPoint prepares the print-out. While this is happening you will see a symbol of a printer on screen.

For a presentation that is several pages long, you can also see how many sides have been printed.

Printing options

Do you simply want to print a single slide or do you want to use specific options when printing? If so, then follow these steps.

1 In the FILE menu choose the *Print* command or press the key combination Ctrl+P.

PowerPoint shows the *Print* dialog box in the display. You can choose the desired printing options here.

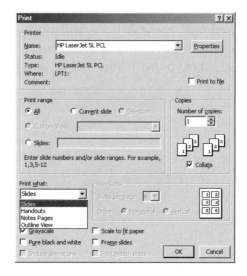

➪ In *Copies* you can determine how many copies of the presentation you want. You can do this by clicking on the 'Number of copies' button.

➪ In the *Print range* box you can decide whether to print the whole presentation, individual slides or a highlighted area.

➪ In the *Print what* box you can decide to print the slide or other document contents by clicking on the list. The rest of the buttons allow you to adapt the printout format (paper size, slide settings, black and white etc.).

2 Click on the *OK* button to start printing.

Some of the options in the dialog box come into operation only when the corresponding document is sent for printing (e.g. the handouts group). Further information about the options can be found under the question in the top right-hand corner of the *Print* dialog box.

We will end the introduction to PowerPoint here. You have got to know the most important PowerPoint functions concerning the creation of presentations. You are now able to create and format slides, save, reload and print presentations, and produce a slide show. An additional example can be found in the next chapter. The PowerPoint Help also supplies you with information about further functions.

Test your knowledge

To test your knowledge you should answer the following questions. The answers are on page 586.

1   How do you insert a new slide into a presentation?

2   How do you delete or move slides around during the presentation?

3   How do you call up an on-screen presentation and how do you move between slides?

4   How do you print out notes to accompany presentation slides?

5   How do you create a presentation with the AutoContent Wizard?

6   How do you assign a presentation design to a slide?

7   How do you change the background of a slide?

Office applications combined

What's in this chapter?

In the previous chapters, you have got to know the most important Office programs. These programs already allow you to carry out many tasks. The strength of Microsoft Office does not come into full effect until you combine the best functions of the individual programs. For example, you can create a mail merge in Word and, in the process, use data from Excel worksheets. Or you can write a letter in Word in which a table is added from Excel. The representation of the turnover figures is not as eye-catching until you transfer the data directly from an Excel Worksheet. This chapter uses knowledge you have already acquired and shows you how to access functions and data from external applications from Office programs.

Mail merge with Excel data

In Chapter 4, you got to know the Mail Merge Word function. In the same chapter, you learnt how to use the data source as a table for the mail merge in Word. Now I would like to show you how to incorporate the data source with the address data in Excel worksheets and access it from Word. In the process, you will learn how to transfer tables from Word documents via the clipboard on to Excel worksheets.

Transferring Word tables in to Excel

For the following steps, you will need a source file in the form of an Excel workbook containing the address data for the mail merge. Do you still have the *Source.doc* source file from Chapter 4? To save typing the address data into the Excel table again, transfer the table from Word to Excel.

1 Start Word and load the *Source.doc* file into the table.

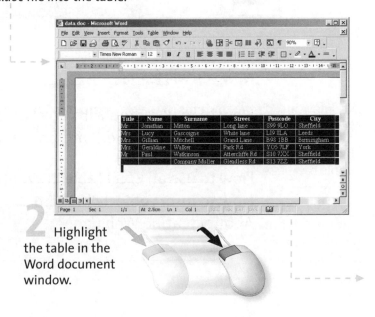

2 Highlight the table in the Word document window.

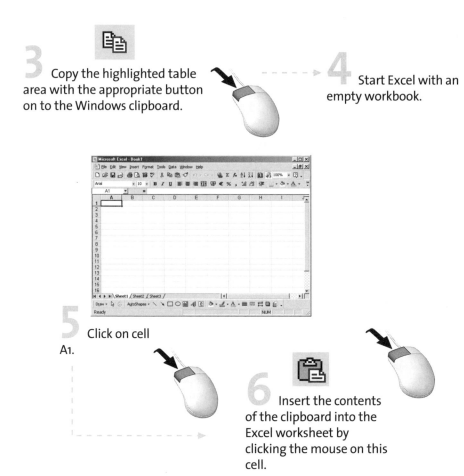

3 Copy the highlighted table area with the appropriate button on to the Windows clipboard.

4 Start Excel with an empty workbook.

5 Click on cell A1.

6 Insert the contents of the clipboard into the Excel worksheet by clicking the mouse on this cell.

Excel now inserts the contents of the clipboard into the highlighted cell. Since a table is being used, its contents are inserted into the worksheet.

The result of using a table can be seen here in the worksheet. You can edit the column widths by clicking on the column headings as required.

367

7 Save the Workbook in the *Addresses.xls* file.

Having followed these steps, the source file is available as an Excel workbook.

Would you like to **sort** a column in the table? Highlight the column in Excel. The table can be sorted in ascending or descending order using these buttons on the Excel toolbar.

You can collect documents in the **clipboard**. Here you highlight the area in the Word document and copy this into the clipboard. You can repeat this up to twelve times. When inserting into the document, the program automatically inserts the *clipboard* toolbar.

If this toolbar does not appear automatically, in the VIEW menu select the *Toolbar/Clipboard* command. For each entry in the clipboard there is a symbol. If you click on the document symbol, the relevant content of the clipboard will be inserted into the document. The symbol gives you a tip on the type of data. The ⊠ button on the toolbar clears the contents of the clipboard. If a section of the document is highlighted, you can click on the *Copy* button to transfer the document section to the clipboard.

Creating a mail merge

After this initial preparation, you can immediately start creating the mail merge. Do you know how to do this?

1 Start Word.

2 Open the prepared letter draft in Word.

You should have a
corresponding draft
available as a result of
the exercise in Chapter 4.

3 In the Word Tools menu choose
the *Mail Merge* command.

Word loads the *Mail Merge Helper* which still contains the old references
to the source file.

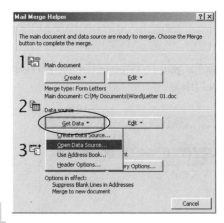

4 Click on the *Get Data*
box in the *Mail Merge Helpe*
dialog box and then on the
Open Data Source option.

5 Select the
data source file. - - - - ▶

369

6 In the *Files of type* box, select 'MS Excel Worksheet'.

7 Double-click on your file (here *Addresses.xls*).

8 And then click on the *Open* button.

Word now opens the dialog box for you to choose the way in which to access the data source (the Excel file).

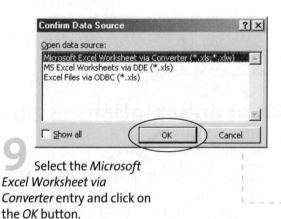

9 Select the *Microsoft Excel Worksheet via Converter* entry and click on the *OK* button.

Open Worksheet

Open document in Workbook:

Sheet1 ▾ | OK

Cancel

Name or Cell Range:

Entire Worksheet ▾

☑ Format for Mail Merge

10 Now choose the name of the worksheet in the *Open document in Workbook* list box and define the cell area if necessary.

11 Select the *Format for Mail Merge* check box.

12 Click on the *OK* button.

The document is now ready for mail merge. If you want to insert or edit the mail merge field, change to the document and edit it accordingly. The mail merge can then start once you click on the *Merge* button in the Mail Merge Helper.

TIP

The relevant steps for mail merge are described in Chapter 4. What's new here is using an external file in Excel format as a source file.

PowerPoint presentations using Excel data

Presentations can be created with PowerPoint very quickly. Even charts can be represented in PowerPoint using the table function. Here in brief are the steps for displaying a chart on a slide.

1 In PowerPoint choose the slide on to which the chart is to be inserted. 'Chart' should have been selected as the AutoLayout.

2 Double-click on the placeholder in the slide which is to incorporate the chart.

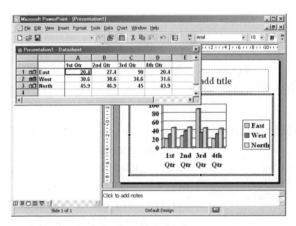

PowerPoint inserts a chart directly into the placeholder. Simultaneously, a table is shown in which you can enter the data of the chart. The chart options (type and so on) can be edited with the CHART menu.

Admittedly, the possibilities of entering data in the table are greatly reduced. However, the data is often already available in Excel. It would therefore be unnecessary to read the corresponding data in Excel and re-type it into the PowerPoint table.

Transfer the data from Excel

Would you like to transfer the data of an Excel worksheet into a chart? This is not a big problem.

Here is an Excel worksheet that contains the turnover data. The worksheet was already created in Chapter 6 and saved as (*Turnover2000.xls*). The area containing the area should now be transferred on to a PowerPoint slide to draw up a chart.

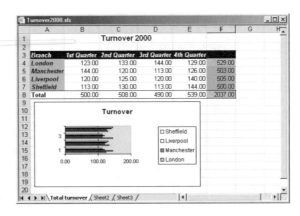

1 Carry out the above steps to insert a chart into the placeholder of the slide.

2 As soon as the table can be seen with the data, click on the *More Buttons* little arrow in the middle of the task bar.

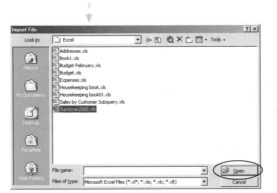

3 Select the desired data in the *Import File* dialog box. The import format can be chosen in the *Files type* box.

4 Click on the *Open* button.

373

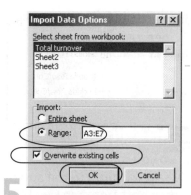

6 Define the area of the data to be transferred in the *Import* group if necessary.

5 Choose the worksheet of the folder in the *Import File* dialog box from which the data is to be transferred.

7 Select the *Overwrite existing cells* check box in order to replace the table with the sample data.

8 Click on the *OK* button.

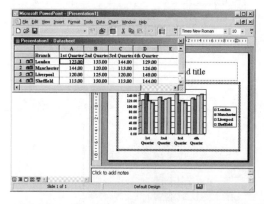

PowerPoint imports the Excel data into the table and edits the chart accordingly.

In the CHART menu, find the commands with which the chart representation is to be edited. PowerPoint shows the same tabs as Excel for the chart. Refer back to Chapter 6 if necessary.

If you have imported too much data from the Excel worksheet, open the FILE menu. This menu offers you commands to exclude data lines or columns of the table from the chart.

Charts transferred directly

Do you not want to edit the chart any further on the slide, but wish to leave it as it is for the presentation? Do you have an Excel worksheet in which the chart is already saved completed? If so, you can save yourself time by transferring the chart from the Excel worksheet on to the PowerPoint slide directly.

1 Open the Excel workbook.

2 Highlight the chart by clicking the mouse.

3 Transfer a copy on to the clipboard with the Ctrl+C key combination.

4 Change to the PowerPoint slide and click on the placeholder for the chart.

5 Insert the contents of the clipboard on to the slide with the [Ctrl]+[V] key combination.

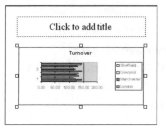

The disadvantage of this approach is that you only have a picture at the end. The font, proportions etc. may not necessarily be right. Furthermore, no edits can be made later.

Using Excel data in Word

Word offers you a table function and even lets you insert data in this table. This approach is, of course, not necessarily suitable for extensive calculations. As described in previous sections, you can insert sections from Excel worksheets into Word.

Transferring an Excel table on to Word

To insert a section of an Excel Worksheet into a Word document, follow these steps:

	A	B	C	D	E	F
1			Turnover 2000			
2						
3	Branch	1st Quarter	2nd Quarter	3rd Quarter	4th Quarter	
4	London	123.00	133.00	144.00	129.00	529.00
5	Manchester	144.00	120.00	113.00	126.00	503.00
6	Liverpool	120.00	125.00	120.00	140.00	505.00
7	Sheffield	113.00	130.00	113.00	144.00	500.00
8	Total	500.00	508.00	490.00	539.00	2037.00

Turnover2000.xls

Total turnover / Sheet2 / Sheet3

1 Highlight the relevant cell range in the Excel worksheet.

2 Copy the highlighted area on to the clipboard with the [Ctrl]+[C] key combination.

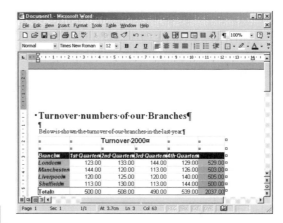

3 Switch to the Word document window and click on the place where you want to insert the data.

4 Press the Ctrl + V key combination.

Word now inserts the contents of the clipboard as a table in the document window. The structure and formatting of the table remains the same during this transfer. However, the calculation formulas are lost. You can try this out easily by changing the values in the table cells. The sums are not modified.

Using an Excel table in Word

A better approach is using the functionality of Excel to make the table accessible in the Word document. Even this is possible in Microsoft Office 2000.

1 Highlight the required cell range in the Excel worksheet according to the example on the previous page.

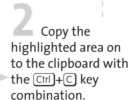

2 Copy the highlighted area on to the clipboard with the Ctrl + C key combination.

377

3 Switch to the Word document window and click on the place where the table is to be inserted.

4 Choose the *Paste Special* command from the EDIT menu.

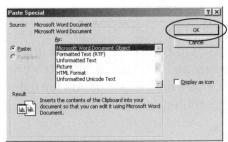

5 Choose the 'Microsoft Excel Worksheet Object' entry in the *Paste Special* dialog box.

6 Click on the *OK* button.

In the status bar, Word shows that you can edit the Excel worksheet by double-clicking the mouse.

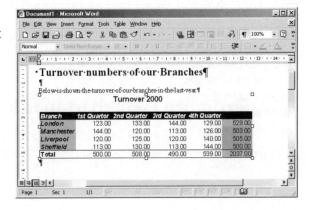

7 Select the object by clicking on it with the mouse

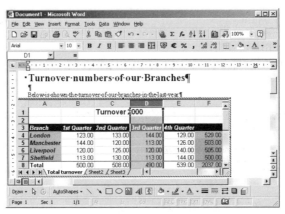

8 Double - click on the relevant object symbol.

Word now inserts the Excel worksheet in to the document area. At the same time, the Excel menu, task and standard bars are displayed.

Word now offers you the Excel functionality. You can change values in the table or correct calculation formulae. To stop editing the Excel object, click anywhere else in the Word document.

Transferring an Excel chart in to Word

Would you like to insert an Excel chart into a report or another Word document? You can do this as described in previous sections.

1 Select the chart in Excel by clicking on it with the mouse.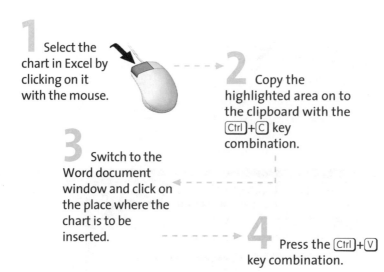

2 Copy the highlighted area on to the clipboard with the $\boxed{Ctrl}$+$\boxed{C}$ key combination.

3 Switch to the Word document window and click on the place where the chart is to be inserted.

4 Press the $\boxed{Ctrl}$+$\boxed{V}$ key combination.

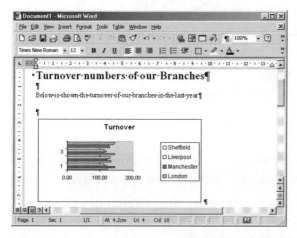

Word inserts the chart as a simple graphic in the document area.

Would you like to insert the chart as an object in the Word document?

5 Choose the *Paste Special* command in th EDIT menu of the Word window.

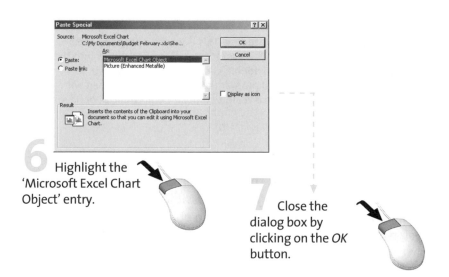

6 Highlight the 'Microsoft Excel Chart Object' entry.

7 Close the dialog box by clicking on the *OK* button.

Word inserts the chart as an object. The image corresponds to the representation. However, double-clicking on the chart will open an Excel object in the background and you can edit the chart.

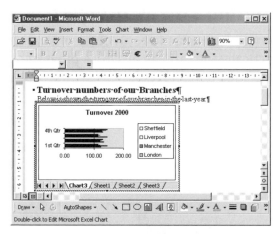

Inserting objects in Word

In the previous section, it is inferred that you have already used the software: the Office programs give you the possibility of using the **functions** of another program in a document. These functions are executed by the Office OLE function.

381

You can insert certain contents of the clipboard as an object in the current document window with the *Paste Special* command in the EDIT menu. Alternatively, Office offers you the possibility of inserting an existing file from an external program as an object. Or you can create a new version of the object directly in the current application. Word or Excel can even offer drawing functions with this technology.

Inserting a file as an object

The insertion of a file as an object into an Office document is practically the same in all Office programs. Accordingly, the method is outlined here in Word.

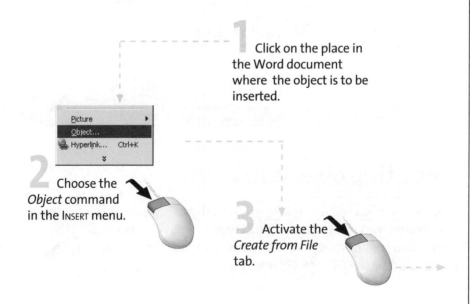

1 Click on the place in the Word document where the object is to be inserted.

2 Choose the *Object* command in the INSERT menu.

3 Activate the *Create from File* tab.

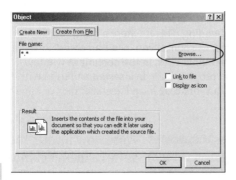

4 Click on the *Browse* button.

5 Choose the folder in the *Browse* dialog box and then the required file.

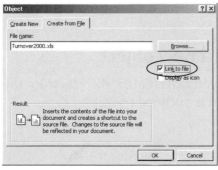

6 Click on the *Insert* button.

7 Highlight the *Link to file* check box.

8 Click on the *OK* button.

383

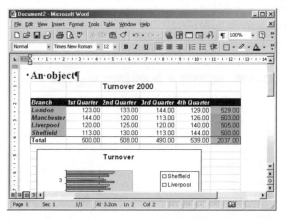

Word now inserts the data as an object into the document. In this example, the Excel Worksheet is displayed. Double-clicking on the object allows editing in the Word window.

Creating and inserting a new object

If the object does not yet exist, you can create it directly from the current application. The method is outlined in Word.

1 Click on the place in the Word document where the object is to be inserted. - - - - - - - - - ▶

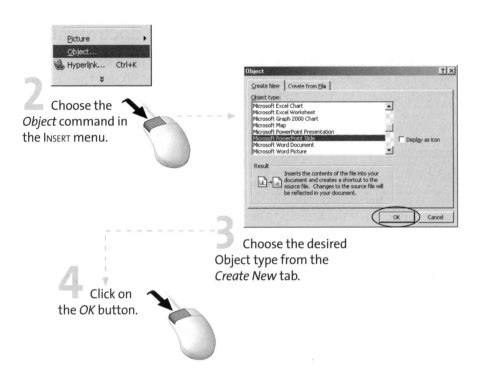

2 Choose the *Object* command in the INSERT menu.

3 Choose the desired Object type from the *Create New* tab.

4 Click on the *OK* button.

Word inserts a new object (here a PowerPoint slide) in the document area. At the same time, the menu and bars of the application (here PowerPoint) generating the object are inserted in to the Word window. You can now create the object.

As soon as you click on a place in the document which is outside the object's parameters, Word stores the object data in the document. If you save the document in a file, the object data will be stored with it. You can edit the object at any time by double-clicking on the object symbol again.

Inserting a sound object into a Word document

As a final example, we wll see how a sound object (or a similar object) can be inserted into a Word document. This allows the owner of the document to listen to the sound object.

1 Click on the place in the Word document where the object is to be inserted.

2 Choose the *Object* command from the INSERT menu.

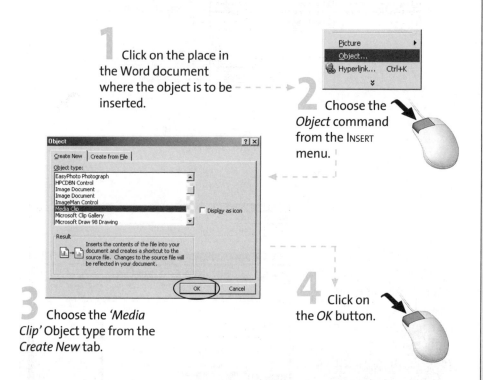

3 Choose the *'Media Clip'* Object type from the *Create New* tab.

4 Click on the *OK* button.

Word displays the *Media Clip* bar and shows the control elements for the sound attributes of the object.

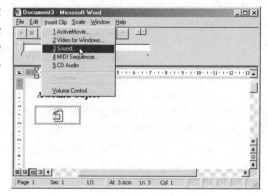

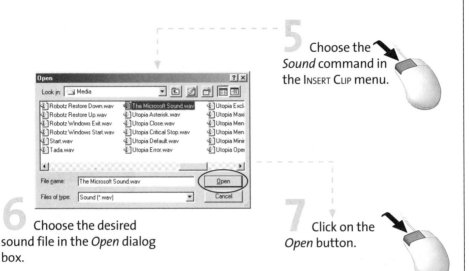

5 Choose the *Sound* command in the INSERT CLIP menu.

6 Choose the desired sound file in the *Open* dialog box.

7 Click on the *Open* button.

As you have changed the inserted object through steps 6 and 7, Word asks if the document is to be inserted. The sound object then appears as a symbol in the document. The symbol is shown as reversed when the above steps are carried out.

The sound file can be represented above the control elements of the media bar. The Word document acts merely as a container.

A sound command can be put directly into the document by using the *Insert as File* tab (*see above*). With the steps shown here, however, Word inserts the name of the sound file as soon as the highlighting of the object is removed. Furthermore, as well as inserting sound files, you can use the media bar to insert video clips into the document in the same way by applying the appropriate format in step 5.

387

Creating Web pages

In the next chapter, you will learn about the Internet and in the process learn which functions Office 2000 provides to display data in a Web format. After that, we will use the example of a small project to create Word, Excel and PowerPoint documents in a Web format and make them available on a local drive. You can then understand the instructions in the next chapter in case you do not own an Internet connection.

The project will be to produce a short presentation that stores certain information about your work and so on in a Web format known as the Home Page. Each user who has access to the files can then learn about your work. The contributions should be created in Word, Excel and PowerPoint.

Creating Web documents in Word

Creating documents in a Web format can be done with a few clicks of the mouse.

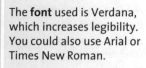 Start Word and create a short document text. ------> Save this document in a Word .doc file.

The document can have the following contents. It concerns a simple report with a chart of the turnover figures.

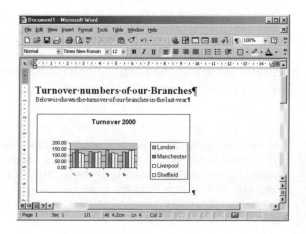

This document is to be saved now in the HTML format used by the Web (*.htm* file). This can be done with a few clicks of the mouse.

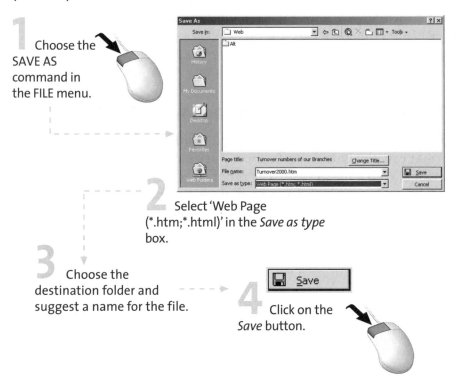

1 Choose the SAVE AS command in the FILE menu.

2 Select 'Web Page (*.htm;*.html)' in the *Save as type* box.

3 Choose the destination folder and suggest a name for the file.

4 Click on the *Save* button.

Choose the *My documentsWeb***destination folder**. Since the *Web* subfolder presumably does not yet exist, create it in the *Save As* dialog box. The relevant steps were introduced in previous chapters. Use the *Turnover 2000* file name. You do not necessarily have to give the full file name – this is completed by Word when saving. Using the *Change Name* button, you can change the title of the Web page, if needed. By default, Word takes the first line of text of the document.

Have you followed these steps? Did everything work? Congratulations. You have just created your first Web page with Word 2000, but perhaps it is not obvious to you as yet. Afterwards, Word still shows the text as before. The *New* button has simply been changed to the *New Web Page* icon in the top left corner. You can create new pages in Web format by clicking on this button and creating them as normal Word documents.

Creating a personal Web page with Word

After you have seen how easy saving a Word document in Web format can be, I would like to show you quickly how you can create a personal Web page in Word. The program is shown with various document drafts which are prepared for Web pages.

1 Choose the *New* command in the FILE menu.

2 Choose one of the presentations in the *New* dialog box on the *Web Pages* tab.

Here select the *Personal Web Page* template.

3 Click on the *OK* button.

Word now creates a Web page based on the template. This page has a default structure where you can insert your text. You can scroll in the document and overwrite the relevant text as in any normal Word document.

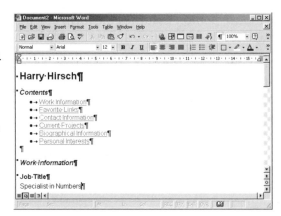

Presumably you noticed the bold underlining at the beginning of the document. These are **hyperlinks,** which Word uses to link to document positions or external documents. You should only remove these hyperlinks when they are no longer needed.

Hyperlink is a special piece of technology from the Internet. A hyperlink provides a link to another document. With just one click of the mouse on the hyperlink you can retrieve the related document.

If you click on a hyperlink, Word shows you immediately the relevant text in the current document or the external document.

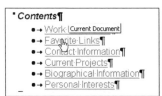

Click on the 'Favorite Links' hyperlink in the document.

391

The mouse pointer assumes the form of a hand when a hyperlink is shown.

Word now shows the text with the previous links. Here a hyperlink is to be entered into the recent Web document.

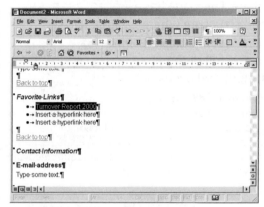

3 Select the 'Insert a Hyperlink here' line and change the text in the 'Turnover report 2000'.

4 Now click on *Insert Hyperlink* in the taskbar.

Word opens the *Insert Hyperlink* dialog box.

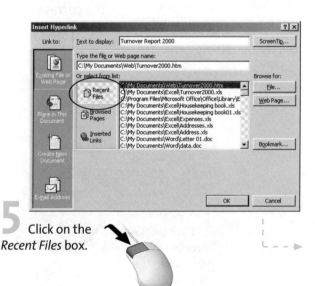

5 Click on the *Recent Files* box.

6 Choose the entry of the previously created Web page example *Turnover2000.htm* in the file list.

If the target file for the hyperlink is not shown in the file list, you can select the *File* command in the *Display Hyperlinks* dialog box. The relevant Office-program opens a dialog box on selection of the object file. In a similar way you can call up hyperlinks to visited Web pages and so on. You simply click on the relevant button and select the required document. You can find details about this in the Help program.

7 As soon as you close the dialog box by clicking on *OK*, the hyperlink is inserted in Word.

8 Click on this hyperlink as a test.

Word starts the Internet Explorer and shows the Web site created in the previous steps.

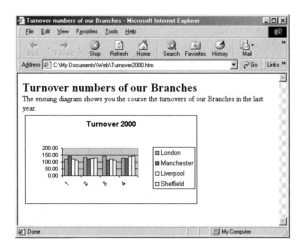

I will explain the function of the Internet Explorer in the following chapter. Word calls up this program as soon as an *.htm* file is given as the link. If you indicate a *.doc* document when creating hyperlinks, its contents will be displayed in Word. With a *.xls* file, Word calls up the Excel program to display the files. The hyperlinks technology is really easy to use. This does not only work with Web pages – you can also insert hyperlinks into Word documents.

Local links

At this point, I must quickly explain how you structure a local link in a current Word document. The prepared document draft contains the words 'Return to the beginning of the page' at various places. Click on these hyperlinks and go back to the beginning of the document.

I have found that these links do not work because a target link does not exist in the used drafts.

So that these references can work, a bookmark must be defined on the relevant reference lines. You can even insert these bookmarks with a few clicks of the mouse anywhere.

1 Click on the place in the document in which the bookmark is to be inserted.

2 Choose the *Bookmark* command in the INSERT menu.

3 Enter the desired names in the *Bookmark* dialog box and then click on the INSERT button.

Use characters and numbers for the bookmark names.

If you would like to insert a local link to such a bookmark, carry out the following steps.

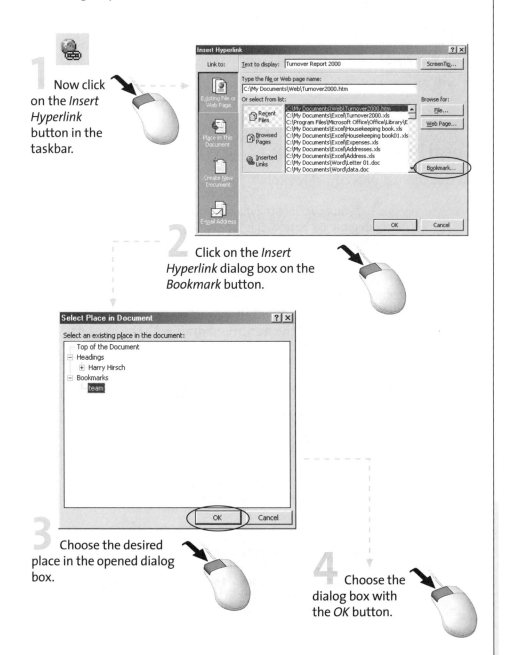

1 Now click on the *Insert Hyperlink* button in the taskbar.

2 Click on the *Insert Hyperlink* dialog box on the *Bookmark* button.

3 Choose the desired place in the opened dialog box.

4 Choose the dialog box with the *OK* button.

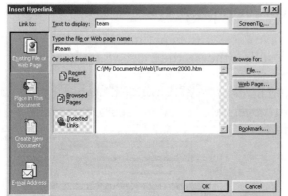

You will now see the name of the bookmark in the *File type or Web page* box with the # sign before it in the *Insert Hyperlink* dialog box. This is the sign for a local link in a document.

5 If you now close the dialog box by clicking the *OK* button, this reference will be entered as the aim.

This way you can insert hyperlinks in a document at any time, which refer to local places in the document in question. The software is ready to create the contents lists of the document draft with the personal Web page.

Saving pages

Have you created the Word document with the information from the personal Web pages?

1 Save the document under the name *HarryH.htm* in the file *My Documents\Web*.

Word comprises additional **document drafts** as well as an assistant for creating Web pages. With the knowledge you have acquired so far, you should be able to use these functions. If necessary, look in the Help program to get tips on individual functions.

The document is still needed in the following pages for a reference.

Storing Excel data as Web pages

As with Word, you can work in Excel with hyperlinks between worksheets and save the results either in the Excel *.xls* format or as an *.htm* Web page. First, the turnover total for the branches individual turnovers should be defined and sorted according to products. The individual turnovers are stored in separate worksheets. Carry out the following steps:

1 Load the sample document created in the last chapter with the branches' turnover data into Excel.

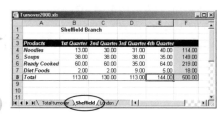

2 Change to the *Table2* worksheet, rename this and insert the following table with the individual data of the branches.

3 Repeat this step for the other branches if necessary.

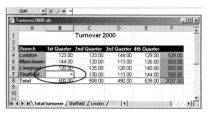

4 Change to the *Total turnover* worksheet and click on Cell *B4*.

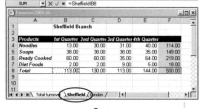

5 Enter an equals sign.

6 Now highlight Cell *B8* in the *Sheffield* worksheet.

Hit the Ctrl
key to confirm.

Excel automatically changes to the
Total turnover worksheet and
shows the 123.00 value in cell *B4*.
This value, however, was
transferred from the *Sheffield*
worksheet!

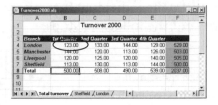

You can easily check this, by highlighting the relevant cell. In the editing menu
Excel gives a reference to the appropriate cell. With this exercise you have
learnt how a cell value from another worksheet can be adopted in a cell. In the
same way you can even show a reference in another workbook.

8 Now repeat the above steps and
insert the cell references for the remaining
three quarters.

If you have done this all right, the turnover data of the Sheffield
branches should now be available in the *Total turnover* worksheet, but
the data for the turnovers has to be entered separately into the *Sheffield*
worksheet. Another link from the total turnover table with the Sheffield
branch worksheet should now be established.

1 Highlight Cell *A7*
in the *Total turnover*
worksheet.

2 Click on the *Insert
Hyperlink* in the taskbar.

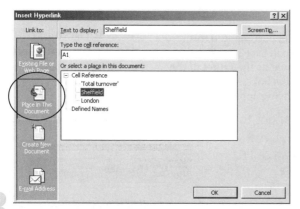

3 Click on the *Current document* symbol of the left bar in the *Insert Hyperlink* dialog box.

4 Choose the *Sheffield* entry in *this document* list.

5 As soon as you close the dialog box by clicking the *OK* button ...

... Excel shows the hyperlink in Cell A7.

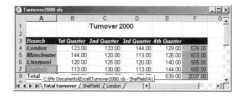

If you click on this hyperlink, Excel automatically changes the specified hyperlink document.

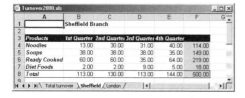

399

Since we have used an Excel document in this example, the display is also in Excel. But if you choose an external document as the target of the hyperlinks, and then click the links, Excel calls up and displays the accompanying application.

You can then see the relevant detailed data. Finally, you have the original worksheet back above the *Sheet* tab.

Do you work frequently with hyperlinks in a

document? If so, insert the *Web* toolbar, using the *Toolbar* command in the VIEW menu.

Using the two left buttons, *Forward* and *Back,* you can flick between visited document pages. Details on navigation with hyperlinks and tips on buttons on the *Web* toolbar are found in the next chapter.

1 Now repeat the above steps and insert the table details for the rest of the branches.

2 Insert the cell references for the branch turnovers in the *Total turnover* worksheet.

3 Insert the hyperlinks to the worksheets with the rest of the branch data in Column A.

You have just carried out the steps for the Sheffield branch. You now have a workbook with the turnover data of the fictitious company.

4 Save this as an Excel workbook.

5 Finally, save the workbook as *Turnover Tables.htm* in the *My Documents\Web* folder.

The last step is performed by the *Save As* command in the FILE menu. These steps were demonstrated in the previous section of Word. Saving is exactly the same in Excel; the dialog box allows you to choose whether the table or the complete workbook is to be saved.

A Web presentation with PowerPoint

The last step is now to create a Web presentation with PowerPoint. This program offers a wizard which makes it possible to edit Web pages attractively for presentation to a division or group.

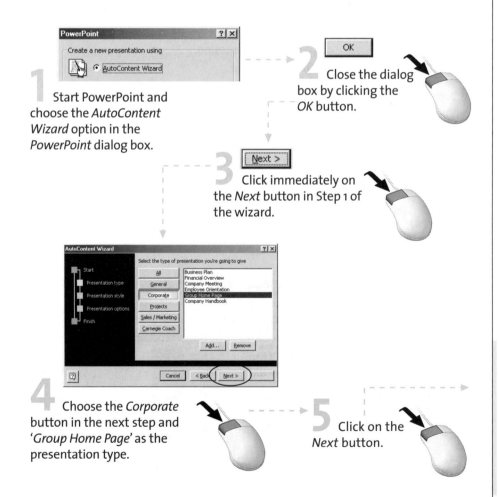

1 Start PowerPoint and choose the *AutoContent Wizard* option in the *PowerPoint* dialog box.

2 Close the dialog box by clicking the *OK* button.

3 Click immediately on the *Next* button in Step 1 of the wizard.

4 Choose the *Corporate* button in the next step and '*Group Home Page*' as the presentation type.

5 Click on the *Next* button.

401

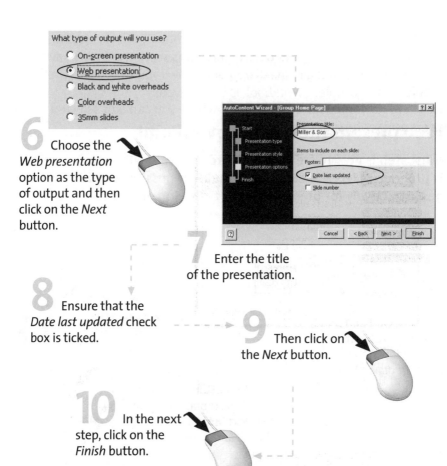

6 Choose the *Web presentation* option as the type of output and then click on the *Next* button.

7 Enter the title of the presentation.

8 Ensure that the *Date last updated* check box is ticked.

9 Then click on the *Next* button.

10 In the next step, click on the *Finish* button.

PowerPoint now creates the slide for the (Web) presentation. You can then see the Web page with individual information. We will now create this as an example.

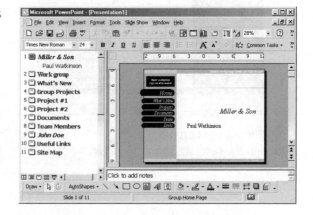

1 Choose the *Master/Slidemaster* command from the VIEW menu.

PowerPoint now opens the *Slide Master* where you can edit selected headers and footers for the slide.

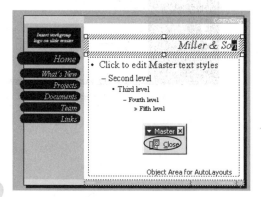

2 Insert the page of the *Slide Master* around the title and name of the group (here Monitoring).

3 Click on the *Close* button of the *Master* taskbar.

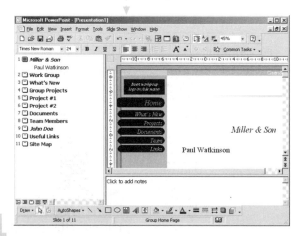

4 Now click one by one on the individual slides and replace the default values with the text which is to be shown later on individual Web pages.

403

In the process, you can use the same software as you did in generating other presentations.

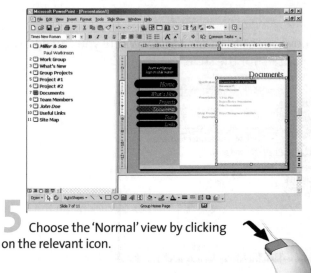

5 Choose the 'Normal' view by clicking on the relevant icon.

Replace the entries in the 'Descriptions' block with your own texts and insert hyperlinks in the Word and Excel created Web pages.

At this point, proceed with the outlines from the previous pages.

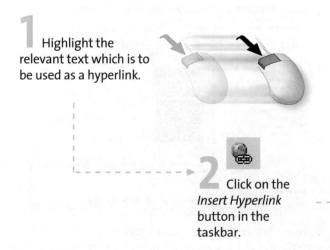

1 Highlight the relevant text which is to be used as a hyperlink.

2 Click on the *Insert Hyperlink* button in the taskbar.

Insert Hyperlink dialog box:

| Link to: | Text to display: | Turnover Report 2000 | ScreenTip... |

Type the file or Web page name:
C:\My Documents\Web\Turnover2000.htm

Or select from list:
- C:\My Documents\Web\Turnover2000.htm
- C:\My Documents\Web\Personal Web Page.htm
- C:\My Documents\Web\Turnover Table.htm
- C:\My Documents\Excel\Turnover Table.xls
- C:\My Documents\Excel\Turnover2000.xls
- C:\Program Files\Microsoft Office\Office\Library\E
- C:\My Documents\Excel\Housekeeping book.xls
- C:\My Documents\Excel\Housekeeping book01.xls
- C:\My Documents\Excel\Expenses.xls
- C:\My Documents\Excel\Addresses.xls

Browse for:
File...
Web Page...
Bookmark...

OK   Cancel

3 Choose the *Recent Files* icon in the *Insert Hyperlink* dialog box.

4 Choose the desired *.htm* file from the list and close the dialog box by clicking on the *OK* button.

In this way, hyperlinks should be left in the *Turnover2000.htm* and *Turnovertables.htm* files in the *\My Documents\Web* folder.

Harry Hirsch

Harry Hirsch is the General Manager of Miller & Son. He is one of the general managers who checks the turnover reports when they are finished.

Telephone: 0403 411881
e-mail: H.hirsch@goldcom.com
Web: Personal Web

1 Now change to the 'John Doe' slide and edit this slide so it becomes the fictitious employee Harry Hirsch.

A hyperlink to a personal Web page of the employee can be found under the 'Web' heading. Above you have created this personal Web page as an exercise, and saved it in the *My Documents* folder. Set up this hyperlink for the slide.

The slide can have the contents shown here. The same software should be used as in previous chapters to edit the slide's contents.

405

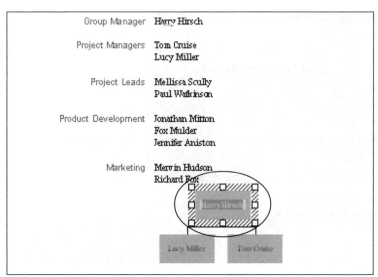

3 Now change to the 'Team members' slide. Replace the names of the employees.

4 Insert the name of the project leaders in the organisational chart and select this text.

5 Click on the *Insert Hyperlink* button in the taskbar.

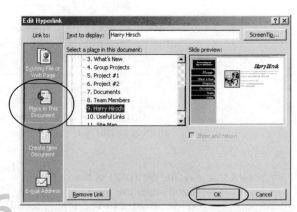

6 Click on *Select a place in this document* in the *Insert Hyperlink* dialog field and choose the '9. Harry Hirsch' entry in the list.

The slide will be shown in preview.

8 Close the dialog box by clicking on the *OK* button.

The hyperlink will be left on the relevant slide in the organisational chart. In this way, you can give the slides text and hyperlinks.

TIP

Alternatively you can select the *Save As* command, and in the dialog box you can choose the 'Web page (*.htm;*html)' file type.

1 Choose the *Save as Webpage* command from the FILE menu.

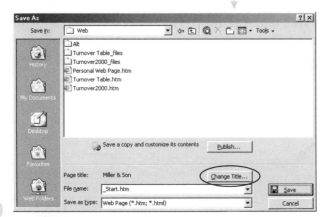

2 Click on the *Change Title* button and enter the title 'Miller & Son' for the Web page.

3 Then save the presentation in the *My Documents\Web* Folders.

As soon as the file has been saved, you can close PowerPoint or other programs which are still open. In the *\My Documents* subfolder there should be a collection of files with the *.htm* extension. How you display these files with the Internet Explorer will be discussed next in Chapter 9.

At this point, we will end the introduction to the Word, Excel and PowerPoint Office programs. You can now use the relevant programs to create documents. Furthermore, you know how to insert the functions from another program as objects in the current document. Even saving documents as Web pages should no longer present you with any great difficulty. Now you are prepared for the next steps. The following two chapters contain an introduction about the Internet and Microsoft Outlook.

Test your knowledge

To test your knowledge, you should answer the following questions. The answers are on page 587.

1   How do you incorporate a Word document into a slide in PowerPoint?

2   How do you insert a Word document into an Excel table?

3   How can a sound object be inserted directly into an Excel worksheet?

4   How can an Excel object exist as an icon in a Word document?

5   Load the personal Web page (*HarryH.htm*), and insert a hyperlink into the *Turnover2000.xls* file in the 'Favorite links' section.

6   Insert a hyperlink in the Microsoft Web page *www.microsoft.com* from the personal Web page in the 'Favorite links' section.

The Internet and intranets and Office 2000

What's in this chapter?

Would you like to know what the Internet, intranet and World Wide Web are? Then read this chapter. Here, you're provided with the basics for viewing Web pages and 'surfing' the World Wide Web. Furthermore, this chapter will tell you in the simplest terms about the Internet and intranets. The program needed for this is already installed in the form of the Microsoft Internet Explorer in Microsoft Office 2000. Do you not have access to the Internet? No problem: use this knowledge to view the HTML documents that are found more and more frequently on CD-ROMs. We saw how to do this in Chapter 8. You can also apply this knowledge to work on intranets, which are used within many companies.

What are the Internet, intranets, the World Wide Web and browsers?

The Internet is changing the worlds of commerce and academia, and daily we hear how it will affect all our lives. But do you really know what is behind this collective term? The word unifies the two terms *Inter(national)* and *Net(work)*. It also has something to do with a comprehensive national network.

A **network** describes a functionality which many computers use to communicate with each other and with managers for transferring files. In this way, computers can exchange files or data amongst themselves. Networks are used frequently in companies. Employees do not need to pass on files such as letters or other documents by disk, but can send these on the net. Alternatively, the files are stored on a central network computer, also often described as a **server**, and can be accessed over the network by people entitled to do so. This way of providing information brings considerable advantages to the company and is, of course, very important in cutting down on the expenditure involved in distributing documents. All documents needed by several employees are placed on the server and can then be edited.

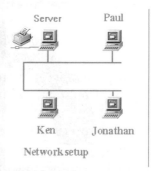

Network setup

This application was taken a step further on the Internet. One can not only connect the company's computers to each other via a cable, but also connect computers based in different cities or countries.

San Francisco
Rome
Rio

A computer in San Francisco can, for example, exchange data with a computer in Rome or in Rio. The systems are, in the process, connected to each other via the public telephone exchange or via data managers (partly by satellite).

Originally, only a few computers in various universities were connected to each other via the Internet. Because exchanging data on the Internet is very simple, quick and cheap, more and more computers were connected to each other worldwide. Today, the Internet consists of many thousands of computers which can be found in institutes, public utilities, government offices and firms. These computers are also often described as **Web servers**. People who have access to such a computer can reach all the other computers on the Internet (and also the users) and request files from them or send files or news to other users. You only need an address, just as with letters.

That is why the Internet functions as a medium for exchanging information. Similarly, as with the post (here you could telephone, send letters, parcels and packages or deal with banks), the Internet offers various services (such as exchanging news, sending files, telephoning and so on). It is, therefore, no problem to visit a NASA computer in the USA from your front room, to find out the weather forecast for Mallorca or to send electronic post to a friend in Australia. In a **chat group**, you can talk with users from all over the world. With the correct equipment, you can even deal with an online conference and hold a conversation over the Internet. The NetMeeting program provided with Internet Explorer 5.0 supports this type of communication. **Newsgroups** allow the exchange of information about the most unlikely subjects.

There is an enormous number of special Internet functions which at this stage do not need to be mentioned. A large proportion of Internet users only really use two functions: sending **e-mails** and 'surfing' the **World Wide Web**. Microsoft Office 2000 supports these functions with Internet Explorer as well as other Internet services such as **chat** and **newsgroups** (which are not, however, dealt with in this book).

The question still remains: how does the World Wide Web work? What is so special about the World Wide Web that it has become so popular? Here are a few thoughts on the subject: on the Internet, there are a few thousand computers which hold a huge amount of files. This creates a few problems when looking for specific documents. Think about searching for a particular file on your own computer. How can this work with so many million users? Have you found the wrong document at the end or can you perhaps not read it because it was created with an

The **World Wide Web** is an additional service on which **Web pages** can be viewed. For example, they can contain the current weather forecast, stock market prices or the advertising of a specific company. We looked at Web pages in the previous chapter, where they were created in Word, Excel and PowerPoint and saved as *.htm* files. To view such Web pages, you need a special program which is called a **browser**. Microsoft Internet Explorer is an example of a browser and comes with Office 2000.

Chat is the English term adopted by the whole world for 'talking' or 'chatting' on the Web. The Internet offers **chat rooms** in which like-minded people can 'meet' and talk about 'God and the Universe'. Chatting, however, is reduced to the exchange of short text. This type of chatting takes place online which means all the users must visit the chat room on the Internet at the same time. The Windows' program **NetMeeting** offers another variant which allows the user to attend Internet conferences via a soundcard and a microphone. Both programs are installed on Internet Explorer in Microsoft Office 2000.

Newsgroups are discussion groups on particular subjects on the Internet. Users can request information on subjects as pages of text and ask their own questions as well as giving answers to existing questions. This allows a worldwide exchange of information. In contrast to chats which take place online, contributions in newsgroups stay there for some time (weeks or months) and can be read by other users at a later stage.

As well as the **Internet**, the term **'intranet'** is used more and more frequently. Intranets are networks that use the same programs as the Internet and are often installed in larger companies. Because only employees of the company can use this network, the name **'inter'** was changed to **'intra'**. Are you familiar with the Internet functions and can you use the company's internal intranet? Microsoft Office 2000 comes with many functions to support the intranet.

unfamiliar program (do you not know which text format someone uses in India and have you installed it by chance on your computer?).

To simplify finding and viewing documents on the Internet, the **World Wide Web** (WWW) was created. Document files are actually scattered worldwide over computers connected to the World Wide Web. Each **document**, however, receives an **address** which clearly determines where the accompanying file is to be found (this address is represented just like a letter address). Furthermore, all **documents** are saved in a special format with the *.htm* or *.html* file name extension. There are programs such as Microsoft Internet Explorer which can read and display these files. These programs are described generally as **browsers**. Both the 'address' and 'file format' allow easy access to the document on the browser. In the previous chapter, you learned that Microsoft Office 2000 program documents are stored as Web pages with the *.htm* or *.html* file name extension. Obviously, Office 2000 already supports the document format of the World Wide Web.

There is another Internet function that you learnt about in the last chapter as an Office function: **hyperlinks**.

An HTML document contains links to access subsequent documents as a rule. If you find such a link in an HTML document, click on the mouse to display the subsequent document.

Have you come across the term **HTML** in connection with creating Web pages? This is the abbreviation for **Hypertext Markup language**. With this 'document description language', documents can be created so that they can be displayed on different computers with a browser. If you create a Web page in Office, this is automatically saved in this HTML format. You can recognise HTML documents by the *.htm* or *.html* file name extension.

Microsoft has also integrated the functionality of hyperlinks into Office 2000. For example, you can leave links to other documents in Word documents (such as Excel tables). Admittedly, you need suitable programs to view these documents. This is the difference in linking Web pages to other Web pages in the HTML format. Internet Explorer then shows the contents of the document.

And now the whole point of the above: if you know the address of an HTML document, state it on the browser. The browser loads the document from the World Wide Web (either from the intranet or from a computer drive) and displays it on your computer.

Internet Explorer – quickstart

As a reader, it makes no difference where these files are saved. If you have tracked down an interesting Web page, get to the other pages via hyperlinks. The browser searches the document of the chosen hyperlink separately on the World Wide Web and loads this from a computer in Rome, Tokyo or Sydney on to your computer if necessary. This switching between different Web pages is known as **surfing the Internet**. You will learn how this works properly in the next section.

Is there only a network at your work place, and not an intranet? If so, leave your documents as Web pages in a space used generally on the server. Other employees can then request these documents with Internet Explorer and use the results of the work. This can be used for all general information, price lists, product information etc.

Does it all sound really complicated? Read the following steps to get you motivated:

➡ The good news: don't worry, because surfing Web pages is really easy and opens a completely new world. Also the browser that you need to surf the Internet comes as **Microsoft Internet Explorer,** which is already contained in Microsoft Office 2000. You can, therefore, start accessing your first Web pages and even have a say if you are knowledgeable about the subject in question!

➡ Microsoft has many Internet functions integrated directly into Microsoft Office. You already know many of the functions (you probably don't realise it yet, but when you use Windows Help, you use a type of HTML document).

➡ The bad news: to 'surf' the Web, you need access to the Internet. This is made available by online providers, such as CompuServe, America Online (AOL), Demon, Virgin, BT, U-NET among others.

➡ If you do not have an Internet connection or are not yet online, you cannot 'surf the Internet' for the moment. But if you have saved HTML documents on your computer, you can retrieve them with Internet Explorer. CD-ROMs will offer the documents in HTML format in future.

> To allow all readers entry with or without an Internet connection, we will follow a 'dry surfing course' for the first steps. Have you worked through the previous chapter? If so, you should now have available several Web pages in the *My Documents\Web* folder. You will now learn your way around Internet Explorer from these files.

To display a Web document, you have two choices:

➡ Start Microsoft Internet Explorer and state where the document is to be found.

➡ Place the Web document as an HTML file on your computer's drive and open the relevant folder window (via the *My Computer* desktop icon or the *My Documents icon*). Then double-click on the HTML file to start Internet Explorer and load the document.

417

Choose the first approach for the following steps, as it allows access to pages on the World Wide Web as well as showing local files. Later, you will find an example to open a Web page directly by clicking on the HTML file.

Starting Internet Explorer

First, you have to start Microsoft Internet Explorer. You will be able to access this program in the Program/Internet Explorer menu in the *Start* menu.

1 Start the program by clicking the mouse on the icon in the status bar.

If there is an icon for the program on the desktop, you can also start Internet Explorer by double-clicking this.

The program opens the window in which the Start page is shown. In this example, the Home Page is empty.

This window is already available in the previous chapter when you select the Web page. The title and menu bars are the same as shown in the file window.

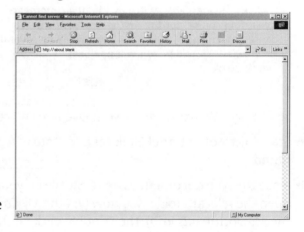

The way you handle the program window also corresponds to the usual operation with Windows programs.

Does Internet Explorer try to make a connection with the Internet immediately after start-up and does it tell you that the address cannot be found via an error message? If so, the wrong **Start Page** was entered. You will learn how to change this below. Do the buttons on the bar at the bottom look different to you (i.e. does the bar show text)? These entries can be inserted via *Toolbar/Customize* in the VIEW menu.

Loading a (local) Web page

Now you must tell the **browser** where it can find the 'Web page'.

1 Choose the *Open* command in the FILE menu or press the ⌈Ctrl⌉+⌈O⌉ key combination.

Explorer shows the *Open* dialog box with an empty *Open* text box.

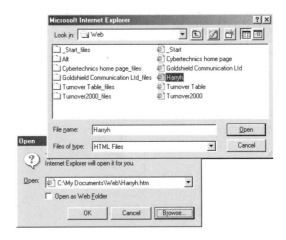

2 Click on the *Search* button.

3 Choose the *My Documents\Web* folder from your Windows drive in the second *Open* dialog box.

The *HarryH.htm* file was stored as a Web page with Word previously in Chapter 8. In the exercises at the end of the chapter, you gave this file a few extra hyperlinks.

 Select the *HarryH.htm* file and click on the *Open* button.

The path to the chosen HTML document now appears in the *Open* box.

5 Click on the *OK* button in the *Open* dialog box.

Internet Explorer loads the appropriate HTML document and displays its contents.

Navigating with hyperlinks

Web pages begin with a sort of list of contents whose entries are executed with hyperlinks.

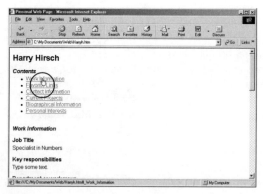

1 Point to one of the hyperlinks.

The mouse pointer takes the form of a stylised hand and the address of the subsequent page is given in the status bar of the browser.

2 Click on the
'Favorite links' hyperlink.

Internet Explorer shows
the relevant section of
the document. If you
have done the exercises
in the previous chapter,
you should have
produced what is shown
here.

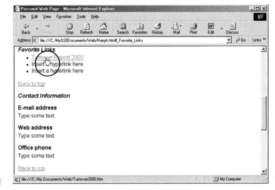

3 Now click on the 'Back
to the beginning of the
page' hyperlink.

If everything has worked, you will now see the beginning of the
document again with the hyperlinks of the table of contents.

You can not only request other documents via the hyperlinks, but also select specific
places inside a longer document with corresponding links. This is easier than
scrolling through the list of pictures inside the document. Whether the technology
for these local links is available depends on the author of the relevant Web page.
Such internal links are usually standard for these pages created with a Word
document.

4 Click on the
'Favorite Links'
hyperlink again.

421

This link was inserted into the Web page during one of the exercises in Chapter 8.

5 Click on the 'Table with turnover data' hyperlink.

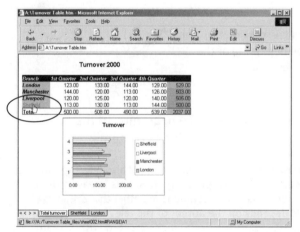

The browser now requests the *Turnover table.htm* Web page created in the previous chapter with the Excel worksheet. Obviously, if the page does not fit into the browser window, the chart is cropped.

6 Change the size of the window as a test.

The browser automatically fits the width of the text to the width of the window. There are NO fixed page **sizes** on Web pages.

7 Now click on the 'Sheffield' hyperlink in the table.

The browser shows the worksheet with the branch data. To change between the pages of the earlier worksheet, you can use the *Sheet* tab in the Web page.

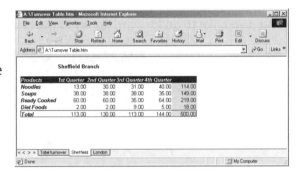

Have you carried out the above steps? Do you have any problems?

However, there are still two other issues which you will run into sooner or later. Suppose you want to return to previously visited pages again. Do you now have to type in the original Web address of the pages in the *Address* box again or do you need to access them using the *Open* dialog box? No, because the browser has thought of this. It automatically displays the address of Web pages you have already visited.

1 Click on the *Back* button in the bar.

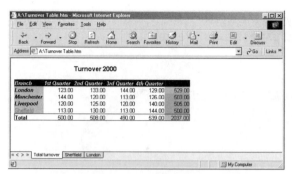 The browser now shows the previous Web pages again. In this example, the browser opens the pages just visited with the total turnovers of the table.

Would you like to go forward again to the branch turnovers?

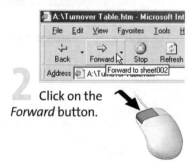

2 Click on the *Forward* button.

The browser can only scroll back or forth page by page with the *Forward* and *Back* buttons, so you may need a lot of clicks to go back to a specific page. Is there perhaps a way to get directly to a Web page which has already been visited?

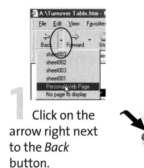

1 Click on the arrow right next to the *Back* button.

The browser now opens a menu with the titles of the visited Web pages.

2 Click on the *Personal Web Page* entry.

The browser now displays the relevant Web page again.

TIP

The same function is available with the *Forward* button. It is very easy to scroll between Web pages with the menu.

Another example

Finally, we will learn how to organise Web pages differently. Do you still remember that we created a Group Home Page in Chapter 8 with PowerPoint?

A **Home Page** is the name for the first page (lead page or start page) of a succession of pages in the World Wide Web. With this Home Page, you can reach the others via hyperlinks.

Let's see how these Web pages are organised. We saved the Home Page in the *\My Documents\Web* file on the Windows drive.

1 Open the *My Documents\Web* file window.

2 Double- click on the *_Start.htm* file symbol.

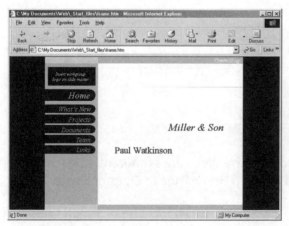

Internet Explorer now shows the Home Page of the Web presentation. The list of contents on the left border contains the hyperlinks to request further document pages.

Until now you have learnt that hyperlinks are shown as blue, underlined passages. Admittedly, this is not that important. In the above steps, hyperlinks are represented as simple green coloured text in the list of contents. Other Web pages use graphics to which hyperlinks are assigned. The type of representation in the Web page depends on the program used for creating it.

1 Point to the list of hyperlinks in the left border.

The mouse pointer takes the form of a stylised hand and the address of the following page is shown in the status bar.

2 Now click on the 'Home Page', 'What's New', 'Projects', 'Documents' and so on hyperlinks one after another.

This representation is used in many Web pages since it allows the user good orientation. The realisation, however, provides specific tools (like PowerPoint) or special technology to structure the Web pages.

The browser requires the document to which it was linked in the hyperlink. The Web pages created by PowerPoint are structured in such a way that the list of contents stays in the left border whilst the contents of the document are visible in the right-hand part of the window. If a page contains a hyperlink in the document part, you click on this instead. The browser then switches to this side.

You see that surfing the Web pages is really very easy. The hardest thing about it all is knowing the right address for the Home Pages (but more about that later).

Accessing the World Wide Web

Were you able to work through the example in the last section? Have you acquired an appetite for more? If so, then it is time to visit your first Web sites on the Internet. This is no more difficult than surfing Web pages saved locally in folders.

Before carrying out the following steps, make sure that your computer's modem is connected with a telephone connection and is switched on. If you access through ISDN, this must be used for online connection.

1 Start Internet Explorer (by clicking the mouse on the button in the *Start* menu).

Now you must tell the browser where the desired document is found. You do this by typing it into the *Addresses* symbol bar. Most addresses look something like:

http://www.xxx.com

http:// shows that a document on the Web is being used (or on the intranet). Then follows a sequence of characters with its own address.

Sometimes the term **URL** is used instead of address. This is nothing more than an English abbreviation for 'Uniform Resource Locator', which corresponds to an address on the Web.

You must know the exact address. For example, you learn addresses of Web pages from companies' adverts. There are also newspapers and other sources which publish such addresses. The following table contains some Web addresses of popular pages (please note these may change over time).

Rolling Stones	www.stones.com
Internet Travel Network	www.itn.net
Internet information	www.freeserve.co.uk
CNN	www.cnn.com
Financial service management	www.finance.com
Choosing a job	www.click-here-now.com/jobs/jobs.htm
BBC	www.bbc.co.uk
Industry	www.industry.net
Job market	www.cyberiacafe.net
CD overview	www.cdnow.com
Job market	www.firstdivisionjobs.com
Cinema information	www.popcorn.co.uk
Ordering books	www.amazon.co.uk
Search engine	www.yahoo.com
Job market	www.jobsearch.co.uk
Search engine	www.lycos.com
The Sun	www.thesun.co.uk
Online games	www.zone.com
Search engine	www.altavista.com
The Times	www.the-times.co.uk
Ordering books	www.whsmith.co.uk
Radio One FM	www.radioone.com
Ordering books	www.blackwell.co.uk
Theatre information	www.whatsonstage.com
Search engine	www.excite.com
Capital FM	www.capitalfm.com

Search engine	www.hotbot.com
PC Pro Magazine	www.pcpro.co.uk
Games	www.gremlin.co.uk
Pearson Education	www.pearsoned-ema.com
Travel	www.americanexpress.com
Microsoft	www.microsoft.com

If you know the address of the document, enter it in the address field of the browser and confirm this with the ⏎ key. The relevant document will then be loaded and you can reach the subsequent pages by using the hyperlinks already mentioned if necessary. Do you want to visit the Pearson Education Web page?

1 Click on the *Address* field in the window of the Internet Explorer.

| Address | 🔁 | http://www.pearsoned-ema.com/ |

2 Enter the URL address shown here.

Have you already visited the page before? The browser notes the Web addresses and adds similar Web addresses in a list box after the entry.

🔁 http://www.cybertechnics.co.uk/
🔁 http://www.pearsoned-ema.com/
🔁 http://www.winzip.com/
🔁 http://www.microsoft.co.uk/
🔁 /Web
🔁 http://www.adobe.com/
🔁 http://www5.metacreations.com/

3 Click on this to transfer such an address.

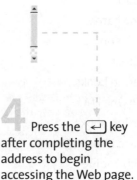

4 Press the ⏎ key after completing the address to begin accessing the Web page.

The browser stores the contents of the pages already visited for a certain amount of time in the cache memory. If the page is not found there, the browser asks whether a connection to the Web should be made.

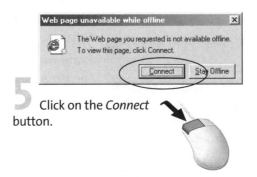

5 Click on the *Connect* button.

If you do not want to have a connection to the Internet, click on *Stay Offline*.

It can now take a couple of seconds until the connection is made and the browser has found the relevant page. Always remember that the document now has to be retrieved from the other side of the world. However, as a user, you do not need to worry about this. You simply type in the correct address in the browser (and confirm the query that you want to go online if necessary).

Sometimes it takes a long time for the computer to connect to the desired page. After you have the document you want, you can abort the browser's inquiry by choosing this button in the bar.

If a page does not load completely, or if you would like to repeat an inquiry, choose the *Refresh* button in the browser's bar. The browser then requests the page again in the WWW.

431

If a valid Web address was given, the browser finds the document and loads the information on to your computer. The relevant page is then built up step-by-step in the browser window. This can take some time depending on the document size and the number of graphics contained in the document.

The picture here shows the Entry page of Babylon 5 at the time this book went to print. This advertisement page was constructed in such a way by the company that it disappears after about 20 seconds. Click on this page instead.

The real Home Page of Babylon 5 appears, showing various options available.

If you point on a link, the mouse pointer takes the form of a stylised hand.

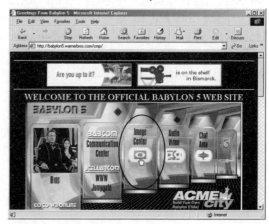

1 Click on the image centre.

Internet Explorer finds the following page (here with pictures of the characters).

2 Click on the button to return to previous pages.

Would you like to chat with other fans?

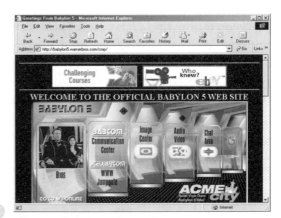

3 Then click on the *Chat Arena* icon in the Entry page.

On the next page, you can chat to anyone who is online or leave a message.

433

In this way you can request Web pages on the Internet. By clicking on hyperlinks, you surf between the pages and request the desired information. This works just like requesting HTML documents from your local drive. The connection is simply slower for the most part and the online time incurs charges as a rule.

Marking Web pages

Is there a Web page that you visit a lot or you especially like? If so, it is really time consuming having to type in the address belonging to it every time. Unfortunately, you often forget the addresses of interesting Web pages. Microsoft Internet Explorer has a function with which you can keep interesting Web pages. This is sometimes also described as **bookmarking** because you insert a 'bookmark' between the pages on the WWW to look up there again later. The relevant function is known as *Favorites* in Microsoft Internet Explorer. There are various possibilities to include Web pages in this list. This is the easiest way to do it:

1 Click on the *Favorites* button.

Internet Explorer now inserts the Explorer bar with the favourites already defined in the left part of the window.

2 Request the desired Web page on Internet Explorer.

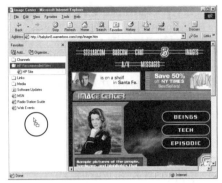

3 Drag the document symbol from the *Address* box of the address bar to the desired place in the Explorer bar.

As soon as you have let go of the left mouse button, the new name is added to the list of favourites. You can request the Web pages later by choosing the relevant entries.

Alternatively you can choose the *Add To Favorites* command in the FAVORITES menu to establish a new entry. Or you can click on the *Add* button in the Explorer bar. Internet Explorer then opens a dialog box in which you can insert the name for the entry.

If you want to define many favourites, it is preferable to sort them into groups (folders). Choose the *File Favorites* in the FAVORITES menu. Or click on the *File* button in the Explorer bar. The *File Favorites* option allows you to clear favourites, rename them and place folders to include the favourite.

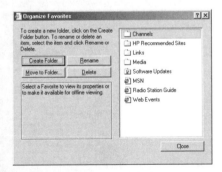

Viewing visited Web pages offline

As long as you have the connection from your computer to the Internet, this is described as being **online**. This is easy to tell since the telephone and online charges accrue. If the connection is terminated, the computer is **off-line**.

Have you forgotten to insert the relevant favourites? Do you want to read a page you have just visited later on?

Microsoft Internet Explorer also provides help for you in this case, by letting you read pages **offline**.

The browser notes the contents of the pages visited by you and stores them in an internal cache memory. This cache memory is kept for a couple of days. If you choose the various pages with the *Back* and *Forward* buttons during an online session on the Internet, the browser can load the contents of the pages from this cache memory. This speeds up viewing Web pages. To view the contents of visited Web pages later offline, carry out the following steps:

1 Click on the *History* button.

Internet Explorer shows the names of the visited Web pages in the Explorer bar, sorted according to days and weeks.

2 Click on *Today* to view the entries.

3 Click on one of the entries.

Internet Explorer now loads the pages from the internal memory. You can then read the pages in peace.

There may be cases, however, when not all the information is available. Sometimes, pictures or other information are missing. Internet Explorer then asks by clicking on one of the hyperlinks whether it should connect to the Internet in order to load the relevant pages. The title bar indicates if there is an online connection. If there is not a connection to the Internet, the title bar states it is offline.

Saving and printing Web pages

Do you want save the text of a page so you can look at it later again? This can be done on Microsoft Internet Explorer in a few steps:

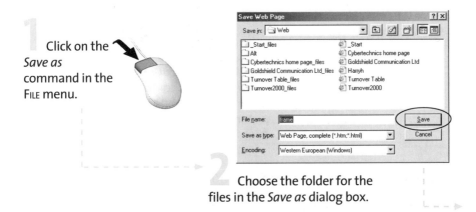

1 Click on the *Save as* command in the FILE menu.

2 Choose the folder for the files in the *Save as* dialog box.

437

3 Correct the file name in the *File name* field if necessary.

4 Click on the *Save* button.

The page's text is saved by Internet Explorer as a file with the above name and *.htm* or *.html* extension in the target folder. At the same time, Internet Explorer 5.0 inserts a subfolder with the same name in which the pictures and help files are stored.

Do you want to save a picture from the Web page?

1 Click on the picture with the right mouse button.

The a

| Open Link |
| Open Link in New Window |
| Save Target As... |
| Print Target |
| Show Picture |
| Save Picture As... |
| Set as Wallpaper |
| Set as Desktop Item... |
| Cut |
| Copy |
| Copy Shortcut |
| Paste |
| Add to Favorites... |
| Properties |

The pictures are automatically stored with their file names (or with the GIF or JPG file name extensions).

2 Choose the *Save Picture As* command in the context menu and enter the name and file for the picture in the *Save Picture* dialog field.

Can you also load a saved document page in HTML format again? Yes: because the HTML document format is becoming so popular, you will find more and more frequently such files on CD-ROMs or on program disks. You learnt how to load these files at the beginning of the chapter.

Printing Web pages

Printing loaded **HTML documents** is really easy.

1 To print a page in Internet Explorer, click on the *Print* button.

Internet Explorer prints the contents of the page.

2 If you need more control over your printing, choose the *Print* command in the FILE menu or press the ⌈Ctrl⌋+⌈P⌋ key combination.

Select the 'Print table of links' check box in the *Print* dialog box. The browser then prints a list of the addresses of all hyperlinks contained in the document at the end of the document page. In this way, you can find out interesting Web addresses.

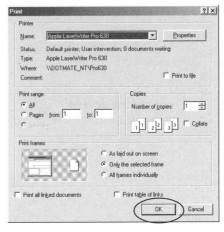

3 Establish the desired options in the *Print* dialog field.

4 Click on the *OK* button.

The browser now prints the contents of the document as well as graphics currently shown. This print-out also includes the parts of the document that are not visible if the viewing window is smaller than the document.

Inserting the Start Page and other options

Starting Internet Explorer automatically loads your own Start Page. This is also known as the **Home Page**.

Clicking on this button in the bar takes you to your Start Page.

If you have lost your way whilst 'surfing' the Web waves, you can get back into chartered waters with this button. Internet Explorer automatically uses a Microsoft Web page as your Start Page. Carry out the following steps to change the Start address (and to edit further options):

1 Load the desired Web page into Explorer.

2 Click on the *Internet Options* command in the TOOLS menu.

Explorer now shows the *Internet Options* character window.

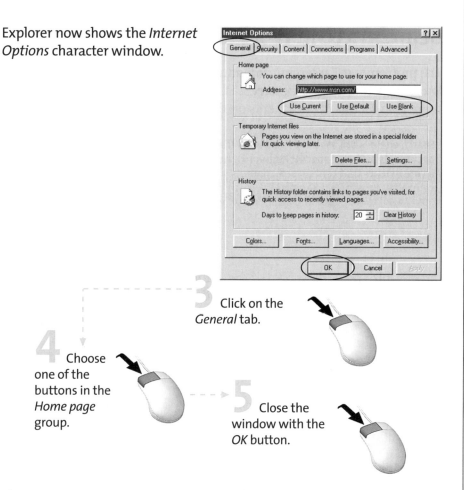

Click on the
General tab.

Choose
one of the
buttons in the
Home page
group.

Close the
window with the
OK button.

The empty page shown at the beginning of the chapter is inserted as the Start Page with the *Use Blank* button. To make the Web document currently loaded the Start Page, select the *Use Current* button. If you choose the *Use Default* button, the address of the Microsoft Home Page is provided.

You can enter a valid address in the Internet as well as a file on your computer as a Start address. Addresses on the WWW on the whole begin with the characters *http://*, whilst a file on the drive of your computer has the address *file// <drive:folder\file>*.

In the *Proceed* group, specify how many days Internet Explorer should store in the cache memory the pages in the *Proceed* folder. Furthermore, you can clear the content of these files using the *Empty 'Proceed'* file button.

Searching the World Wide Web

The problem with accessing individual Web pages is that you have to know the addresses. At the very least, this is a quantitive problem as there are millions of documents on the World Wide Web. Fortunately, there are **search engines** which you can use to search for specific document contents.

You could enter the URL address of a search engine directly into the *Address* field of the address symbol bar. But Internet Explorer supports you in the search with the help of a predefined page.

1 **Search**

Click on the *Search* button in the Explorer bar.

Internet Explorer makes a connection to the Internet and loads a Search page in the Explorer bar of the window.

2 Type in the search term into the entry box.

3 Select the *Search a Web page* options box.

4 Click on the *Search* button.

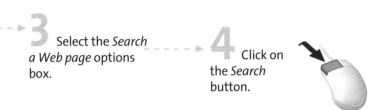

The search engine shows the documents found in the window of the Explorer bar abbreviated along with the hyperlinks.

4 Click on one of the hyper links to open the document in the right-hand part of the window.

You will also find options in this window to limit the search (for example, by language) or to set the number of search results displayed.

Does the search engine not come up with any satisfactory information? If so, you can open a menu with names of other search engines and make an entry with the *Other* button in the Explorer bar.

Here you see the page of the Excite search engine. Search terms can be entered as well as setting search options in the relevant pages.

1 To reduce the number of search engines used, click on the *Edit* button in the Explorer bar.

You can define which search pages of the user are offered in the *Customize* dialog box using a check box.

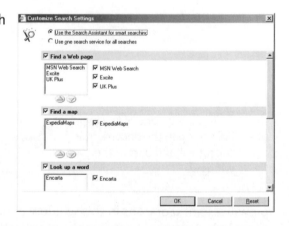

This option, however, can only be used as long as the browser is connected online with the Microsoft Web page.

The disadvantage of this solution is the constraints in terms of search engines provided by Microsoft. I avoid searching using the Explorer bar. Furthermore, I type the Web address of the desired search engine (such as www.yahoo.com, www.altavista.com or www.eule.com) directly into the *Addresses* box. The browser then shows the Web page of the relevant search engine and the search term can be entered.

You can search the Internet using keywords very easily using search engines. It depends on the search engine in question as to how these keywords are entered. Many search engines expect a plus sign between the terms of several key words. Other search engines need quotation marks around the search terms. The Yahoo search engine has the advantage that you have access to the information of other search engines such as Altavista. You may possibly get the results as a page of this search engine.

Downloading files

Sometimes files (e.g. from programs) are stored on the Web server and you may want to store them on your local computer. To do this, use the hyperlink that offers to **download** the file.

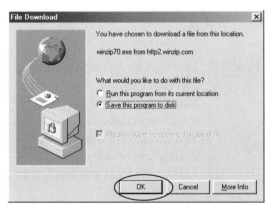

Download WinZip 7.0 SR-1 (winzip70.exe - 943,835 bytes)

1 Click on the relevant hyperlink.

Internet Explorer opens a dialog box in which you can choose the desired action.

445

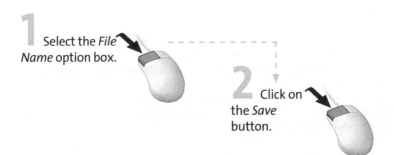

1 Select the *File Name* option box.

2 Click on the *Save* button.

The browser opens the *Save As* dialog field.

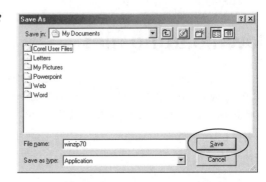

3 Choose the goal folder and correct the file name if necessary.

4 Start the downloading by clicking on the *Save* button.

During a longer downloading, Internet Explorer informs you about the current status of the loading process in a dialog box. You can also find out in this dialog box how long the loading process still has left to go.

The downloading can be stopped at any time using the *Cancel* button. the *Close this dialog box when download completes* check box was selected, Internet Explorer closes the dialog box after downloading.

During loading, you can deal with other tasks with Internet Explorer (for example, choose other Web sites). To check the downloading status, click on the button of the downloading dialog box in the Windows task bar. The dialog field then appears in the foreground.

Internet Explorer also has buttons to exchange e-mail and to edit Web pages. Dealing with e-mail is discussed in Chapter 10. How you create and save Web pages was outlined briefly in Chapter 8. At this point, we will end your introduction to Internet Explorer and the main terms used on the Internet. For further training, just surf the Web or request local HTML files.

What's in this chapter?

Microsoft Outlook 2000 is your work organiser. Use Outlook 2000 to organise your office work day-by-day. The following functions are available in this program: calendar, notes, tasks, contacts, journal, and a central mail office for electronic messages. This chapter contains an introduction to the basics of Outlook 2000. It shows you how you can use this tool in the office on a day-by-day basis. You will learn how to record and retrieve appointments or notes with Outlook. It shows you how to edit electronic messages and manage your list of contacts with the program. After reading this, you will understand Outlook 2000 and will be able to use it for your most important tasks.

Outlook – a quick overview

Microsoft Outlook 2000 is installed with Microsoft Office 2000. Use Outlook 2000 to organise your office on a day-by-day basis. The program contains a collection of helpful functions, including a calendar, a note book and an address book, with which you can organise your work every day. Outlook 2000 can create journals, and includes a central mail office to send and receive electronic mail.

Starting Outlook

When you install Microsoft Office 2000, Outlook 2000 is also set up. Office sets up the program symbol on the desktop or in the *Start* menu.

Double-click on the *Outlook* icon on the desktop to start the program.

Alternatively, you can also call up the program with PROGRAM/ MICROSOFT OUTLOOK in the *Start* menu.

Microsoft Outlook

The program is started and displays the program window.

An assistant appears when you first call up Outlook 2000 after installing Office, which Outlook sets up for sending e-mails. Furthermore, you may need to manually set up the in- or outbox for mail. If Outlook 2000 is not installed, refer to Chapter 11. There, you will receive basic information on how to configure the program.

Outlook overview

As soon as you start Outlook, the program opens the applications window. The layout of this window is configurable. This is the default layout.

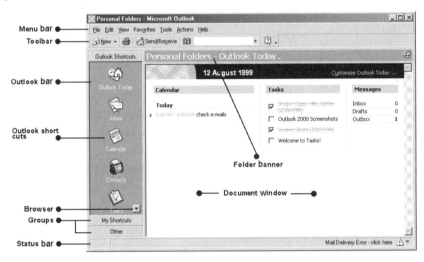

The program uses symbol and menu bars known to other Office applications in the applications window.

⇒ In the document area, the **Personal Folders** - **Outlook Today** window is displayed. In this folder, the tasks to be dealt with are clearly listed. You will see a column with the entries for the appointment calendar. Another column lists tasks to be carried out with the deadline for completion. The number of messages in the in- and outboxes is listed on the right in the *Messages* column.

The **Personal Folders** - **Outlook Today** window is structured as a Web page. If you point on a text entry, this is marked as a hyperlink. By clicking on the individual entries, the relevant window is opened (for example, to show the inbox). This type of representation is configurable and can therefore look different in your system. Use the **Outlook Today** function, in the top left-hand corner, to edit the way personal folders look with various options (*see* Chapter 11).

⇨ The Outlook bar is now in the left pane of the window. The various Outlook folders can be requested by clicking on their icon in the bar.

The status bar contains general information about the chosen folder (such as how many entries are available in the appointment calendar).

Working with the Outlook bar

Outlook stores the information in various folders (inbox, outbox, notes, calendar etc.). The information can be requested and edited with the Outlook functions from these folders. The Outlook bar is displayed on the left side of the Outlook window. This bar allows you access to individual Outlook folders.

Is this bar missing from your Outlook window? Then tick the *Outlook Bar* command in the VIEW menu. As soon as the command is selected with a tick, the bar is shown in the Outlook window. You can also use this command to delete the bar.

The Outlook bar is sub-divided into several groups: *Outlook Shortcuts*, *My Shortcuts* and *Other*.

1 Click on the horizontal bars to open the group

Here you will see the *Outlook Shortcuts* group. Each group consists of a row of icons which stand for various folders (or functions). If the space in the bar is not sufficient to show all the icons, you can scroll with the ▾ arrow in the group. The arrow is either at the top or bottom of the bar.

Does Outlook display the window described above when opened? If so, you are then ready to get to know the individual Outlook functions. First, two tips: as long as you do not use all the Outlook functions, simply go on further with the next steps. If there is a function available on the Outlook bar which is not in the described format, refer to Chapter 11. This describes how to set up specific icons in the Outlook bar groups.

E-mail

'Just give me your e-mail address.' This is becoming a very common request and sending e-mails is becoming an increasingly important part of office and even personal life. Outlook offers a function for managing incoming and outgoing electronic mail. As long as your system has a connection to the Internet or an intranet and is set up appropriately, you can use the e-mail functions of Outlook to create and edit mail.

What is e-mail?

What hides behind the term e-mail and how do you use this Internet function? An **e-mail** is nothing more than a **letter** which you send in the form of an electronic message to a recipient. As with normal mail, you have to include the sender's and recipient's address. These will be in a specific form, such as *name@transport.com.*

The message written by you is then sent as a text file on the Internet (or by an electronic mail system on the intranet) and stored in the recipent's **mailbox** (on the Web server). The recipient can then download the message from the mailbox on to his or her computer and read it. If you have your own e-mail address, other users can send you electronic messages in the same way.

The Outlook program has functions to exchange incoming and outgoing mail with the mailbox on the Internet or intranet server. You can, therefore, send and receive messages with the program. New or received messages are saved in the cache memory locally on your computer in their own files with the name *Inbox* and *Outbox*. This allows you to edit the electronic mail with continuous connection to the Internet. If the mail is edited, you can call up the function to send/receive message. The rest is done by Outlook.

Send and receive messages

To send or receive e-mails, you need an e-mail account. This is similar to a bank account; you can neither receive payments or carry out transfers without your own account. An e-mail account is set up on the intranet by the network administrator. If you have set up access to the Internet by one of the online services or another provider, you will receive an e-mail address together with the right to access an Internet server. At the same time, the relevant provider will set up an e-mail account with a mailbox for incoming messages on a server. Outlook exchanges electronic mail with this server. Consequently, you will have an e-mail account on the Internet or intranet and your computer is set up to have access to this account.

If Outlook is configured correctly, you can exchange electronic mail through the Internet/intranet. Have you written a message and want to send it? Or do you want to know if you have already received mail? You must then call up the function to receive or send messages.

1 🖳 Send/Re̲ceive

Click on the *Send/Receive* button in the standard bar of the Outlook application window.

Your user name as well as your password is checked when accessing the Internet. You will see a dialog box which prompts you to enter your user name and password.

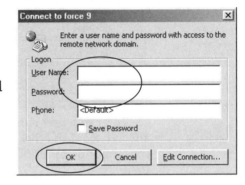

2 Enter your user name and password and click on the *OK* button.

The system then makes a connection to the Internet server of your Internet provider.

The exact amount of time required to connect depends on the Outlook version as well as the access used to the Internet/intranet. As a rule, however, access to e-mail is protected by the user's name and password. Consequently, some time must be spent authenticating the exchange on the Internet.

You will find the *Save Password* check box in the registration dialog boxes. If you select this check box, Windows records the instructions you have supplied regarding the password and the dialog box will not be displayed in future. Admittedly, there is a danger that unauthorised people will read this saved information and misuse it. If you are using a shared facility, it is safer not to save your password.

Even access to your Internet mail box is protected, as a rule, by a user name and password. This prevents unauthorised people from reading your mail.

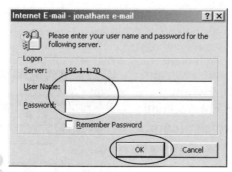

3 Enter your user name and password and click on the *OK* button to confirm them.

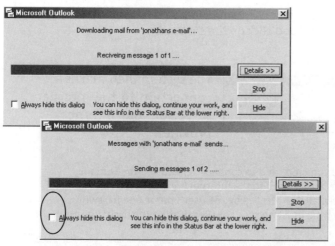

Outlook then delivers the messages written by you to the server and also empties your Internet mail box. This is shown through the dialog box. If required, you can select the check boxes in these dialog boxes. The dialog will then be hidden.

Furthermore, you can configure Outlook so that it automatically interrupts the connection to the Internet, after messages have been exchanged.

The process of exchanging mail works in a similar way to normal mail. To mail a letter, you have to take it to the post office, or place it in the internal mailbox or outbox of your company. If you want to edit incoming mail, you check with the branch of your mail office (and for this you need a PO box key). Delivery of the letter is then a job for the post office. Outlook works in exactly the same way. The Send/Receive function gives your written message to the sub post office of the server for forwarding. At the same time, it checks in the mailbox of the server to see if new messages have arrived and transfers these, if necessary, to the local mailbox of your computer.

Reading received messages

Have you carried out the following steps and want to read the mail received in the local mail inbox? The Outlook bar should display the icons for the in- and outboxes in a group.

According to the Outlook configuration, you will find the icons for the mail in- and outboxes in various groups. For example, in my system, I have left both icons in the *My Shortcuts* group. If the mail in- and outbox icons are missing, check in Chapter 11 to see how you set up this icon in the Outlook bar.

You can view the folder with your mail which has been saved locally on your computer with both these icons.

1 Look for the *Inbox* icon in the Outlook symbol bar.

The number in brackets shows you the messages contained in the inbox which are unread.

2 Click on the *Inbox* icon.

Outlook 2000 shows you the number of messages received in the *Inbox* folder window. The messages received are listed in the upper part of the inbox in the inbox bar.

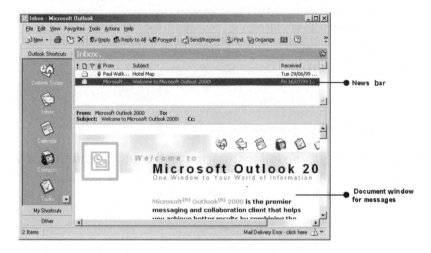

News bar

Document window for messages

Even if you do not have Internet/internet access, a message from Microsoft is already stored automatically in the inbox when installing Outlook.

A line is reserved for each message in the bar in which the status of the message, the sender, subject and date received are shown.

1 Now click on one of these lines with the received message.

Outlook shows the content of the message currently selected in its own message window (underneath the inbox bar). Do you want to increase or reduce the space for displaying the message?

2 Drag the horizontal part of the window (between the inbox bar and window) vertically in the desired direction.

Do you want to see the message in its own window? This is probably advantageous if you have attachments to the message or want to reply to the message (we will learn about these later).

3 Double-click on the message in the bar.

Outlook now opens its own window to edit the message. The top part contains the details of the sender, subject and so on. If necessary, a window with the symbols of the attached files appears in the lower part of the page which you can choose to edit by double-clicking on it.

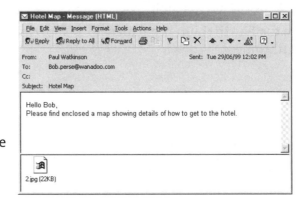

You can close this window with the *Close* button ☒ in the upper right corner of the window.

The symbols of the message bar

The message bar of the mail inbox contains further helpful information next to the details of the sender and the subject.

At the start of the line of the message bar, you will find four columns with symbols.

→ The first column with the exclamation mark ⚡ shows the priority of the message. The sender can allocate a normal, high or low priority with Outlook. This column usually remains empty as messages are generally given normal priority.

→ The second column ◻ with an envelope shows whether this message has been read ◁ or is still unread ✉. Furthermore, this will also show you whether a message is encoded or protected.

→ In the third column, a stylised flag ⚑ shows that the relevant message is to be flagged for follow-up (for example, because clarification is still required).

→ In the fourth column, a paperclip 📎 shows that the message has an attachment.

You will find a detailed list of all the symbols along with accompanying descriptions in Outlook Help under the 'Inbox Symbols' heading.

You can recognise the status of the message in these columns at a glance.

Changing the status of a message

As soon as you have clicked on a message in the message bar, its symbol in the status column is changed to 'read' (i.e. the symbol changes). Have you clicked on a message by mistake but do not have the time to read it? Simply set the status back to 'unread'.

1 Click on the line with the message in the message bar with the right mouse button.

2 Choose the *Mark as Unread* command in the context menu.

In the second column of the message bar, Outlook re-sets the symbol for the relevant message to ✉.

Do you want to follow a message until it is finally completed?

1 Click on the message in the message bar with the right mouse button.

2 Choose the *Flag for Follow Up* command in the context menu.

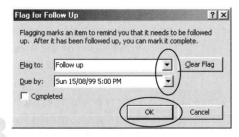

3 If necessary, define the *Flag to* and the *Due by* categories. Close the dialog box with the *OK* button.

Both pieces of information appear later when showing the message (*see later*).

The message then displays the 🚩 flag symbol on the message line.

Opening an attachment

An advantage of e-mail over fax is that other files can be sent with the message as attachments. A message with an attachment is marked with a paperclip 📎 in the message window or message bar. Do you want to open this attachment and save it as a file?

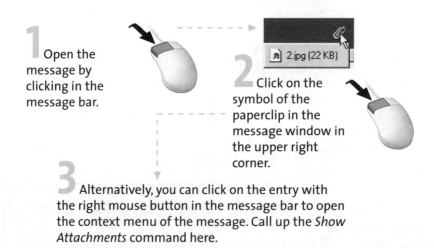

1 Open the message by clicking in the message bar.

2 Click on the symbol of the paperclip in the message window in the upper right corner.

3 Alternatively, you can click on the entry with the right mouse button in the message bar to open the context menu of the message. Call up the *Show Attachments* command here.

A message can carry several attachments. Outlook adds the names of the attached files in a submenu in both instances. You can then open the attachments to edit the relevant file. Or you can save the file for further editing in a folder.

4 Choose the name of the desired attachment in the menu.

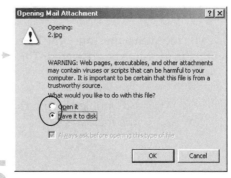

You should only choose the *Open* option if you are sure that the message contains 'non-dangerous' contents.

5 Select one of the option boxes and click on the *OK* button.

Save the attachment as a file to edit it.
As a result of this, the *Save As* dialog box appears.

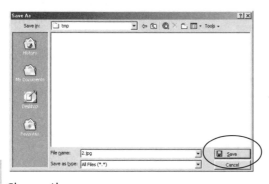

1 Choose the destination folder.

2 Click on the *Save* button.

The symbol of the attachment also shows the type of file attached, and which program is available to edit it. If you do not have the relevant program, the symbol of an unknown file is shown. In the above example, there is a JPG file presented as an attachment which you can open with the Windows Editor. It is recommended that attachments should be stored in files in case the message comes from an unknown source. You can then check the file with a virus scanner before opening.

Replying to or forwarding a message

Have you received a message which you want to forward to a third party? Should the message be answered? This is no problem for Outlook.

1 Double-click on the message in the message bar.

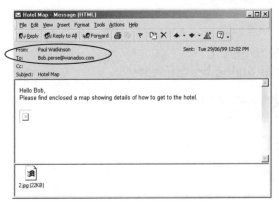

Outlook now opens the window to edit the message. The top part contains the details of the sender, subject etc.

In this part, there is information about possible attachments to the message with the chosen category. A window appears in the bottom part with the symbols of the attached files which you can choose by double-clicking to edit.

You can now prepare to reply to or forward the message with the three buttons in the standard bar.

2 Click on the *Reply* button.

Outlook opens a new window in which the text of the received message is displayed. This makes it easier for you to create your answer, since the subject of your message is delivered along with it. This is an extremely useful option if you receive many e-mails a day.

Furthermore, the *To* box of the recipient's address is already filled out.

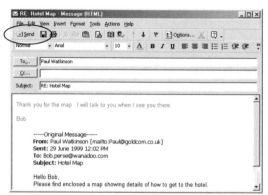

3 Now add the text of the reply to the message.

4 Click on the *Send* button in the symbol bar.

Outlook closes the window with the message and stores this in the outbox.

According to the individual configuration, the outbox can be either the mail outbox on the e-mail server or the local mail outbox. Collecting outgoing messages is recommended when sending messages on the Internet. This is then transferred on to an Internet Server in an online session (*see later*). An introduction to the Outlook configuration can be found in Chapter 11.

The standard bar has two further buttons to edit the message next to *Reply* button. An electronic message can be sent to several recipients *see later*). If you receive such a message, you can, if necessary, send an answer to everyone who is on the list of recipients.

The *Reply to All* button [Reply to All] does this.

If you choose this button, Outlook shows the window to edit the message. The *To* box then contains several recipients who will all receive a copy.

The *Forward* ⬅️🐾 For**w**ard button allows you to send the message on to one other person.

If you click on this button, the received message is 'mirrored' in a new window. You then have to choose the recipient's address in the *To* box, making sure you write it correctly (*see* page 478).

Techniques for handling messages

Messages received are displayed in the message bar. You can delete messages that are no longer needed, print out contents, and store important messages in separate folders.

1 Double-click on the message in the message bar.

Outlook opens the window to show the message.

2 Click on this button to print a message.

If you want to use special options when printing out, choose the *Print* command in the F<small>ILE</small> menu. Outlook opens the *Print* dialog box with the available options. You already know this dialog box from other Office programs.

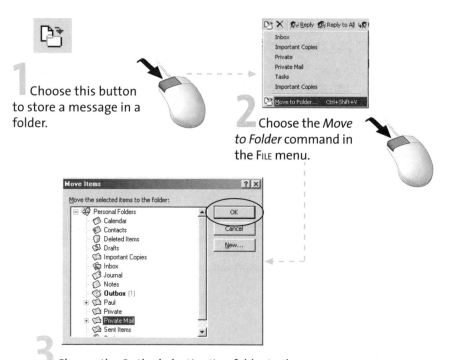

1 Choose this button to store a message in a folder.

2 Choose the *Move to Folder* command in the FILE menu.

3 Choose the Outlook destination folder in the *Move Items* dialog box and then close the dialog box in the *OK* box.

You can set out your own folder in Outlook with the *New* button.

The program then moves the message into the chosen folder. The entry disappears into the message list of the *Inbox* folder. Have you chosen the option to forward a message? You can then change the status of the forwarded message directly in the message window if necessary.

1 Click on this button.

Flag for Follow Up ? X

Flagging marks an item to remind you that it needs to be followed
up. After it has been followed up, you can mark it complete.

Flag to: Follow up   ▼   Clear Flag

Due by: Mon 30/08/99 5:00 PM   ▼

☐ Completed

OK   Cancel

2 Adjust the flag or the due date in the
dialog box for the message.

Have you opened the received message to read it in its own
window? If so, you can then use both the buttons shown
here to scroll through the message list. Clicking the mouse
on the buttons shows the following or previous message in
the window one at a time.

If you do not need a message any more, you can delete it with the ⊠
button. Outlook moves the message into the *Deleted Items* folder which is
called up with the Recycle Bin symbol in the Outlook bar.

Creating a message

Do you want to write a new message? In Outlook you can do it in a
few steps.

1 Click on the
arrow next to the
New button in the
standard bar of the
Outlook window.

Outlook adapts the meaning of the
New button depending on the folder
opened. If you have opened the
Outbox folder, the button creates a
new message.

2 Choose the *New Mail Message* command in the menu.

Microsoft Outlook opens the window to create the message. The layout depends on the e-mail editor. Usually, Outlook is used to edit the message and the window looks as it does here. You can now write your message.

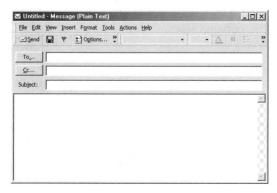

3 Click on the *To* box and enter the recipient's address in this box.

If the e-mail address is invalid, you will receive the message back as undeliverable. If you wish, you can enter several addresses in the *To* box to send the message to several recipients. The messages are separated by a semi-colon (;).

Is entering e-mail addresses manually too much work for you? In the following pages we will see how to use the *Contacts* function to manage an address book. Often, the recipients and e-mail addresses in the contacts list are already entered. The e-mail address can be transferred into the *To* box very easily.

469

1 Click on the *To* button.

Outlook shows the *Select Names* dialog box with the entries of the contact list.

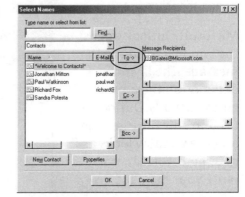

2 Choose a name with a valid e-mail address in the contact list.

3 Click on the *To* -> button.

The chosen addresses are transferred into the *Message Recipients* list. You can carry out the above steps repeatly and enter several recipients. As soon as you close the dialog box with the *OK* button, Outlook transfers the address details into the message window.

Perhaps you are wondering what the three *To, Cc* and *Bcc* boxes in the *Select Names* dialog box are for. Is a *To* box not enough? In principle, you can work with a *To* box and ignore the other fields. Letters are, however, often sent as a copy to another addressee as well. The *Cc* box stands for 'Carbon Copy'; if you enter one or more recipients in this field, they will all receive a copy. To prevent recipients from seeing the names of other recipients, use the *Bcc* field ('Blind Copy').

Have you entered the recipient's address? Your address is included automatically by Outlook.

1 Click on the *Subject* box and enter a short subject for the message.

2 Click in the text area below and type in the text of the message.

The result could then look like this: here the *To, Cc* and *Bcc* boxes and *Subject* were used. The text area contains a simple message.

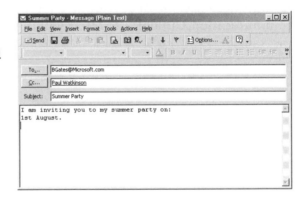

Specific rules (known as netiquette) have been developed in e-mail communication which you should observe.

Time is money. Because e-mail is a very fast communication medium, the rules that apply here are different from standard business correspondence. The purpose of e-mail is to provide fast information about something. E-mails should, therefore, be brief (the recipients who receive many messages every day will thank you for this). You can save youself typing time by using abbreviations that have become standard practice, such as BTW (by the way) and FYI (for your information).

The message on page 471 consists of simple text with no additional formatting. Since e-mail develops from previous methods of communication, Outlook also offers you the option to format the message.

1 Open the FORMAT menu ...

The *Plain Text* command is selected in the menu.

2 ... and choose the *HTML* command.

As soon as the *HTML* command is selected with a tick, Outlook releases the Format functions. The e-mail is then presented in the style of a Web page.

You can then select text entries and format them with the buttons of the formatting bar. You have already learnt the relevant techniques in Word. The background of the message or the graphics coding can be inserted with the commands in the FORMAT menu.

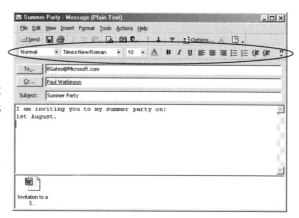

If the message is finished, you can spell check it with the *Spelling* command in the TOOLS menu or by pressing the F7 key .

The priority of the message can be made higher or lower with one of the symbols in the standard bar.

This changed priority is shown to the recipient in the message bar. Do you want to attach one or more files to a message and send it?

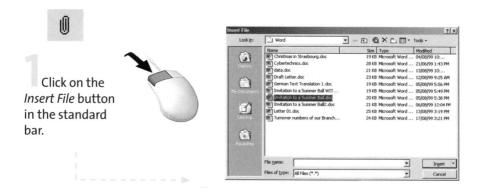

1 Click on the *Insert File* button in the standard bar.

2 Choose the desired file(s) in the *Insert File* dialog box.

473

Select several files by clicking on them with the 仓 key depressed.

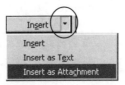

3 Click on the arrow next to the *Insert* button and choose the *Insert as Attachment* command in the menu.

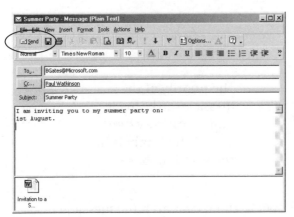

The window with the message then looks like this. In the bottom pane, you will see the symbol of the attached files.

4 If the message is complete, click on the *Send* button in the standard bar.

Viewing the Outbox

Do you want to view the contents of the *Outbox* folder?

1 Find the *Outbox* symbol in the Outlook bar.

2 Choose this symbol by clicking the mouse.

Outlook now shows the message list of e-mails ready to send. By double-clicking on an entry in the list, the message is loaded into the edit window again.

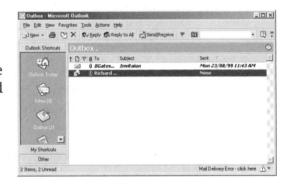

It is beyond the scope of this book to cover all the e-mail functions in Outlook. Also note that Outlook cannot work with every online service. An AOL user must use the e-mail function of the AOL access software. You will find details in the program's help and in the additional literature.

Managing contacts

Outlook has its own function for managing contacts. The approach is the same as for any well-kept address books. The contact function has been very well developed. It does much more than simply recording contacts with an address and a telephone number: the function also manages e-mail addresses of existing contacts and allows you to collect a variety of data relevant to your contacts.

Looking up contacts

Do you quickly need to use the address of a business partner? Do you want to look up a telephone number? All this is possible as long as the relevant people are entered in the contact list.

1 Click on the *Contacts* symbol in the *Outlook Shortcuts* group of the Outlook bar.

Outlook now opens a window with the contacts already entered. As with a visiting cards record, these contacts are listed and sorted according to the first letter of the entry in this window. All contacts are displayed in the window.

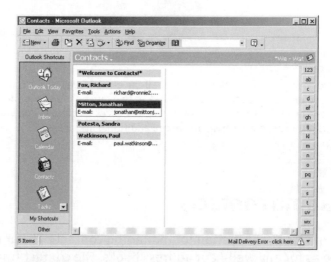

Just like a telephone directory, you can look up a specific entry in an extensive contact list.

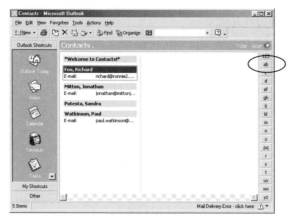

2 Simply click on one of the buttons on the right side of the window.

Do you need more detailed information on the relevant person?

3 Double-click on the entry in the list.

Outlook opens the *Contact* dialog box with various tabs.

You will find the most important details such as addresses, telephone numbers, e-mail addresses etc. in the *General* tab. Boxes can be filled with various details.

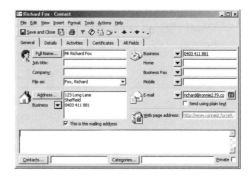

477

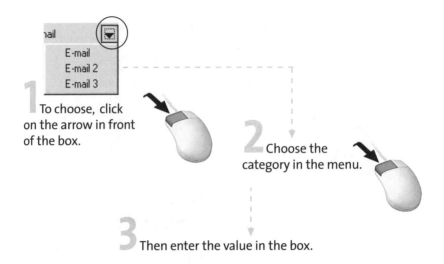

1 To choose, click on the arrow in front of the box.

2 Choose the category in the menu.

3 Then enter the value in the box.

When you have entered new data in the tab, this can be stored directly with the *Save and Close* button.

Creating contacts

If you want to create a new contact, you can use the *New* button in the Outlook standard bar.

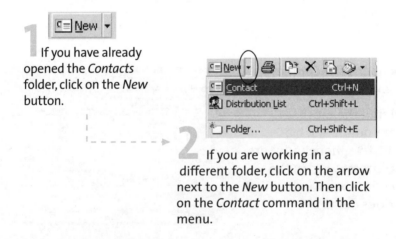

1 If you have already opened the *Contacts* folder, click on the *New* button.

2 If you are working in a different folder, click on the arrow next to the *New* button. Then click on the *Contact* command in the menu.

Outlook opens the dialog box with the tabs to define the new contact. Fill in the boxes with the available data.

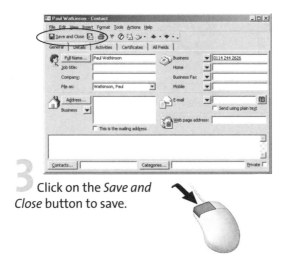

3 Click on the *Save and Close* button to save.

The *Name* box can record forename as well as surname. Since Outlook sorts the contents of the *Contents* folder according to the first letter, you should list surname before forename. You can check the entries in the telephone number and address fields according to specific criteria for validity with the *Name* and *Address* buttons. You will learn how to delete contacts at the end of the chapter.

Notes in Outlook

Have you ever experienced the situation where your desk is covered with small notes and post-it notes? Everyone makes notes in some form as *aides-mémoire*. Outlook has a function for looking after such notes.

Calling up notes

To call up existing notes, you only need to click the mouse a few times.

1 Click on the *Notes* symbol in the Outlook bar in the *Outlook Shortcuts* groups.

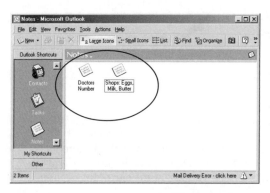

Outlook shows the contents of the *Notes* folder. You can see the notes already defined as a small, yellow symbol. The beginning of the note is added as a label to the icon.

Shops: Eggs, Milk, Butter

19/07/99 12:17 PM

2 To view the whole contents of the note, choose the symbol by double-clicking on it.

You can supply the text of the note at any time. You can close the window with the ⊠ button in the top right corner.

Do you want to request other functions to edit notes?

 Click on the
Open note icon.

Outlook now opens a menu with commands
to print, delete, save or forward the note by e-
mail. You will also find a command in this
menu to draw up a new note or change the
colour of the note.

Create a note

Outlook offers you various ways to create notes. You can use the *New*
button in the standard bar of the Outlook window next to the
command shown in the previous section, or you can do the following:

Click on the *Notes*
symbol in the Outlook
bar in the *Outlook
Shortcuts* group.

481

Outlook opens the *Notes* folder.

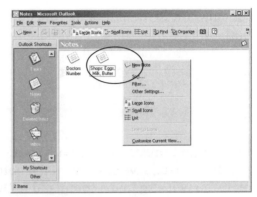

2 Click on an empty space anywhere in the folder window with the right mouse button.

3 Click on the *New Note* command in the context menu.

4 Then enter the text for the note.

As soon as you leave the window with the *Close* button ⊠ in the upper right corner of the window, Outlook stores the note.

Managing tasks

Another daily problem is completing tasks that are allocated to us in our office every day. A report must be produced, maybe on a regular basis, according to a specific timescale. Appointments must be kept, cheques must be written to settle invoices and so on. In a well-managed office, there is a schedule for every event. You can now let Outlook look after the scheduling. Enter the tasks in the program. Outlook shows a list of tasks to be carried out on the *Outlook Today* window as soon as you open it (*see* page 451).

Looking at the due tasks

Do you need an overview of the tasks in hand? In the *Outlook Today* folder window you can access all defined tasks.

1 Click on the *Tasks* symbol in the Outlook bar in the *Outlook Shortcuts* group.

Outlook shows the contents of the *Task* folder. The *Due Date* column indicates the deadline by which the task is to be completed.

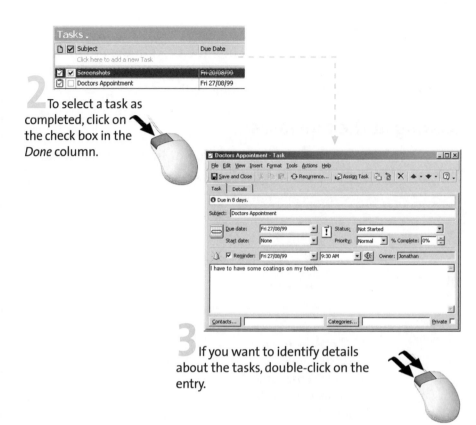

2 To select a task as completed, click on the check box in the *Done* column.

3 If you want to identify details about the tasks, double-click on the entry.

Outlook opens a dialog box with boxes for editing the task status. Do you want to be reminded of the due date of the task?

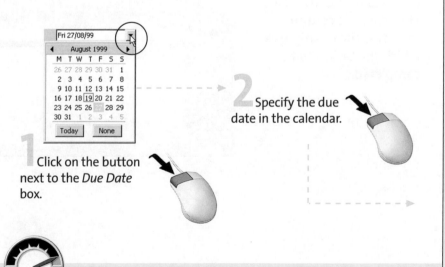

1 Click on the button next to the *Due Date* box.

2 Specify the due date in the calendar.

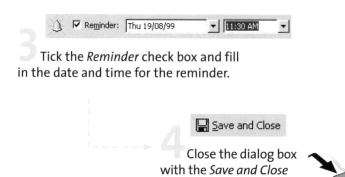

3 Tick the *Reminder* check box and fill
in the date and time for the reminder.

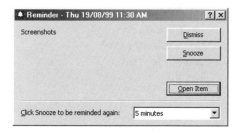

4 Close the dialog box
with the *Save and Close*
button.

Outlook oversees appointments in the future and reminds you of
their due date as required.

If the set deadline is reached,
Outlook reminds you with the
dialog box shown here of the
task still outstanding. You can
place the event on the remind
schedule with the *Remind again*
button.

The Reminder time must to be set with the calendar of the *Reminder*
box. The *Categories* button opens the dialog box with the task
description. If you click on close, the reminder is ended. You will
receive no further reminder – thank God, peace at last!

Creating a task

Do you want to add a new entry to the task list? Outlook offers
several options for this.

If the folder with the tasks is opened, you only need to click
the mouse on the *New* button.

485

Or click with the right mouse button on one free place in the folder and use the context menu of the file to establish a new task. In both cases, the *Task* dialog box shown in the previous section appears along with the *Tasks* and *Details* tabs for entering the subject as well as setting the due date and the editing status.

Task lists are usually made so that a note and, if necessary, a due date are given. And exactly this method can be used in Outlook.

In the *Subject* line, Outline shows a box to enter a new task.

1 Click on the box and enter the subject for the entry.

2 Click, if required, on the box in the *Due Date* box and enter a due date.

A calendar may be opened with the button on the right side of the box in which you can choose the date.

You can select an edited task and remove it from the list with the *Delete* button.

The *Print* button allows you to print out the list of tasks on the printer.

You can look up a telephone number quickly, for example, with the address book symbol.

Working with the calendar

The calendar function is the central part of Outlook. You can plan your appointments with this calendar, manage tasks and so on. To call up the *Calendar* folder, proceed with the following steps:

1 Click on the *Calendar* symbol in the *Outlook links* group on the Outlook bar.

Outlook then opens the *Calendar* folder. You will also see the appointment calendar for the chosen day next to the calendar page of the current month.

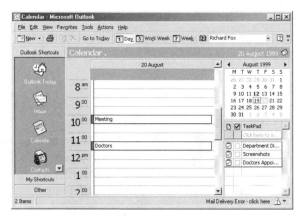

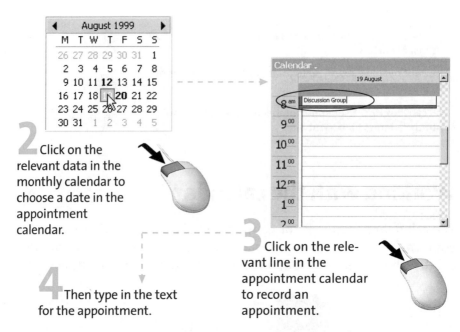

2 Click on the relevant data in the monthly calendar to choose a date in the appointment calendar.

3 Click on the relevant line in the appointment calendar to record an appointment.

4 Then type in the text for the appointment.

The appointment frame is subdivided into 30-minute sections.

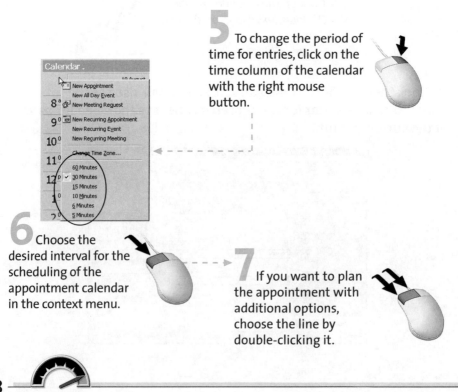

5 To change the period of time for entries, click on the time column of the calendar with the right mouse button.

6 Choose the desired interval for the scheduling of the appointment calendar in the context menu.

7 If you want to plan the appointment with additional options, choose the line by double-clicking it.

Outlook opens a dialog box with the *Appointment* and *Attendee Availability* tabs.

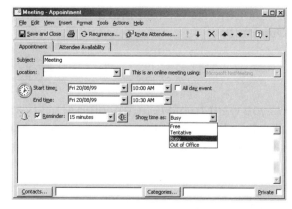

Enter the subject in the appointment box in the *Appointment* tab. You can also enter the start and end times of the appointment. With the *Reminder* option, you can place this appointment in the reminder schedule. The *Show time as* list box allows you to designate a status.

8 Close this dialog box with the *Save and Close* button.

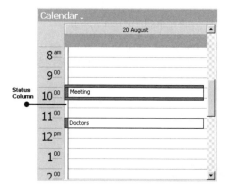

Outlook emphasises the work time with colours in the appointment calendar at 24-hour intervals. The status column between the time and entries is colour coded. The colours give you information as to the status in the *Show time as* list box (Free, Busy, Out of Office, Tentative).

You can fit in a lot of text into one line. The text scrolls to the left when you type it in to the line. With longer texts, however, it is no longer legible in the appointment page.

1 To request a longer entry, point to the line with the mouse.

489

Outlook inserts the text into a QuickInfo.

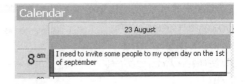

Do you want to move an appointment? If so, click on the relevant line and drag it with the mouse up or down. Additional functions of the calendar are described in the programs Help.

And here are a few tips for time management and organising the running of the day (with or without Outlook):

- Collect the tasks for your day and assess the time needed.

- Analyse the activities according to the ABC principle (A = important task, B = averagely important, C = less important) and set the priority.

- Bring the tasks into a sequence according to the Pareto principle: 20% of the time needed to complete a task brings 80% of the results, so do the important ones first!

- Reserve time for recurring tasks (such as weekly meetings). Make a week or monthly plan for tasks to be done. Specify the time allocated in the course of the day and eliminate them.

- Complete your communication rationally (by e-mail, for example).

- Leave extra time in your appointment to allow for the unforeseen (use the 60:40 rule, i.e. 60% of the time is planned, but the rest is free for unexpected and spontaneous activities).

- Use the possibilities of Outlook to check over and be reminded in good time.

Deleting Outlook objects

In Outlook, data (e-mails, notes, tasks etc.) are described as objects. Deleting objects works just the same as all functions. As soon as you click on the function symbol in the Outlook bar, the program opens the relevant folder in the document window. At the same time, a standard bar is inserted into the applications window. To delete an object, the following steps are required:

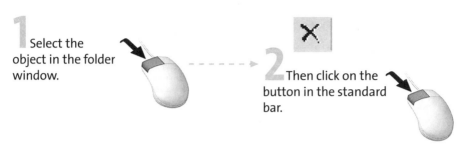

1 Select the object in the folder window.

2 Then click on the button in the standard bar.

The program moves the relevant object into the Recycle Bin – the *Deleted items* folder.

This folder is represented with the symbol for a wastebin in the Outlook bar.

If you click on the *Deleted items* symbol, Outlook shows the contents of the folders.

You can select an object in this folder. Its contents are then shown in a window.

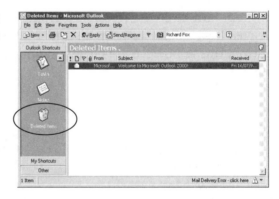

Have you deleted an object by mistake? Do you want to restore an object from the *Deleted Items* folder?

1 Drag the *Objects* symbol from the *Deleted Items* folder to the symbol of the desired folder in the Outlook bar. If you let go of the mouse button, Outlook moves the object.

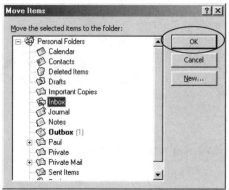

2 Alternatively, you can click on the object with the right mouse button and choose the *Move to Folder* command in the Context menu.

3 Then choose the target folder in the *Move Item* dialog box and then click on the *OK* button.

Since Outlook saves the deleted object into a folder, you must empty this regularly to create free space on the disk. If you have opened the *Deleted Items* folder, you can discard a selected object with the *Delete* button. This is, however, really long-winded if you have many deleted objects.

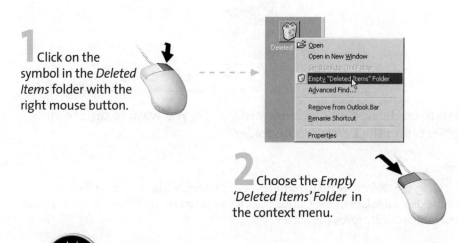

1 Click on the symbol in the *Deleted Items* folder with the right mouse button.

2 Choose the *Empty 'Deleted Items' Folder* in the context menu.

Here, we will end the introduction to Outlook. The program is so powerful that only a rough introduction at this point is possible. Some functions, such as faxes, have been omitted completely. For further information, please refer to the program's Help or to the manual that comes with Outlook 2000.

Test your knowledge

To check your knowledge, you should answer the following questions. The answers are on page 588.

1   Create a note.

2   Enter an appointment for the 17th April at 9.00 am.

3   Draw up a task with active reminder.

4   Check the received e-mail.

5   Set a read E-Mail back to 'unread'.

6   Delete a note.

What's in this chapter?

Before you can use Office 2000, you will have to install it. After installation, you can insert or delete functions or repair Office. Furthermore, the Office program allows you to adjust things by using many options. Is a toolbar missing or is it in the way on the screen? In this chapter, you will learn how to correct these problems with only a few clicks of the mouse. You will also practise setting specific options for the Office program. This allows you to tune the program to your needs.

You can already:

Now you will learn:

Installing and maintaining Office

Before you can start using Office 2000, you need to install it and set up the required programs. The range of individual components depends on which version of Office you have bought (*see also* the explanation in Chapter 1). Perhaps later on you would like to insert or delete components. You can also call up the maintenance functions with a few mouse clicks.

Installing Microsoft Office 2000

As a rule Microsoft Office 2000 is delivered on a CD-ROM that contains all the necessary functions. During the **installation**, the **program data** will be copied to the **hard disk** of your computer and established in the *Start* menu. For the installation, the computer must satisfy the minimum requirements for Office both in terms of hardware and software:

⇥ An operating system must be installed on the computer (Windows 95, Windows 98 or Windows NT 4.0).

⇥ You will require a Pentium Processor with 133-MHz clock speed or better, and 32 Mbyte or more of RAM.

> **TIP**
> Before installation, you should save all important data on the hard disk. In addition, you should quit all programs currently loaded.

Furthermore, the computer should be equipped with the normal accessories such as a mouse, graphics card and a CD-ROM drive. And there must be enough free **storage space** on the hard drive (about 200 Mbyte or more) for the installation of the Office program. The exact requirements depend on the size of the installed software. Your Office pack will specify the minimum requirements. Bearing in mind what we have said so far, your computer must exceed the minimum specifications provided on the pack itself.

The actual installation is quite simple as a wizard leads you through the few steps.

1 Put the Office CD-ROM in the drive.

Windows recognises the CD-ROM and automatically starts the installation program. If this doesn't work at once, call up the *Setup.exe* program in the main file of the CD-ROM by double-clicking on the file icon in the file window.

The program announces itself with a dialog box and prepares the installation. At the same time, the system is checked.

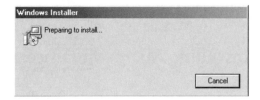

Then the Setup Wizard appears, and accompanies you through the installation steps. The installation steps are shown to you in the left hand column.

2 Click on the *Next* button.

In the 'Customer information' step, the wizard asks for your name, initials, the organisation and the CD key.

3 Enter the information, then click on the *Next* button.

The CD Key is found on the CD case and is necessary for checking your licence. You are only entitled to use the program with a valid Office licence. Enter your real name as well as your initials (if you like). These details are used in many Office programs for automatic completion of specific information (such as sender's details).

In this dialog box, you have the opportunity to read the licensing conditions.

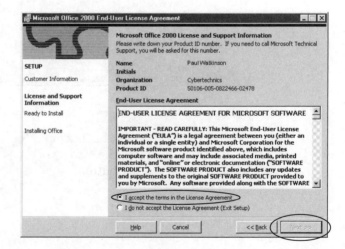

4 After you have accepted the conditions by clicking on the corresponding highlighted option box, click on the *Next* button.

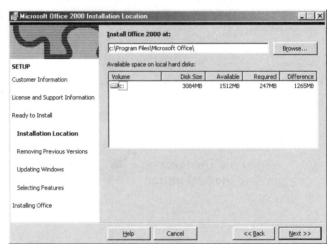

5 At this point, choose the drive into which the Office program will be set up.

The available saving space will be given for each drive. If necessary, use the *Search* button to choose a new drive.

6 Click on the *Next* button.

If you have previous Office versions installed on your system, tell the wizard in a separate step whether these should be overwritten or kept. This step is not performed here.

499

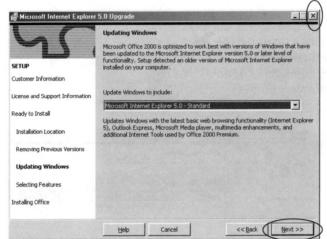

You can set the installation range of Internet Explorer here, by clicking on the list.

7 Then click on the *Next* button.

This step allows you to specify the installation range.

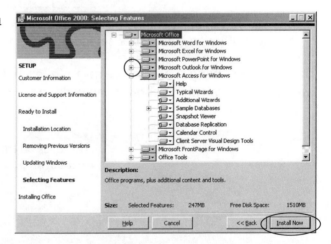

8 If necessary, click on the plus sign in front of an Office component and specify the installation options.

9 Click on the *Install Now* button.

For every Office function you can specify whether to exclude it, install it, start it from CD-ROM or if it should be installed automatically when it is first requested. To do this, click on the arrow next to the symbol of the component, and choose an option from the menu shown.

As soon as you close the previous dialog box by clicking on the *Install* button, the Setup program begins the installation. This may take some time.

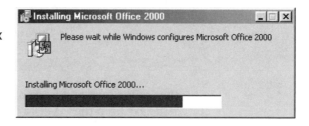

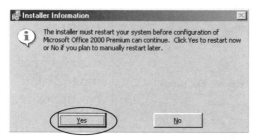

During installation, Setup will need to re-start your computer.

10 Confirm this new start by clicking on the *Yes* button.

After the new start up, Setup closes the installation and shows the success in a dialog box. At this point you can call up and use the Office program from the *Start* menu.

What to do if Office 2000 is damaged

When installing different programs, or when a system crashes, or when deleting files, the functionality of Office 2000 may become damaged. When working with an Office program, if you get the feeling that something is damaged, you can simply update the last installation.

1 Exit all current running Windows applications.

2 Put the Office 2000 CD-ROM in the drive.

3 If the Setup program doesn't automatically appear, start *Setup.exe* from the CD-ROM main index (with a double-click on the file symbol in the open file window).

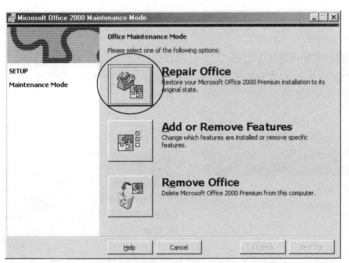

Setup analyses the system and registers it with the maintenance mode dialog box opposite.

4 Click on the *Repair Office* button.

5 Confirm by clicking on the *Next* button.

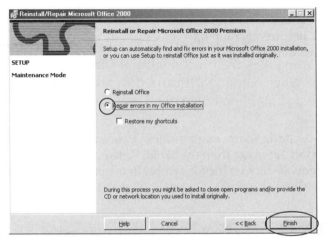

In this dialog box choose the
Repair errors in my Office installation
option and click on the *Finish* button.

The Setup program then checks the installed components and
updates all files for the current installation.

Inserting/deleting components

Microsoft Office 2000, according to the pack you have purchased,
consists of various programs. In the installation, only the basic
functions are normally set up on the hard disk. Using the options
described in the previous section, you can explicitly decide which
components are to be installed. If the status 'Install on First Use' is
active for a function, then when the corresponding function is
required for the first time, Office automatically asks for the CD-ROM
to be inserted. Then the component will automatically be installed.

If you have a component set on the status 'Not Available' in the
installation, then the corresponding function or the respective
program is not available. At any time, you have the opportunity to
add certain functions to the program or delete functions that are no
longer necessary (this saves space on the hard disk).

1 Exit all currently running Windows applications.

2 Put the Office 2000 CD-ROM in the drive.

3 If the Setup program doesn't automatically appear, start *Setup.exe* from the CD-ROM main index (with a double-click on the file symbol in the open file window).

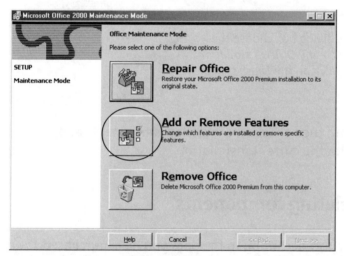

Setup analyses the system and registers it with the maintenance mode dialog box opposite.

4 Click on the *Add or Remove Features* button.

5 Click on the *Next* button.

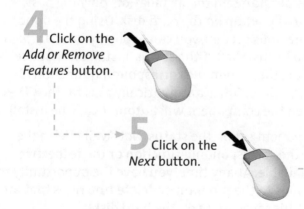

6 In the dialog box above, click on the plus sign in front of the name of the relevant program, in order to show the branch with the program functions.

7 Click on the arrow to the right-hand side of the component symbol, and choose the installation option.

If you set the status of a component to 'Not Available', this will then be deleted from the system. 'Run from CD' lets you operate the program directly from the CD-ROM. You can install non-available components by setting their status to 'Run from My Computer' or 'Installed on First Use'.

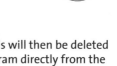

8 Then click on the *Update Now* button .

Setup analyses the adjustment and fills up the system with the missing program files. During this process, superfluous files will also be deleted.

Setting up programs on a desktop

Do you use the Office program often? If so, then calling it up from the *Start* menu is perhaps something of a chore. A more elegant solution is to put the program icon on the desktop. Internet Explorer or Microsoft Outlook 2000 will automatically be given an icon on the desktop. You can also set up these icons on the desktop for the remainder of the Office applications.

1 In the *Start* menu open *Programs*.

2 By holding down the right mouse button, drag the entry of the corresponding Office application to the desktop.

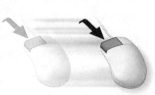

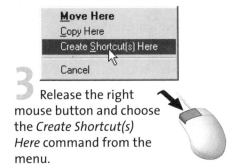

3 Release the right mouse button and choose the *Create Shortcut(s) Here* command from the menu.

Windows sets up an icon for the corresponding program on the desktop. To start the program, just double-click on the *Desktop* icon.

Customising toolbars

In previous chapters, I have introduced the Office program toolbars to you. At this point we will learn how the toolbars in Office applications can be adapted to suit your needs.

Suspended toolbars

The standard toolbar and the formatting bar of Office programs are usually positioned in rows. This leaves more room to view the document in the program window. But, this also means that, when the window is smaller, not all of the buttons are visible.

This is where you can give Word, Excel or other Office programs a hand. Position the toolbars where you want them. Would you like to display the formatting bar on a separate line? We will see what you are allowed to do with the toolbars.

1 Point to the left edge of
the toolbar with the mouse.

The left edge of the toolbar contains the **move handle**. If you have
done everything correctly, then the mouse pointer takes on the form
shown here. You can now move the bar as you like.

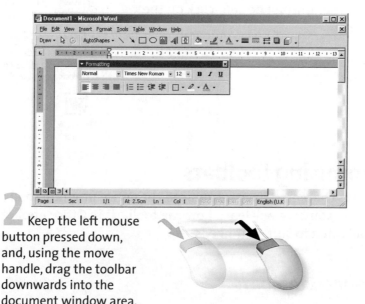

2 Keep the left mouse
button pressed down,
and, using the move
handle, drag the toolbar
downwards into the
document window area.

Suddenly, the toolbar will become visible as a small window. You will
recognise all the buttons, and in the title box of this window the
name of the bar is displayed. This type of representation is described
as a **floating toolbar**.

You can handle a floating toolbar in the same way as any other window. You can move the bar by using the title bar. By dragging the border of the window, you can determine the size of the bar. The program always adapts the bar so that the buttons lie in one or more rows. Click on the *Close* button ✖ in the right corner of the bar and the toolbar will disappear. To insert a toolbar again at a later point, in the VIEW menu choose the *Toolbars* command and a list of toolbars will appear. One mouse click on the name of the missing toolbar and it will be inserted again. The toolbars that are ticked are already displayed.

Floating toolbars are good for seldom needed functions, so that you can call them up when you need them. Unfortunately, most of the floating toolbars have the knack of always covering exactly the piece of the document on which you want to work. To avoid this anchor the toolbar on the edge of the window, where there is enough room.

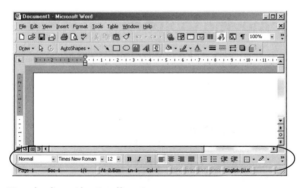

1 Simply drag the toolbar to the bottom edge of the window and let go of the mouse button.

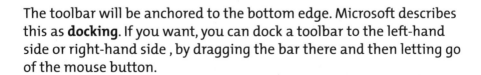

The toolbar will be anchored to the bottom edge. Microsoft describes this as **docking**. If you want, you can dock a toolbar to the left-hand side or right-hand side , by dragging the bar there and then letting go of the mouse button.

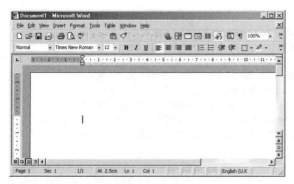

In this book, the formatting toolbar will be positioned in a row directly under the standard toolbar, as shown in this picture.

Inserting/removing toolbars

To insert/remove toolbars, take the following steps:

1 Open the VIEW/TOOLBARS menu.

In the submenu, you will see the names of all the toolbars that the program has at its disposal. A tick before the corresponding name signals that the relevant toolbar is visible.

2 Click on the name of the desired toolbar.

If the command was highlighted with a tick, this will disappear and the toolbar will be removed.

Otherwise, the program will insert the toolbar. The next time the menu is opened, the toolbar name will be marked with a tick.

Entering/removing buttons

The Office program only shows the most important or most often used buttons in the toolbar. You also have the opportunity to set up your own individually configured toolbar. Perhaps you don't use some of the buttons and maybe others are important to you.

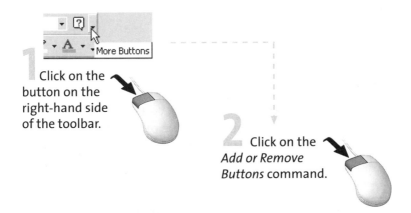

1 Click on the button on the right-hand side of the toolbar.

2 Click on the *Add or Remove Buttons* command.

An additional menu will appear with the available buttons for this bar. Visible buttons are highlighted with a tick.

✓	Standard
✓	Formatting
	AutoText
	Clipboard
	Control Toolbox
	Database
	Drawing
	Forms
	Frames
	Picture
	Reviewing
	Tables and Borders
	Visual Basic
	Web
	Web Tools
	WordArt
	Customize...

3 Click on a command to either insert or remove the corresponding button in the toolbar.

A visible button will be removed and vice versa.

Inserting/deleting buttons

Using the steps from the previous section, you can insert or remove buttons from the toolbar. You also have the opportunity to completely delete buttons from the toolbar or to insert new buttons in the bar.

1 Click on VIEW/ TOOLBARS/CUSTOMIZE.

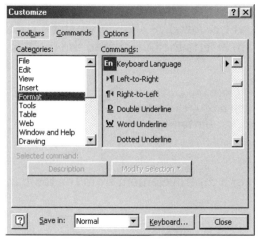

2 From the *Commands* tab choose an entry from the *Categories* section.

In the *Commands* list you will then find a list of buttons and control elements for this category.

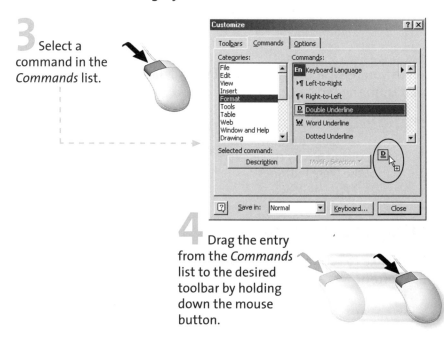

3 Select a command in the *Commands* list.

4 Drag the entry from the *Commands* list to the desired toolbar by holding down the mouse button.

As soon as you let go of the mouse button, the entry is moved to the user defined toolbar (*see later*). As soon as you let go of the mouse button, the program inserts the button into the toolbar.

5 Close the *Customize* dialog box by clicking on the *Close* button.

To delete a button or a control element from the toolbar, carry out the following steps:

1 Click on VIEW/
TOOLBARS/CUSTOMIZE.

2 By holding down the left mouse button, drag the button from the toolbar into the open *Customize* dialog box.

As soon as you release the left mouse button, the button will be removed from the toolbar.

3 Close the *Customize* dialog box by clicking on the *Close* button.

Creating a new toolbar

Would you like to set up your own toolbar with the buttons that you use most often?

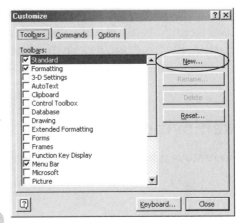

1 Click on VIEW/TOOLBARS/CUSTOMIZE.

2 On the *Toolbars* tab, click on the *New* button.

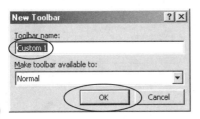

3 Enter the name of the toolbar, and close the dialog box by clicking on the *OK* button.

Depending on the Office program, the *New Toolbar* dialog box could look a little different to the representation shown here. In Word, for example, you are able to choose which document template to set the toolbar on. With the *Normal template* the new toolbar is available in all documents. PowerPoint or Excel do not have any document template, therefore this field is missing.

 The new toolbar then appears on the desktop. You can then move this toolbar and provide it with buttons (*see earlier*).

4 In the *Customize* dialog box, click on the *Close* button, to end the customisation.

Removing a toolbar

To remove a toolbar, you need only a few mouse clicks.

1 Click on VIEW/ TOOLBARS/CUSTOMIZE.

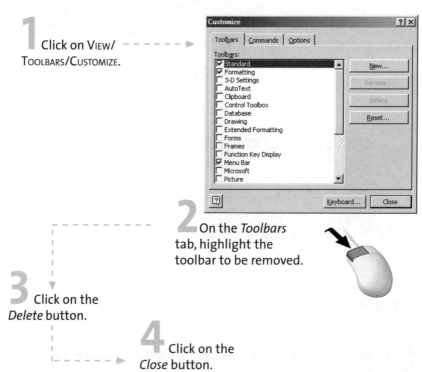

2 On the *Toolbars* tab, highlight the toolbar to be removed.

3 Click on the *Delete* button.

4 Click on the *Close* button.

The original settings of a changed or deleted toolbar are restored as soon as you click on the *Reset* button. This is not valid, however, for user defined toolbars or buttons. After deleting, these stay deleted.

Changing print options

For printing, all Windows programs fall back on the **printdriver** of **Windows**. This driver is a **program**, which takes over the outputs of programs, prepares them for the printer and then passes them on to the printer. In the previous chapters, you have learnt how to use specific program settings for printing e.g. landscape printing.

You can also influence various print driver settings. Windows supports the running of several printers at the same time. These can be available locally or in a network. If the corresponding driver is installed for these printers, you can choose which printer to print on.

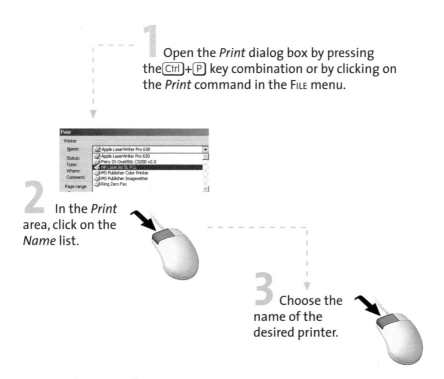

1 Open the *Print* dialog box by pressing the Ctrl + P key combination or by clicking on the *Print* command in the FILE menu.

2 In the *Print* area, click on the *Name* list.

3 Choose the name of the desired printer.

When you start printing, this will happen on the chosen printer.

In Windows, one of the printers will be used as a default printer. The choice of another printer stays valid until you change it or until you exit the program. The next time you start the program, it will use the default printer again. You can set the default printer in Windows in the *Printers* file (*Start* menu *Settings/Printers*). Click on the printer symbol with the right mouse button, and then in the menu choose the command *Set as Default*.

Would you like to change the settings (paper tray, print direction and so on) for your printer? This is also possible in the *Print* dialog box.

1 Open the Print dialog box by pressing the [Ctrl]+[P] key combination.

2 In the *Print* dialog box, click on the *Properties* button.

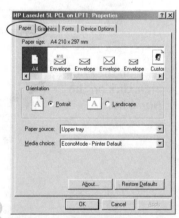

3 In the *Properties* dialog box, there a several tabs. Choose the desired options on these tabs.

However, notice that the set-up of this tab is dependent on the printer used. You will find details on dealing with printing in *Windows 2000 In No Time*, also published in this series.

From the *Paper* tab you can set the orientation of the sheet or the tray for the paper feed

Word settings

The display options for Microsoft Word can be usually set in the VIEW menu.

The top three commands determine the display option. The corresponding modes can also be set using the buttons in the bottom left corner of the document window.

Using the *Ruler* command, you are able to insert or remove the horizontal and vertical rulers.

Setting the Word properties is done using several tabs of the *Options* properties window.

In the TOOLS menu, choose the *Options* command.

The tabs of the *Options* dialog box brings the properties together in various categories.

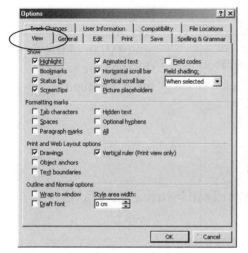

In the *View* tab, you will find all the Word properties that have to do with display.

For example, highlight the *Horizontal* and *Vertical scrollbar* boxes to display both scrollbars.

By clicking on the *Status bar* button, the Word status bar is either inserted or removed.

Customising file lists

Office applications show the names of the last four loaded documents in the FILE menu. You learnt this in previous chapters. But you can adjust this for most of the Office programs.

1 In the TOOLS menu choose - - - - - - - - - ►
the *Options* command.

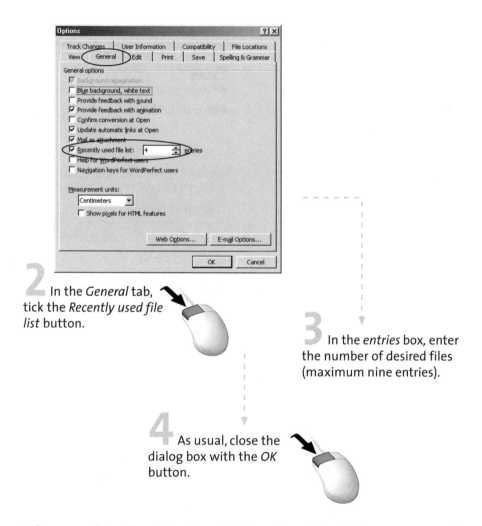

2 In the *General* tab, tick the *Recently used file list* button.

3 In the *entries* box, enter the number of desired files (maximum nine entries).

4 As usual, close the dialog box with the *OK* button.

When you close the dialog box, Word or the active Office program will list the relevant number of files in the FILE menu.

Setting user initials and address

When constructing a piece of writing, occasionally the user initials are used. Furthermore, when writing a letter, Word can automatically fill in the sender's details. You can set the corresponding information.

521

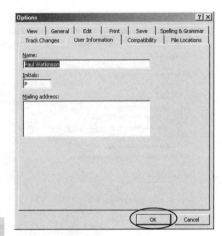

1 In the Tools menu choose the *Options* command.

2 Activate the *User Information* tab, and enter the address as well as the initials.

3 Close the dialog box by clicking on the *OK* button.

Setting edit options

Have you ever wondered why Word automatically enters a space when you enter a word when you do a drag-and-drop for a word or a character? Or don't you like the drag-and-drop function, when moving text? When you press the ⇥ key, does the sentence jump to the right? Would you like to prevent a highlighted piece of text being overwritten by an entry? You can set these as well as other properties in the *Edit* tab.

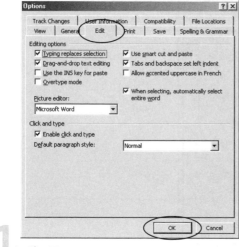

2 Activate the *Edit* tab, and highlight the desired options there.

1 In the Tools menu, choose the *Options* command.

3 Close the dialog box by clicking on the *OK* button.

Details about the individual options are contained in the Help sections of the individual tabs.

The above tab shows the standard settings of Word. Remove the tick on the *Typing replaces selection* control button and then a selected text will not be overwritten by an entry. You can stop the insertion of spaces by removing the tick on the button for *Use smart cut and paste*.

Setting print options in Word

A few pages back, you learnt about the print options of the print driver. Word also has a *Print* tab, on which you can specify various settings. As an example, would you like to prevent Word from printing in the background?

523

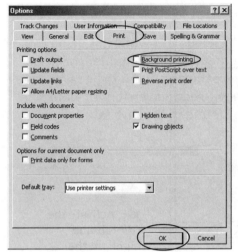

1 In the Tools menu choose the *Options* command.

2 Activate the *Print* tab, and remove the tick on the *Background printing* control button.

3 Close the dialog box by clicking on the *OK* button.

Switch off background printing if your system has only a small main memory. Before printing, tick the *Draft output* control button. Word will then print the document with a reduced resolution. This is quicker, and also saves toner or ink when printing.

Before printing, Word will now open a dialog box, in which the the printed pages are listed (you know this from Excel). Only when Windows has taken over the printout can you continue working on Word.

Setting save options

Word can automatically save a document while it is being worked on. This prevents the loss of documents if the computer crashes. Furthermore, Word 2000 allows the document to be saved in several forms that can be worked on with earlier versions of Word. The corresponding options can be found in the *Save* tab.

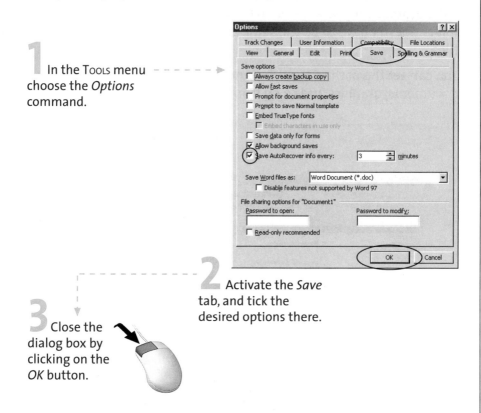

1 In the Tools menu choose the *Options* command.

2 Activate the *Save* tab, and tick the desired options there.

3 Close the dialog box by clicking on the *OK* button.

The *Allow background saves* control button saves the document as soon as you choose this function. However, you can still work on the document while it is saving. If you would like to make a backup copy ready for system crashes, highlight the *Save AutoRecover info every* control button and enter the time interval in minutes. In the event of a crash, Word will try, when next called up, to automatically open a restored version of the last document.

When starting a new file, Word uses a document template. You can use the command *New* in the FILE menu, in order to choose further templates. If you choose the command *Open* from the FILE menu, Word will show the folder from which the last document was loaded. After starting Word though, you can set another folder. Would you like Word to already know at the start into which folder you would like to save your document? Also, when entering graphics, a specific folder will automatically be entered in the corresponding dialog box. This folder doesn't have to be the same as the folder for saving graphics files.

You can set the path to the drive and folders for templates, Word documents, graphics and so on from the *File Locations* tab.

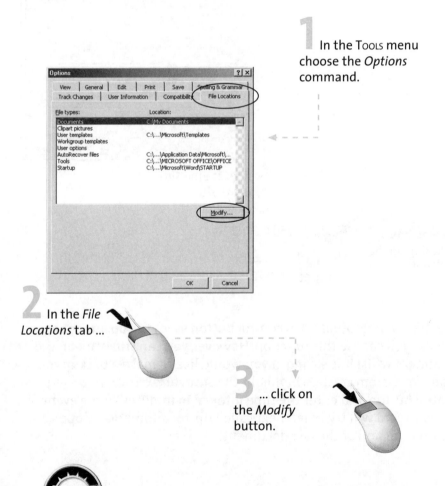

1 In the TOOLS menu choose the *Options* command.

2 In the *File Locations* tab ...

3 ... click on the *Modify* button.

4 In this dialog box, enter the desired folder.

5 Close the dialog box by clicking on the *OK* button.

6 Close the tab by clicking on the *OK* button.

The next time you start, Word will use the relevant folder as the setting.

Customising the spell check

AutoCorrect and the spell checker in Word (and in the other Office programs) can be influenced with specific instructions.

1 In the TOOLS menu choose the *Options* command.

2 Activate the *Spelling & Grammar* tab from the *Options* dialog box.

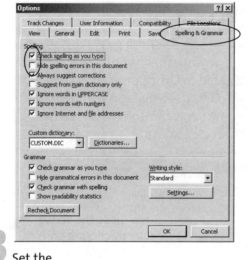

3 Set the options on the tab.

4 Close the tab by clicking on the *OK* button.

If you would like to stop Word checking for spelling mistakes as you type, remove the tick from the *Check spelling as you type* control button.

Correction of Internet and file addresses is prevented as soon as you tick the corresponding button. Choose the *Writing style*, if you wish, according to the type of document you are writing (Casual, Standard, Formal, Technical and so on).

> Word remembers if you have used a spell check on a document. So, if you check the document again, it will only check the part that is new or has been modified. Do you need to check the document again (for example, because you have mistakenly classified a spelling mistake as correct)? If so, click on the *Recheck Document* button. Word then resets the spelling and grammar checker and rechecks the spelling of the entire document.

The marking of spelling mistakes in the text with a wavy line can be removed by highlighting the *Hide spelling errors in this document* control button.

Using AutoCorrect

AutoCorrect checks your entries for spelling mistakes, and if needed, it will automatically correct any misspelt words. This correction takes place by default and is available in Office programs such as Word, Excel, PowerPoint and so on. Office is provided with a predefined list of correction proposals. At any time, though, you have the opportunity to adjust the settings for AutoCorrect.

1 In the Tools menu choose the *AutoCorrect* command.

You will find this command in the Tools menu in all Office programs that support AutoCorrect.

The program opens the *AutoCorrect* dialog box which, in the title box, states the language. The number of tabs varies in the Office programs. Word shows several tabs.

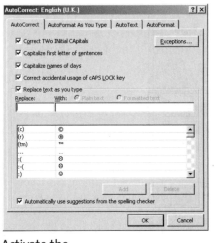

2 Activate the *AutoCorrect* tab.

3 Tick the control buttons, according to your desired options.

In the bottom half of the tab, you can see a list of correction terms.

1 In order to delete a correction entry, choose this from the list. If you need to, you can use the scrollbars to see more.

2 Then click on the *Delete* button.

The misspelt word appears in the left-hand column, while the right-hand column contains the correction. If you want to correct a word, then choose this too.

In order to add a new term to the list, the following steps are needed:

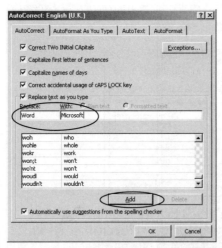

1 Enter the wrong word into the *Replace* box.

2 In the *With* box, enter the correctly spelt text.

3 Click on the *Add* button.

4 Close the tab by clicking on the *OK* button.

Useful as AutoCorrect can be, in some cases corrections can go badly wrong. True, you can undo the corrections by pressing the Ctrl+Z key combination. But, at the very least, this is still annoying. Here, it helps to pay attention to the *AutoCorrect Exceptions*.

1 On the *AutoCorrect* tab, click on the *Exceptions* button.

The corresponding program then opens the *AutoCorrect Exceptions* dialog box, with several tabs.

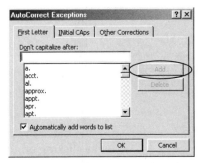

2 Activate the desired tab, type in the text for the exception, and then enter it on the list by clicking on the *Add* button. Close the dialog box.

With the *Delete* button, you can remove a highlighted entry from the list.

The *AutoFormat* tab in the *AutoCorrect* dialog box offers you various options for formatting Word text while you are typing.

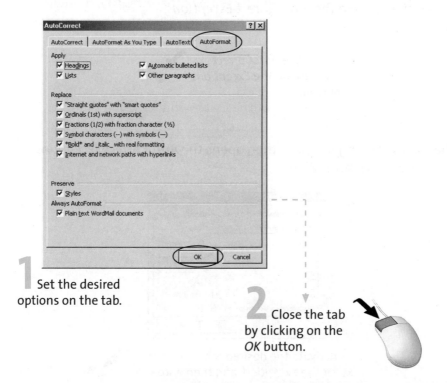

1 Set the desired options on the tab.

2 Close the tab by clicking on the *OK* button.

Word then automatically carries out a formatting, when a certain key combination is pressed.

You will find hints on the individual options in the *Help* of the tab.

532

Customising Excel

Similar to Word, Excel also allows you to set several properties using tabs.

1 To call up the Excel properties dialog box, choose the TOOLS menu and the *Options* command.

Excel then opens the *Options* dialog box with several tabs. On these tabs you will find the properties sorted by categories. The following will give you a quick overview of these properties and the relevant tabs.

Excel View options

You can influence the display of the Excel window, using the *View* tab.

To remove the status bar, remove the tick from the *Status bar* control button. Gridlines can be inserted or removed by using the control button with the same name.

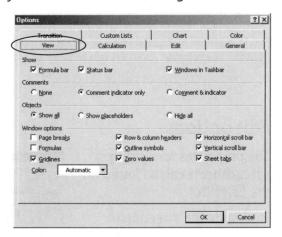

The sheet tabs can also be removed, by removing the tick from the control button with the same name.

General Excel settings

Would you like to set the list of recently opened files? Do you need more than three spreadsheets in a workbook?

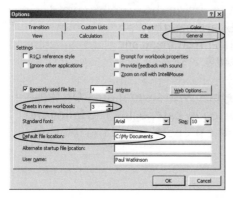

If so, choose the *General* tab. With the *Sheets in new workbook* option, Excel lets you choose between 1 and 255 spreadsheets in a new book. The *Default file location* box allows you to set the path for the file that Excel uses when the *Open* dialog box is chosen.

In the chapter on Excel, I explained that cells are labelled with letters and numbers. This reference style is called A1 reference style, after the first cell. If you tick the *R1C1 reference style* control button, the columns and rows will be labelled with numbers.

Edit options

The properties for editing spreadsheets can be found on the *Edit* tab.

To change the direction in which the active cell moves when you press Enter, specify the direction in the *Direction* field on the tab. Remove the tick from the *Edit directly in cell* control button, then corrections can only be carried out in the formula bar.

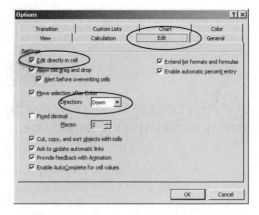

You can also switch off the drag-and-drop cell option.

Defining AutoComplete lists

In the chapter on Excel, I showed you how you can fill in rows and columns elegantly with default values using the AutoComplete. However, the function needs to have information about sequence building. This is easy to confirm with numbers, such as 1, 2, 3 etc. but more difficult with word sequences such as days or months. It is also conceivable that you have a list of names of employees in a department. If you need a table with the names of employees in a department, then the AutoComplete function could be of service.

Would you like to set up your own list for AutoComplete? If so, follow these steps in Excel.

1 Open the *Options* dialog box by clicking on *Options* in the Tools menu.

2 Activate the *Custom Lists* tab.

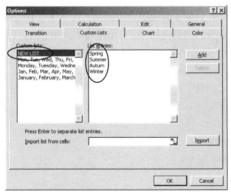

3 In the *Custom lists* column, click on *New list*.

4 Click on *List entries*, and type in the desired terms.

5 Close the tab by clicking on the *OK* button.

Now the new list is available to you in the AutoComplete function.

Calculations options

Normally, Excel goes through the calculation every time there is a new entry in a cell on the spreadsheet. This is no problem with simple cells. If, however, a spreadsheet has many formulas, the new calculation can take some time. You can switch off automatic calculation.

1 Open the *Options* dialog box by clicking on *Options* in the TOOLS menu.

2 Activate the *Calculation* tab.

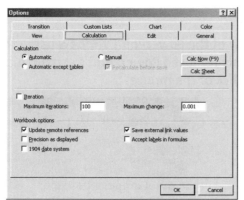

3 Click on the *Manual* button in the *Calculation* section.

4 Close the tab by clicking on the *OK* button.

You can find information about individual tab options by using the *Help* option. The button can be found in the top right-hand corner of the dialog box.

Then, after entering data, you have to press the F9 key to run the new calculation.

Customising PowerPoint

Just like Word or Excel, PowerPoint also lets you set options by using tabs.

1 In Powerpoint, choose *Options* in the TOOLS menu to call up the *Options* dialog box.

In these tabs, you will find the properties sorted into categories.

View options

You can influence the display of the PowerPoint window using the *View* tab. Have you mistakenly removed PowerPoint's startup dialog? You can correct this with a click of the mouse.

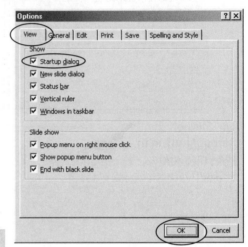

1. In the *View* section tick the *Startup dialog* control button.

2. By using the remaining control buttons, you can enter or remove further window elements.

3. Close the tab by clicking on the *OK* button.

General options

When setting up a presentation using the AutoContent Wizard, you can insert the username into the footer of a slide. Do you know how to do this?

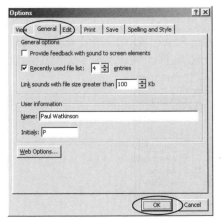

1 Open the *Options* dialog box (TOOLS/OPTIONS command), and activate the *General* tab.

2 On this tab, set the desired options and then click on the *OK* button.

You can also set the number of entries for the recently opened files in the FILE menu, on this tab.

Saving options

When saving, PowerPoint can save the file in a number of formats. This allows you to do further work on older versions of PowerPoint. The default file location for saving, the *Save AutoRecover info every (x) minutes*, and other options, can be set using the *Save* tab from the *Options* dialog box.

539

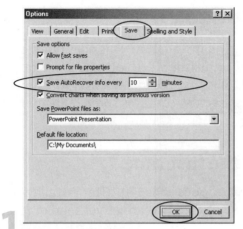

1 Tick the option, or enter the value in the field.

Using the *Save AutoRecover info every* you can set it so that PowerPoint saves at specific time intervals.

2 Close the tab by clicking on the *OK* button.

The *Spelling and Style* tab contains options for controlling spell check properties. This is managed by using control buttons, similarly to Word. You can set the corrections PowerPoint needs to do on entry, activate spell check and specify style. The *Print* tab has specific options regarding the printout. You can get further details about the options from the *Help* menu.

Customising Outlook

Outlook 2000 is set up during installation. This does not mean, however, that there aren't adjustments or settings to make. On the contrary, when the program is first called up, it asks for specific information. The following section contains some hints for setting up Outlook.

Using Outlook for the first time

The first time that Outlook 2000 is called up after installation, there will be a (small) problem. The program cannot yet send or receive e-mails, as the relevant information is missing and the program doesn't know how it should send or receive electronic news.

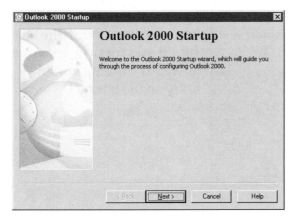

On the first call up, Outlook 2000 shows the dialog box for the *Start* window, as shown here.

1 Click on the *Next* button.

In the following step, the wizard asks for the e-mail upgrade options.

2 If there is an e-mail program already installed, then choose this option and click on *Next*.

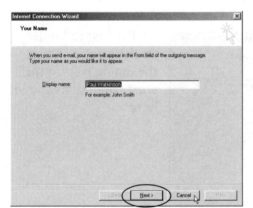

Depending on the chosen options, the wizard starts the Internet entry and, in the next step, it asks for the user name as well as the date of your entry on the Internet.

3 Enter your user name and then click on the *Next* button.

In this way, the wizard leads you step-by-step through the dialog pages for Internet entry and the Outlook start options.

Because there are various ways to set up the Internet, current literature states that this option is available and that Outlook 2000 is set up and ready on your system. Consult your system administrator or your Internet provider for details on how to set up Outlook entry to the Internet.

Handling folders

Outlook structures the symbols of the Outlook bar into folders. These groups are displayed horizontally. You can define some folders and also delete them.

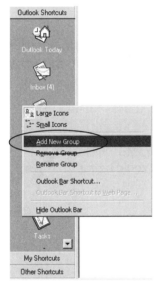

Click with the right mouse button anywhere in the Outlook bar.

In the menu call up the command *Add New Group*, in order to set up the new group.

3 To delete the current group, choose the *Remove Group* command from the menu.

4 After setting up the new group, type in the group name.

To rename a group, repeat the above steps, but then choose the *Rename Group* command

Setting up a new group

Outlook allows you to access the various folders by clicking on the symbols in the Outlook bar. When adjusting this bar, you can set up shortcuts to the folders. Perhaps you would like an inbox and an outbox for your e-mails.

1 Open the group in the Outlook bar, into which the new symbol is to be inserted. This could be, for example, *My Shortcuts*.

ᴅᴅ Large Icons
Small Icons
Add New Group
Remove Group
Rename Group
Outlook Bar Shortcut...
Outlook Bar Shortcut to Web Page...
Hide Outlook Bar

2 With the right mouse button click on a free place in the Outlook bar.

3 From the menu call up the *Outlook Bar Shortcut* command.

4 In the dialog box shown here, choose the *Outlook* option in the *Look in* box.

5 Click on the symbol for the *Outbox* folder, or choose this name in the *Folder name* box.

If *Personal Folders* is closed, click on the plus sign next to the symbol and the symbol will be highlighted in the Folder hierarchy.

6 Close the dialog box by clicking on the *OK* button.

Outlook then enters the Outbox symbol into the group.

To add an Inbox, repeat the above steps, but choose the *Inbox* symbol.

To delete a link, choose the option *Remove from Outlook Bar*.

Outlook Today

The Start Page 'Outlook Today' shows you an overview of tasks, appointments and mail. The folder content is shown in the style of a We site. You can, however, configure the appearance of this folder.

1 In the Outlook bar click on the *Outlook Today* symbol to open the folder in the document window.

2 In the window click on *Customize Outlook Today*.

Outlook opens another page in the document window, where the options are listed.

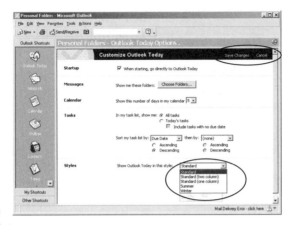

3 Set the desired options.

The representation can be set, using the list on the bottom bar of the page, to either two columns or Summer/Winter.

4 Close the page by clicking on the *Save Changes* button.

Outlook then shows the 'Outlook Today' page, but with the new options.

Other Outlook options

For the various functions, Outlook allows you to set the properties for editing and viewing.

1 To set the rest of the Outlook options, choose the *Options* command from the TOOLS menu.

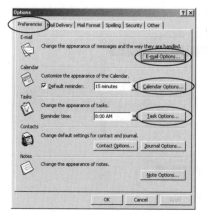

On the *Preferences tab*, you will find the individual options.

2 Click on the button for the individual option and set the properties on the shown tab.

Format for your e-mails can be set in the *E-mail Options* dialog box, in the *E-mail* field. You can set the output to plain text, to HTML pages or to a special Outlook format.

You will find other options for the program settings on the other tabs.

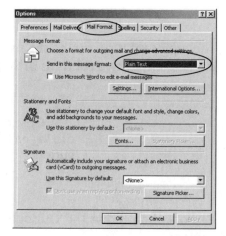

TIP

You can find detailed information on the options in the *Help* tab.

Internet Explorer options

The settings for Internet Explorer can be influenced with various buttons. For example, would you like to remove the saved Web sites that you have visited? This prevents anybody from checking which Web sites you have visited. In order to do this, complete the following steps:

1 In the Tools menu choose the *Internet options* command.

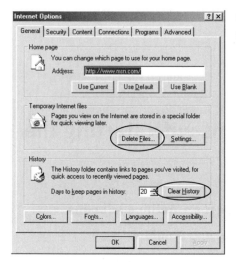

On the *General* tab you will find options for the startup page.

2 To empty the *History* folder, click on the *Clear History* button.

3 If you would like to delete temporary loaded internet files, then choose the *Delete Files* option.

4 Close the tab by clicking on the *OK* button.

The time span for saving visited Web sites can be set using the field *Days to keep pages in history*.

On the *Security* tab, you can set the safety levels for surfing the Internet. You will find more on this theme and the rest of Internet Explorer options in the program *Help*.

Problems with starting the computer

After switching it on, nothing happens

Check the following points:

⇥ Are all plugs plugged in at the socket?

⇥ Is the screen switched on?

⇥ Is there any electricity?

The computer reports: Keyboard Error, Press <F1> Key

Check the following points:

⇥ Is the keyboard switched on?

⇥ Is something lying on the keyboard?

⇥ Is one of the keys jammed on the keyboard?

Next press the function key F1.

The computer reports: No System or Drive Error...

Presumably there is still a disk in the A: drive. Remove the disk and re-start the computer.

Problems with the keyboard and mouse

■ **Having started, the keys on the number pad are not working properly**

On the right of the keyboard there is a keypad where numbers can be entered. If no numbers are appearing when using these keys, press the ⌈Num⌋ key. This is also called the **Numlock** key and is found in the top left corner of the number pad. As soon as the *Num* light is on, you can type in numbers on the keyboard. If you press the ⌈Num⌋ key again, the Numlock is off, and you can use the cursor keys on this keypad.

■ **When pressing a key, several characters appear suddenly**

The keyboard has a repeat function. If you press a key for a little longer than necessary, the computer repeats the character pressed. Perhaps you are holding the key down for too long. You can change the time that it takes Windows to activate this repeat function.

1 In the *Start* menu click on *the Settings/Control* Panel.

2 In the control panel window double-click on the *Keyboard* icon.

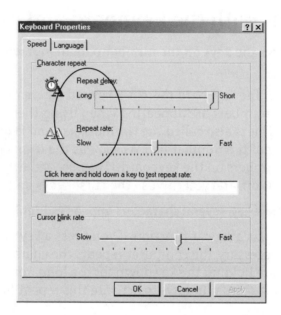

3 In the *Speed* tab, change the settings for *Repeat rate*.

You can check the settings in the test box, and then close the window by pressing the *OK* button. If the problem is not solved by doing this, please check whether a key is jammed or the keyboard is damaged (e.g. the switch for the key 'bounces', so for each character typed, many appear).

■ **When pressing the keys, only capital letters appear**

You have presumably pressed the ⬇ key. Press it again to re-set the mode.

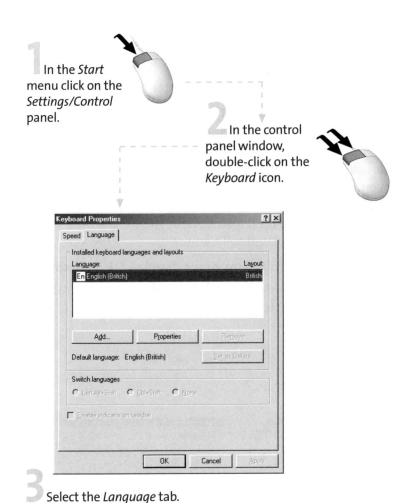

1 In the *Start* menu click on the *Settings/Control* panel.

2 In the control panel window, double-click on the *Keyboard* icon.

3 Select the *Language* tab.

Here the keyboard language must be set on *English (British)*.

If several languages are available, select *English* and close the window. If the *English* entry is missing, you must install it again using the *Add* button. Windows will lead you through the appropriate steps.

■ **The mouse pointer either does not move at all, or does not move properly**

Check the following points:

⇛ Is the mouse plugged into the computer correctly?

⇛ Is the mouse on a mouse mat?

⇛ Is the ball of the mouse dirty?

If the mouse has been used for a long time, the part that recognises the movement of the mouse gets dirty. Remove the ball from underneath the mouse. You will see a few small wheels. If these are dirty, clean them. You should also not put the mouse on a smooth surface, because the ball will roll badly.

■ **The mouse buttons are mixed up, or the double-click does not work**

This is usually because you have a left-hander's mouse. Train yourself to be a left-hander, or take the following steps:

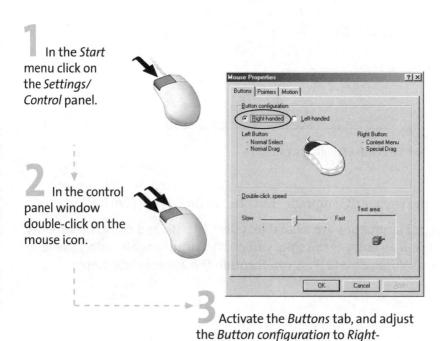

1 In the *Start* menu click on the *Settings/Control* panel.

2 In the control panel window double-click on the mouse icon.

3 Activate the *Buttons* tab, and adjust the *Button configuration* to *Right-handed*.

Are you working with a laptop? If so, activate the *Move* tab and check the *Mousepointer* check box. Furthermore, in this tab you can also adjust how quickly the mouse pointer moves.

As soon as you close the window, the mouse buttons should start working properly. Do you have problems with **double-clicking**? In this tab you can also alter the speed of the double-clicking, in order to work better with the mouse.

Windows desktop and Office

■ **On the desktop the text 'Safe Mode'appears**

When starting up, Windows recognised a problem and started the computer in a safe mode. This occurs when Windows has not been exited properly. Exit Windows and attempt to re-boot the computer. This will usually solve the problem.

■ **The icons on the desktop cannot be moved**

If the desktop icons automatically spring back to their old position after moving the mouse, take the following steps:

1 Click with the right button on an empty place on the desktop.

2 In the context menu choose the *Arrange Icons* command.

3 Undo the *Autoarrange* command in the submenu with a mouse click.

Now icons can be moved.

■ A link has been erased by mistake

If you have mistakenly erased a link, you can immediately open the context menu with the right mouse button and select the *Undo:Delete* command. Otherwise the link must be created afresh (*see* Chapter 11).

■ An Office program is missing from the *Start* menu

You must repair Office (*see* Chapter 11).

■ An Office program function is missing

Is a program missing, although it is listed in the Office package? The program or function has been switched off with the Setup. You must add the function to Office (*see* Chapter 11).

■ The taskbar is missing, has moved, or is too big

The taskbar can be moved on the desktop. You can drag it with the mouse to any of the four sides of the screen. The taskbar can also be pushed to the edge so you see only a grey line. Drag the taskbar with the mouse to the required position. Sometimes it disappears when the window is maximised. You can make adjustments to the taskbar with the *Properties/Task bar* command in the *Start* menu. In the *Task bar Options* tab, check the *Always in Foreground* check box.

■ A window has disappeared

Check in the taskbar. Usually, the window has just been hidden by another window. Otherwise press the [Alt]+[⇆] key combination repeatedly to change between windows. In Excel, a document window can also be concealed by another. Choose the window entry in the Window menu.

■ **A document window cannot be placed in the foreground, or worked on**

If you click on the document window in the background and nothing happens, or a document window does not allow any input, a dialog box is probably open, which is concealed by another window. Minimise the window in the foreground and close the dialog box. Then the program window can be selected, and the required document can be worked on.

■ **You cannot see everything in a window**

Sometimes a window is too small. You can scroll in the window with the scrollbar to display the contents which are not visible.

■ **The toolbar is missing in a program window**

In many programs you can use the VIEW menu to insert or remove the toolbar and the task bar. The *Toolbar* command opens a submenu with the names of the bars. Click on the desired names. If the toolbar is missing in the menu, it has been erased. To bring it back refer to Chapter 11.

■ **A menu command is missing**

Office programs contain only the most important commands in the opened menu. If you click on the symbol at the bottom edge of the menu, Office inserts all the commands of the menu.

■ **A menu command is displayed in grey and does not work**

Although the Office programs display the commands in the menu, this does not mean that a particular command makes sense in the current context. For example, in Excel, many commands are blocked off when inputting information into cells. Finish off the last operation, and then try to re-select the command.

■ **The buttons are too big**

In the Office programs, you can adjust various options on the toolbar.

557

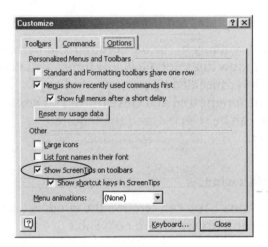

1 In the VIEW menu select the *Toolbar/ Customize* command.

2 In the *Options* tab you will find the *Large icons* check box, which you must switch off.

3 Click on the *Close* button.

■ **A button is missing**

Maybe the button has been erased or cut out. Add the button, or insert it (*see* Chapter 11).

■ **A program can no longer be operated on**

Sometimes a program will not react to keyboard input or mouse clicks.

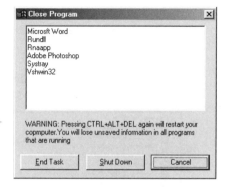

1 Press this key combination simultaneously: $\boxed{Ctrl}$+$\boxed{Alt}$+$\boxed{Del}$.

2 Click in the *Close Program* window on the programs which are not working anymore.

3 Click on the *End Task* button.

Windows now attempts to forcibly end the program. If this does not work, a further window will appear with the advice that the program is not reacting. You must then select the command to end the program.

Folders and files

■ **File extensions do not appear**

Are extensions for some file names missing in the folder windows in Explorer, or in the *Open* or *Save As* dialog boxes?

1 In the VIEW menu select the *Folder options* command.

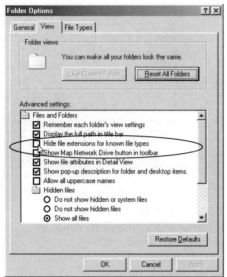

2 In the *View* tab undo the *Hide file extensions for known file types* check box.

3 Close the window.

- **Certain files are not displayed**

  Are you sure that a certain file is in a folder, but it is not appearing in the folder window or in Explorer? If so, you must open the *View* tab (VIEW/FOLDER OPTIONS menu). In the *Hidden files* group, the *Show all files* option box must be marked. After closing the tab you will see all hidden files. If necessary, press the [F5] key to update the window display.

- **Every folder is displayed in a single window**

  For every folder icon which is selected in a folder window by double-clicking, Windows opens a further window immediately. Select the *Custom, based on settings you choose* option box in the *General* tab, and click on the *Settings* button. In the *Custom settings* dialog box, select the *Open each folder in its own window* option box.

■ **The floppy disk or CD-ROM cannot be read**

On double-clicking on the drive symbol, a box appears with the advice that the drive is not working. Check the following points:

⇉ Has a disk or CD-ROM been inserted in the drive?

⇉ If it is a CD-ROM, open and close the drive and wait a few seconds. Usually Windows then recognises the change of the CD-ROM.

⇉ Has the disk been inserted correctly into the drive?

⇉ If you are using a new disk, perhaps it hasn't been formatted yet. In this case you must format the disk before using it (*see* Appendix B). If you find a mistake, remove it.

1 Click on the *Retry* button.

Sometimes it is necessary to repeatedly click on the *Retry* button. Alternatively, you can click on the *Cancel* button and repeat the whole action.

■ **Nothing can be written on the disk**

When attempting to save a file on to a disk, a window appears with this error announcement:

Remove the disk from the drive and remove the read-only property (see the Appendix). If the read-only is not set, it could be an unformatted disk. How to format a disk is described in the Appendix.

■ A file cannot be changed

You have loaded a document file in a program, changed the content of the file and then selected the *Save* command. However, the program opens the *Save As* dialog box and suggests a new name for the file. If you give the old name of the file, the program announces that the file is read-only. With files of a CD-ROM it is clear that its contents cannot be changed. If CD-ROM files are copied, these files keep their read-only property, but you can remove the read-only from such files.

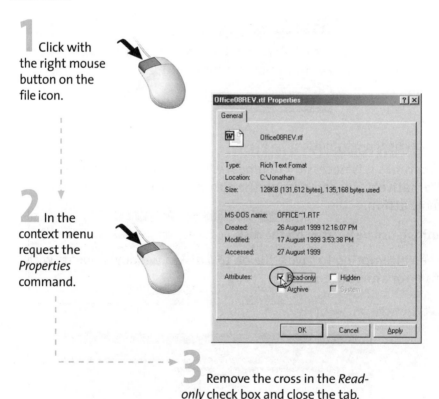

1 Click with the right mouse button on the file icon.

2 In the context menu request the *Properties* command.

3 Remove the cross in the *Read-only* check box and close the tab.

A read-only can also have other causes. If someone else is working on the same file in the network, and you open it at the same time, Windows will not allow any overwriting. If you exit the program and wait until the other person has finished working on the file, you will be able to carry out your changes to the file. You can also select the *Read-only* option when loading the document, using the *Open* menu.

■ **A file is mistakenly deleted**

Double-click on the desktop on the paper basket icon, then click with the right mouse button on the required file, and select the *Restore* command in the context menu.

■ **A file cannot be found**

Maybe you have saved the file in another folder. In the *Start* menu chose the *Search/Files/Folder* command, and type the file name, or part of it, in the *Search* dialog box in the *Name* field. Click on the *Start* button. If the file is found, open it with a double-click on the file symbol.

Problems with printing

■ **The printer does not work**

When printing, the message displayed here is given. The printing is disrupted. Remove the fault and click on the *Retry* button.

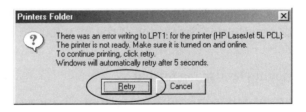

You can stop printing by pressing the *Cancel* button. To sort out the printing fault you must check the following points:

⇥ Is the printer switched on and plugged in?

⇥ Is the cable between the computer and printer connected correctly?

⇥ Is the printer set to **Online**?

⇥ Has the printer got enough paper, toner and ink?

⇥ Is there an obstruction in the printer (e.g. a paper jam)?

⇥ Have you selected the wrong printer?

⇥ Is the printer driver set up properly (for example, the choice of printer connection)?

■ **The printer is not working**

In the *Print* dialog box change the printer driver. These steps are described in Chapter 11.

■ **The print-out contains only strange symbols**

Does the print-out only contain cryptic symbols? If so, you have probably installed the wrong printer driver. Change the driver in the *Print* dialog box (*see* Chapter 11). If no other driver is available, install a new printer driver in the *Print* folder window which does fit your printer. This can be done using the *New printer* symbol. An assistant leads you through the steps of the installation of the printer.

■ **Removing landscape format**

The print-out is in landscape format. Change the print option from landscape to portrait format as shown in Chapter 11.

■ **The printer takes the paper from the wrong tray**

Change the printer options for paper insertion. This is described in Chapter 11.

■ **On the print-out the graphics appear too coarse**

On a print-out, sometimes graphics can appear really coarse.

In the properties window of the printer, you can often adjust the print options. For example, set the colour mixture in the *Graphics* tab on *Fine*. Adjust the content of the *Resolution* list box. In the *Device Options* tab you can also change the quality of the printing.

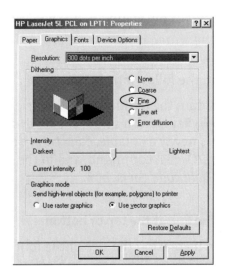

Click on the *Print* dialog box on the *Properties* button (or Ctrl + P).

Word, Excel and PowerPoint problems

■ **Word: graphics are only printed as borders**

If this happens, the *Picture placeholder for graphics* function is switched on, or you have chosen the concept print-out. In the TOOLS/ OPTIONS command open the *View* tab. Remove the cross in the *Picture placeholder* check box.

■ **Word: table borders are missing in the print-out**

The gridlines for tables are only displayed on the screen. If you would like to see them in the print-out, highlight the table and, using the *Boundaries* button, allocate an appropriate framing to the table (*see* the chapters on Word).

■ **Word, Excel: the gridlines for tables are missing in the display**

In Word, in the TABLE menu, select the *Insert gridlines* command. In Excel select the TOOLS/OPTIONS command and in the *View* tab, mark the *Gridlines* check box.

■ **Word: in the document, the following text appears{ ... }**

The curved brackets contain the definition of the field code. Highlight this, and press the Alt+F9 key combination. The field value is now inserted. If the display is newly available, each time the document is loaded, choose the TOOLS/OPTIONS command, and in the *View* tab remove the tick in the *Field code* check box.

■ **Word: text is cut off in the line at the top or bottom**

This effect occurs when increasing the size of the font in Word. Click with the right mouse button on the paragraph, select the *Paragraph* command in the context menu, and in the *Indents and Spacing* tab, change the value in the *Line spacing* list box from 'exactly' to 'at least'.

■ **Excel: cells contain the value ####**

The cell is not wide enough to display the value. Enlarge the table column.

■ **Excel: the value keyed in is displayed in another way**

This effect occurs when the cell contains another cell format (e.g. because you entered a time earlier, and then deleted the value). Highlight the cell, choose the FORMAT/CELL menu command, and set the cell format back to standard (*see* the chapters on Excel).

■ **Excel: the places after the decimal point disappear in the print-out**

Excel holds back places after the decimal point when the value is 0. Highlight the cell and allocate it two decimal places in the *Add decimal places* button (*see* the chapters on Excel).

■ **Excel: formulae appear in the table cells**

Select the Tools/Options command. In the *View* tab delete the mark in the *Formula* check box.

■ **Excel: when inputting, the table will not do any new calculations**

The automatic calculation is switched off. Press the F9 function key, or go to Tools/Options. In the *Calculate* tab set the *Automatic* option box (*see also* Chapter 11).

■ **PowerPoint: the start dialog to select the AutoContent Assistant does not appear**

Go to Tools/Options. In the *View* tab select the *Start dialog* check box.

■ **PowerPoint: the *New Slide* dialog does not appear**

Go to Tools/Options. In the *View* tab select the *New Slide* dialog check box.

In this appendix you will find additional explanations for naming folders and files, and for dealing with drives and disks. Read this appendix if you are not yet clear on these issues, or if you want to deepen your knowledge from Chapter 1.

Folders and files

Folders and files are two terms that you often meet in Windows and when working with Office programs. When you use a program to write a letter, create a drawing, or design an invoice table, and then save your results, a file is created. This contains all relevant data (for example the text of the letter, a picture, a calculation table, or a program. Every file carries a name and a symbol. This name allows you and the computer to find the required file again.

> **Folders and files**
>
> The **names** of files must satisfy certain rules in Windows. A filename can be up to 255 characters long. You can use the letters A to Z, a to z, the numbers 0 to 9, spaces and other characters. A valid name would be *Letter to Smith*. However, the characters "/<> are not permitted in the filename.

Files are displayed in the folder window (*see* Chapter 1). It is not only the name that is displayed here, but also the symbol. This symbol advises you on the content of the file (e.g. a text file, a graphics file etc.). In documents, the symbol is defined by the program and is used when the file is saved. The difference between contents of a file, and also the **Save As Type**, occurs in the **file name extension**. This is an appendix separated from the file name by a dot, and usually contains three letters (for example *.txt*, *.bmp*, *.exe*, *.bat*, *.ini*, *.doc*). This extension fixes the type of file, i.e. fixes which programs can be used to work on the file. A text file set up in Microsoft Word could, for example, be labelled as *Statement1-99*.

> Whether the extension is displayed in windows depends on the set options (VIEW/FOLDER OPTIONS menu, *View* tab, *Remove file name extensions for know file types* option).
> You can write the file name and the extension with upper or lowercase letters. Windows does not distinguish between these. This means that the names 'Letter to Smith.doc' and 'letter to smith.doc' are treated the same in Windows. The MS-DOS and Windows 3.1 limit of eight letters to a file name and three characters for the extension no longer exists in Windows 95/98 and Windows NT. But to save unnecessary typing file names should not really be longer than 20 characters.

In Windows, the files are allocated various symbols, depending on the type of name extension used. You will now see a few examples of such file names.

Symbol	Comment

Picture.bmp

This is a graphics file with the *.bmp* extension. Such files can be created with the *Paint* program in Windows and added later to Office documents. According to the program used, graphics are left in files with different file name extensions and symbols.

Word.txt

This symbol and the *.txt* extension stand for files that contain only text. Such files could be created in the *Editor* Windows program (which is not further explained in this book).

test.doc

Files with the *.doc* extension contain text with additional specially formatted words or letters (e.g. bold, italic), pictures other. The symbol on the left is used when the *Word* Office program is installed on your computer.

Access.xls

Files with the *.xls* extension contain spreadsheets and are worked on in the *Excel* Office program.

Access.mdb

Files with the *.mdb* extension are produced in the Access Office Program, and contain data and documents of a database.

Pres1.ppt

Documents produced in PowerPoint and saved in a file are labelled with the *.ppt* extension and the symbol on the left.

Test.htm

Files with the *.htm* or the *.html* extension contain Internet documents that are displayed by the Internet Explorer (*see* Chapter 9).

hh.chm

The *.chm* extension stands for help files.

Symbol	Comment
Command.exe	The *.exe* extension stands for program files. If it is an older MS-DOS program, the window symbol on the left is displayed.
Calc.exe	Windows programs also have the *.exe* extension in file names. But here each program has its own symbol (on the left, the symbol of a Windows calculator is shown).

There are many other symbols for files which depend on the file name extension and the program installed in Windows.

> **TIP**
>
> Like files, **folders** are given a **name** and a folder **symbol.** For allocating folder names, the same rules apply as for file names. But as a rule, folders do not have the file name extensions. Sometimes folders are called **directories.**

> **CAUTION**
>
> Files and folders must be given a clear name. You cannot have two files or folders with the same name. A file can, however, be saved with the same name into different folders.

Dealing with drives

To save files and folders, the hard disk, floppy disks or CD-ROMS are used. Individual labelling of the drive can differ, depending on the computer (for example, *data1 (D:), System (C:).* But all drives are named according to a simple scheme, which applies to all Windows computers.

⇨ The drives are numbered with letters from A to Z, followed by a colon. You can recognise these letters in the *Workplace* window.

⇒ The **floppy disk drive** is usually recognised as the first drive, and is therefore given the letter **A:**

⇒ If a **second floppy disk drive** is available, this is labelled **B:**

⇒ The **first hard drive** is given the letter **C:**

If further **CD-ROM** and **network** drives exist, these carry the labelling **D:, E:, F:** and so on.

The symbols below advise you on types of drive.

Symbol	Comment
  3.5" Floppy(A:) 5.25"Floppy (A:)	These symbols are used for floppy disk drives. The disk symbol shows which **type of disk** the drive supports. Generally with new computers, only the **3.5 inch floppy** can be used. These are disks with a width and height of 3.5 inches, placed in a plastic casing. Older computers often use the **5.25 Inch floppy** with a diameter of 5.25 inches, and placed in a flexible plastic cover.
  System (E:)	**Hard disk drives** are given this symbol. They are built into the computer and, unlike a floppy disk, cannot be changed. A great deal more data can be saved on the hard disk than on the floppy.
  (F:)	If the computer has a CD-ROM drive, it is given this symbol.

Sometimes drives are shown with a stylised hand in the bottom left corner. This hand shows that the drive is networked, which means that other users in the network can access the drive. This hand is also used for released printers or folders. More on this function can be found in *Windows 2000 In No Time* and *A Simple Guide to Windows*, both published by Prentice Hall.

System (C:)

Dealing with disks

When working with Office documents you might want to save them on floppy disks before deleting them. You can then copy your deleted documents from the floppy disk back onto the hard disk (*see* Chapter 1) if necessary. If you are not used to using floppy disks, here are a few hints.

When working with floppy disks, there are a few things to be careful of. Here you see a 3.5 inch floppy, which is in a firm plastic cover.

The paper sticker (also the label) allows you to label your disk. You should always use this sticker.

The metal slide on the bottom edge protects the magnetic strip from dust, dirt and finger prints.

In the top right corner, the disk has a small rectangular opening, which can be closed up with a slide. If this opening is blocked, files can be copied on to the disk. By opening the gap the disk can be protected from being written over. An opening on the left side of the disk means that it is a 1.44 Mb disk. A 720 Kb disk would not have this opening.

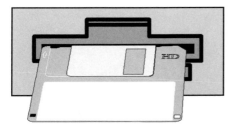

When inserting the disk, touch the paper sticker and use the scheme shown opposite (metal slide first, paper sticker on top) to insert it into the drive.

To remove the disk, press the eject button which is on the drive.

Formatting disks

Before you can use a **floppy disk**, it must be **formatted**. When formatting, Windows summons all information to the management of the files, and an empty content directory to the data carrier. Furthermore, Windows checks the disk for mistakes. Normally, newly bought disks have already been formatted by the manufacturer (which is displayed on the disk packaging). In this case, you do not have to think any more about all this. But, if Windows or a program is missing a certain formatting, you can format the disk yourself, following just a few steps.

To **format** a (new) **floppy disk**, do the following:

1 Insert the disk in the drive. Make sure that it is not read-only.

2 Open the *Workplace* window, and click with the right mouse button on the disk drive symbol.

3 In the context menu choose the *Format* command.

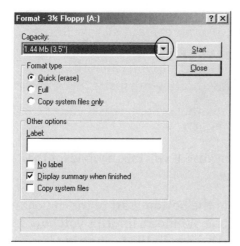

Windows opens the dialog box to format the disk.

4 Adjust the various options in this dialog box.

In the *Capacity* list box there are two types of memory density to be selected. 3.5 inch disks can store data with a capacity of either 720 Kb or 1.44 Mb. If you format a disk with 1.44 Mb, more data will fit on it. In the section *Format type* decide how the disk is to be formatted.

If you want to, you can give the disk another name (maximum 11 characters) in the *Label* box.

New, unformatted disks are always formatted using the *Full* format. A disk that has already been used can be erased using the *Quick* choice in the option box. In this case, the table of contents will be erased and all the files lost, but the formatting takes place considerably quicker.

5 Click on the *Start* button.

Windows will now start formatting the disk. It will take a while for the full formatting process to be complete.

In the bottom part of the dialog box, Windows informs you how far through the formatting it is.

If the *Display summary when finished* check box was marked, Windows will display detailed information about the disk, after it has finished formatting.

6 Close the message box by clicking on *Close*.

7 Click on *Close* to close the formatting dialog box.

Finally, use the disk to save files and folders.

Opening documents quickly

When working with documents in Word, Excel, PowerPoint or any other program, you can proceed by following the instructions in the previous chapters. In the *Open* dialog box, choose the required document names and open these in the program. Windows and Office, however, offer a few tricks to help you open files quicker.

Double-click on the symbol of a document name and Windows will start up the file type assigned to the application. This application will automatically load the document name and indicate when it is ready.

The symbols of the last 15 documents to be loaded by double-clicking are listed in the *Documents* menu in the *Start* menu.

In this menu, one mouse click on the document name is enough to load the document, together with its accompanying application.

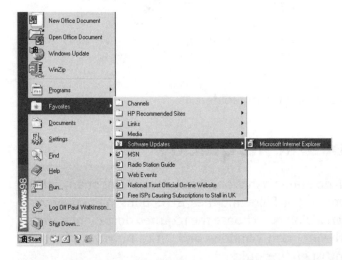

The *Favorites* menu in the *Start* menu or in the folder window also allows you to access frequently used document files. To set up an entry like this, drag the file icon, with the mouse, to the *Favorites* menu, wait until the menu has opened and then move the icon to the desired position. As soon as you let go of the mouse button, it will be inserted.

In the *Open* dialog box you can open the *History* folder as well as the *Favorites* folder. This folder contains the names of the last files to be worked on. Highlight the required document file and click on the *Open* button. The document will be opened.

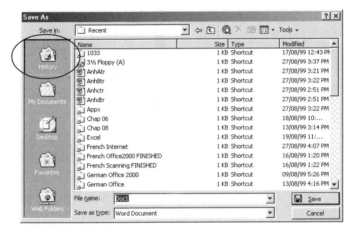

There are therefore many roads to 'Rome'. Which one you take is up to you. Further tips on dealing with files and folders can be found in Chapter 1.

Chapter 1

1   Click on the *Maximize* ⬜ button. With some Office programs, the F11 key also works.

2   Click on the *Close* ✖ button, or choose the FILE/ EXIT command.

3   Begin with *Programs* in the *Start* menu. Alternatively, double-click on the program icon on the desktop, or double-click on the document file that was created with this program.

4   Highlight the file icon, click on the right, select *Rename* in the Context menu, and type the new name. Finally press the ⏎ key.

5   Drag the icon from one folder window to the second, by holding down the right mouse button. In the context menu select *Copy*.

6   Drag the file icon to the wastepaper bin.

7   Press the F1 key, or select the first command in the HELP menu.

8 Click on a free place in the folder window with the right button, select the *New* command in the context menu, and then select the command with the document name of the desired Office document.

Chapter 2

1 In the FILE menu select the *Save as* command; in the *Save As* dialog box give the new file name.

2 Type in the text in paragraphs. Then highlight the paragraphs and click on the *Center* button ≡ in the format toolbar.

3 Highlight the passage, and enter a high value in the *Font Size* list box in the format toolbar.

4 Highlight the paragraphs, click with the right mouse button on the highlighted area, and then select the *Paragraph* command in the context menu. On the *Indents and Spacing* tab, change the value of the *Before* and *After* fields in the *Spacing* group.

5 In Word, do not press the ⏎ button to get to the next line.

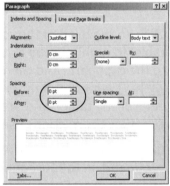

Word will automatically go to the next line when you have reached the right margin.

6 Highlight the text and drag it with the mouse to the new position. Or cut the highlighted text with Ctrl + X, click on the new position, and paste the text with Ctrl + V .

Chapter 3

1 Draw up the invoice as a document, as described in this chapter. Choose the FILE/SAVE AS command. In the *Save As* dialog box, select 'Document Template (*.dot)' in the *Save File As Type* box. Give the name of the template and save this as a file in the *Templates* subfolder.

2 Select the FILE/NEW command, or press Ctrl+N. In the *New* dialog box, look for the tab that contains document templates for the letter. Mark the symbol of the document template and click on the *OK* button. Write the letter and save it as a normal document.

3 Open a new text page with the *New* button. Add a few sales changes. Click on a paragraph, and then on the *Insert Table* button. Fix the number of lines and columns using the table palette.

4 Click on the head of the column (gridlines on the top edge of the table) to highlight the column. Copy the column with Ctrl+C on to the clipboard, and then paste the contents into the table with Ctrl+V. Now highlight the header (click on the gridline on the left edge of the table), and press the described key combination again. To remove corrections use the key combination Ctrl+Z.

5 Click on the table, and in the TABLE menu choose the *Sort* command. In the *Sort* dialog box, and in the *Sort By* box, enter the last column.

6 Enter the columns by pressing the ⇆ key. Set the tab as shown opposite.

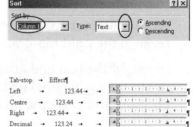

7   Enter the text 'Dear Madam' and highlight it. Select the INSERT/
    AUTOTEXT/NEW menu command. In the *Create AutoText* dialog box
    enter 'dm', and click on the *OK* button.

8   Draw up a table as in exercise 3. Highlight a table line, and in the
    Borders palette select the ▦ button. Repeat this with the rest of
    the lines.

9   Click on the lowest cell of the column. On the toolbar, click on the
    ▦ button. On the Tables and Borders toolbar select the Σ
    button.

10 Write the text and highlight the superscript part. With the right
    mouse button, click on the highlighting, and in the context menu
    choose the *Symbols* command. On the *Font* tab, mark the
    Superscript check box in the *Effects* group. Close the tab.

11 Highlight the superscript part of the text and press the [Ctrl]+[___]
    key combination. Otherwise repeat the steps from solution 10, but
    without marking the check box.

Chapter 4

1   The main document with the letter content and the mail merge
    fields. The data source (source file with addresses).

2   From the Mail Merge box select an *If-Then* condition, which
    evaluates the 'Sir' or 'Madam' form of address to provide the set
    phrase 'Dear'.

3   Click on the place and select the INSERT/PICTURE command and the
    Clipart or *File* command in the submenu. Then choose the
    graphics file from the dialog box.

4   Click on the *Draw* button ▨ . On the drawing toolbar choose the
    desired drawing tool, and draw lines, figures and AutoForms.

5 With the right mouse button click on the enumeration paragraph, and in the context menu select the *Bullets and Numbering* command. In the following dialog box, the bullets and numbers can be selected.

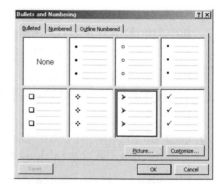

6 Click on the table and in the TABLE menu select the *Sort* command. In the *Sort by* box in the *Sort* dialog box, enter the desired

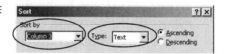

column with the numbers. In the *Type* list box, select the *Number* entry.

Chapter 5

1 In the FILE menu, select the *Save as* command, and in the *Save As* dialog box, enter the new file name.

2 Highlight the cells in the worksheet, and click on the *Center* button ≡.

3 Highlight the area of text and in the *Font* dialog box in the format toolbar, choose a higher value.

4 Click on the cell where the sum should appear. Click on the *AutoSum* button Σ. Highlight the cells to be totalled up, and then press the ⏎ key.

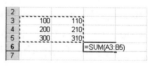

5 Click on the cell, and enter the formula shown opposite in the formula bar. Press the ⏎ key.

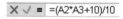

6   Click on the top left cell of the area, and drag the mouse to the bottom right cell of the area.

7   Click on the cell. Click on the *Add decimal place* button ⁺⁰₀₀ .

Chapter 6

1   Highlight the cell of the target worksheet and type in the equals sign. Excel starts the mode to enter a formula. Now change to the source worksheet and click on the cell whose value is to be taken. Press the ⏎ key. Excel automatically swaps to the target sheet and displays the adopted value in the cell. The formula used to do this is displayed in the formula bar, e.g. 'Table1!A2'.

2   Enter some values into a column. Click on the first target cell, and select the *Function Wizard* ƒ* button. In the *Add Function* dialog box select the *All* function category and the *MIN* function name. Click on the *OK* button.

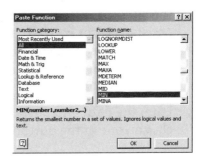

In the formula palette, enter the cell area containing the cells to be evaluated (or just highlight the area with the mouse). Close the formula palette.

Repeat these steps for the maximum value, in which you will use the *MAX* function name.

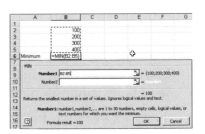

3 Create a column with amounts in euros, and a column with amounts in foreign currency. Enter the euro values, and format them in the euro currency format. Click on the

desired cell in the column of the amounts in foreign currency. Enter the EUROCONVERT formula and set the parameter for conversion from euros into the required currency. To convert euros to French francs, the following formula applies: =EUROCONVERT (A2, 'EUR', 'FRF'). Here the A7 cell is converted. Allocate the correct currency format to the result cell.

4 Enter into a column the market share as a percentage, and the name into another column. Highlight these cells and click on the 🏛 button. In the Chart

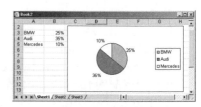

Assistant enter *Pie chart* as the type of chart. If need be you can carry out the remaining steps (for example, you can select the *Display percentage* option box on the *Data description* tab).

5 Enter the data into the table. Highlight the desired column, and click on one of the buttons on the standard toolbar ♉ ♊ .

Chapter 7

1 Click on the 🗐 button and select AutoLayout.

2 Highlight the slide in the *Slide Sorter View*. To delete, choose the EDIT/DELETE SLIDE command. To sort, drag the slide icon to the required position, or move the slide in the slide sorting view.

3 Press, for example, the F5 function key, or select the *Screen Presentation* in the bottom left corner of the document window. To scroll, click on the slide with the right mouse button and call up the appropriate command in the context menu.

4   Press the [Ctrl]+[P] key combination. In the *Print* dialog box and the *Print* list box, select the *Notes Pages* option.

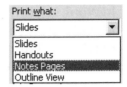

5   Select the FILE/NEW command, and click on the *AutoContent Wizard* on the *General* tab of the *New* dialog box. Select the *OK* button and follow the steps of the assistant.

6   Click on the slide in the Slide Sorter View. Click on the *Common Tasks* button in the *Format* toolbar. Choose the *Apply Design Template* command from the menu. In the dialog box displayed, select the outline template.

7   Click on the *Slide Sorter View* of the slide. On the format toolbar, click on the *Common Tasks* button. Select the *Slide Layout* command from the menu. Select the desired layout from the open dialog box.

Chapter 8

1   In PowerPoint select the INSERT/OBJECT command. In the *Add Object* dialog box click on the *Create from File* option box. Select the *Search* button and enter the desired Word *.doc* file.

2   In Excel, choose the INSERT/OBJECT command. In the *Add Object* dialog box, click on the *Create from File* tab. Click on the *Search* button and select the desired Word *.doc* file.

3   In Excel, select the INSERT/OBJECT command. In the *Add Object* dialog box, click on the *Create from File* tab. Click on the *Search* button, and select the desired sound file.

587

4 In Word, select the INSERT/OBJECT command. In the *Object* dialog box activate the *Create from File* tab and enter the file. Or, on the *Create New* tab, choose the *Microsoft Excel Worksheet* object type. Before closing the *Object* dialog box, mark the *Display as Icon* check box.

5 Start Word, and using the FILE/OPEN command load the desired file. Look for the passage with links, and enter the text of the hyperlinks. Then highlight the text and click on the button. In the *Add Hyperlink* dialog box, select the *File* button. Finally, look for the desired file.

6 Start Word, and using the FILE/OPEN command, load the desired file. Search for the passage, enter the hyperlinks text. Then highlight the text and click on the button. In the *File Type or Web page* box, enter the *www.microsoft.com* hyperlink. Close the dialog box.

Chapter 10

1 In the Outlook bar, click on the *Notes* icon. Select the *New* button, and enter the text in the note window.

2 In the Outlook bar, select the *Calendar* icon. In the calendar page, look for '17 April', and highlight the date with a mouse click. In the calendar, you can flick through the months using the buttons. Click in the appointment calendar on the 9:00 line, and enter the appointment.

3 In the Outlook bar, click on the *Tasks* icon. In the tasks list, double-click on a free line. Enter the subject on the *Tasks* tab. Activate the *Reminder* check box, and fix the reminder time.

4 Load the new post by clicking on the *Send/Receive* button from the Internet. Click on the *Post Delivery* icon in the Outlook bar. Double-click on news if you want to read it.

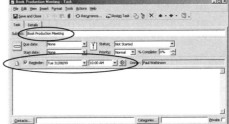

5 Click with the right mouse button on the News in the News bar. In the context menu select the *Mark As Unread* command.

6 Click on the *Notes* icon in the Outlook bar. Mark the note icon and click on the ✕ button.

Access

Microsoft Database program; not contained in all Office versions.

Account

Entitlement to establish an online connection with a service provider and, for example, to surf the World Wide Web.

Address

Memory place in the directory (main memory) of the computer, or information of where to find a **Web page** or the receiver of an **e-mail.**

ANSI symbols

ANSI is the abbreviation for American National Standards Institute. ANSI symbols define the symbols used in Windows.

AOL

Abbreviation of the firm America Online, which provides access to online services.

Applications program

Programs that are useful for working on the computer (e.g. Word, Excel, Access, CorelDraw).

Arithmetic processor

Special calculating chips for mathematical calculations.

ASCII symbols

ASCII is the abbreviation for American Standard Code for Information Interchange. The ASCII character set contains 127 characters (letters, numbers and a few special characters).

Assistant

Program that helps the user solve a task.

AutoCorrection

A function in Office programs that recognises typing errors as they occur and corrects them automatically.

AUTOEXEC.BAT

A batch processing file (*.BAT) which gives the computer basic DOS commands when you turn it on. You can display and work on these files with any editor. With the help of these files and the CONFIG.SYS file, you can analyse and remove memory problems and many other system problems.

AutoFormat

A function in Word and Excel that lets a document or table be formatted automatically.

AutoText

A Word function whereby contractions can be used to call up whole expressions (e.g. 'ys' for 'yours sincerely').

Backslash

The \ symbol is used to separate folder names.

Backup

Term describing the safeguarding of data (files are saved on a floppy).

Basic

Abbreviation for **Beginners All-purpose Symbolic Instruction Code.** Basic is a simple and easily learnt programming language.

Baud

Speed instruction when transferring data over serial lines.

Bit

This is the smallest unit of information in a computer (the value can be 0 or 1). There are 8 bits in a byte.

Bitmap

Format for saving pictures or graphics. The picture is divided up into individual points (like on the screen), which are saved by the line.

Boot

Start the computer.

Browser

A program with which the pages in the World Wide Web can be displayed.

Bug

A software error in a program.

Byte

The information unit consisting of 8

bits. A byte allows numbers from 0 to 225 to be displayed.

C

A programming language.

Character set

The characters that can be used on the computer (*see also* ASCII and ANSI).

Chat

An Internet service where participants can talk in 'chat rooms'.

Check box

Square in a dialog box, which can be marked with a cross if you click on it. A crossed check box corresponds to a chosen option.

Chip

General term for an electronic component.

ClipArt

Graphics file with stylised motifs. A wealth of ClipArts are contained in Office 2000, which can be added to any documents.

Clipboard

Memory in Windows which is used to exchange data between programs.

CIS

Short name for the CompuServe firm, which provides access to online services.

COM

Name of the serial interface of the PC (e.g. COM1).

Command

An instruction to the computer.

CONFIG.SYS

A configuration file that gives the computer basic DOS memory and system commands. You can display and edit these files with any editor. With the help of this file and the AUTOEXEC.BAT file, you can analyse and remove many memory problems, and a great deal of other system problems (*see also* AUTOEXEC.BAT).

CPU

Abbreviation for **central processing unit**, the calculating unit of the computer.

Cursor

The position pointer of the screen (shown as an arrow, hand, vertical line, egg-timer etc.).

Database

Programs to save, manage and query data (e.g. Microsoft Access).

Desktop publishing (DTP)

Editing documents (e.g. brochures, books) on the computer.

Dialog box

A window in Windows, in which inputs are requested.

Document template

Template files used in Word to create new documents.

Download

Using a modem to extract data, for example, from the Internet to your computer.

DPI

Abbreviation for dots per inch, which is the resolution of the printer.

Drag-and-drop

A technique in Windows where an object can be dragged to another icon (like a window or the wastepaper bin) by pressing the mouse button. If you let go of the mouse button on an icon, Windows carries out an action (for example a file might be deleted or copied).

Editor

A program to create and edit simple text files.

Electronic mail (e-mail)

News that can be sent electronically (*see* Chapter 8).

Ethernet

Technique of transferring data in networks.

Excel

A spreadsheet program from Microsoft.

Extranet

Network to do business on the Internet (for example, ordering on the Internet).

FAT

Abbreviation for **file allocation unit,** the method by which Windows stores files on a floppy disk or hard disk.

File

Data is saved in a file on floppy disks or hard disks (*see* Chapter 1).

Font

Name of the style of writing used to portray letters of a text (e.g. Arial, Times, Courier).

Formatting

Marking of the text in a document (with bold, underlining etc.). For a floppy disk or data carrier, formatting means preparing it for saving files.

Format template

see document template

Freeware

Software that is free and can only be passed on for free.

FTP

File Transfer Protocol – a function of the Internet whereby files can be transferred between computers.

Gb

Abbreviation for gigabyte (1000 megabytes).

GIF

Graphics format used for graphics in Web pages.

Gopher

A search service in the Internet.

Graphics card

Card that slots into the PC and manages the display on the screen.

Hardware

All physical parts of the computer that can be touched. (The opposite is software.)

High Memory Area (HMA)

Part of the memory, which lies above the 1-megabyte limit.

Homepage

The first page of a Web site in the World Wide Web. From this page there are hyperlinks to other Web pages.

HTML

Hypertext Markup Language, the document format in the World Wide Web.

Hyperlink

Access in an HTML document to another Web page.

Internet

Worldwide link of computers in a network (*see* Chapter 9).

Intranet

A firm's internal network, using the Internet technology (*see* Chapter 9).

Italic

A text format where the letters are displayed sloping.

Joystick

The control column used in game programs.

JPEG

Graphics format, used for graphics in Web pages.

Kilobyte

The unit of measure for 1024 bytes.

LAN

Local Area Network – a network within a firm. (The opposite is a Wide Area Network.)

LCD

Liquid Crystal Display – a special display on laptop computers.

Link

A technique of Windows, in which an object in another folder or document can be accessed. By clicking the link, the object is opened.

List box

A box containing a list, allowing you to select a given option.

Lotus 1-2-3

Spreadsheet program of the Lotus firm.

Macro

Module that contains recorded or typed-in commands to service the program. In macro reproduction, commands are automatically carried out. It allows the automating of certain processes.

Mb

Abbreviation for megabyte (1 million bytes).

Modem

Additional device with which data from a PC can be transferred and received. A modem is needed for Internet access.

MS-DOS

An older operating system from Microsoft.

Multimedia

Technique whereby text, pictures, videos and sounds can be integrated into the computer.

NetMeeting

Windows program where meetings can be held on the Internet.

NetShow

Windows program to show video transmissions from the Internet.

Network

Connection between computers to share data.

Newsgroups

Discussion groups on certain subjects on the Internet.

OLE

Abbreviation for Object Linking and Embedding, a technique that allows the insertion of objects (data and functions) of a program into a document.

Online service

Services for access to the Internet, e.g. T-Online, America Online and CompuServe.

Operating system

The program (for example, Windows) that runs after the computer has been switched on.

Option box

Round elements in a dialog box, which, when clicked on, are marked. Option boxes always occur in groups. Only one option box per group can be marked.

Outlook

Windows program to create, forward, read and receive e-mails. It also contains notepad, calendar, task lists etc. to organise the office work load.

Output unit

Device that can receive the output of the computer (e.g., screen, printer).

Paragraph

Text that is joined together in Word, and is completed with a paragraph mark by pressing the Enter key.

Parallel interface

Connection between a computer and a piece of equipment (usually a printer).

Path

Indicates the path on a hard disk to a file in a certain folder (for example C:\Text\Letters).

Processor

Another name for the CPU.

Public domain

Software that is publicly accessible, and can be freely copied or passed on with permission from the author (*see also* Freeware).

QWERTY keyboard

Describes the keyboard (the first six keys of the second row spell 'QWERTY').

RAM

Random Access Memory – the components of which the main memory of the computer is made up.

Recording density

You can distinguish between floppy disks by their recording density: DD (Double Density) and HD (High Density).

Resolution

This measure gives the number of pixels needed to construct a picture (arranged as rows of pixels). The resolution defines the number of pixels per line, and the number of lines per picture (this also applies to screen resolution).

Save File as Type

Determines from which program a file can be worked on (e.g. *.doc* files for Word, *.exe* files are programs, *.xls* files belong to Excel).

Scanner

An add-on with which pictures or documents can be read into the computer.

Screen saver

A program that prevents 'burning' of the screen when the computer is not being used.

Serial interface

Interface for operating a piece of equipment (modem, mouse).

Server

The main computer in a network.

Shareware

Software that can be freely passed on and can be set up for test purposes. When used regularly, the software must be registered with the program author and a small fee paid. This gives the user the opportunity to test the software extensively beforehand. The author can do without costly sales paths, so the software is usually offered at a good value.

Software

Another name for the program.

Spreadsheet

Program with which calculations in the form of a table can be made very easily.

TrueType font

Special technology developed by Microsoft for illustrating fonts.

Typography

The teaching of forming documents.

Unix

An operating system on which many computers run.

URL

Abbreviation for **Uniform Resource Locator**, the address of a Web page).

User interface

The way the computer accepts information from the user and displays the information. For example, Windows has a graphics surface with icons and windows.

VBA

Abbreviation for Visual Basic for Applications. This is the programming language in Office in which macros are recorded or programmed.

VGA

Graphics standard (16 colours and 640 times 480 pixels). Today Super VGA is used, with more colours and pixels.

Virus

A program that spreads and copies itself into another program. Sometimes a virus will disrupt the computer at a definite time (for example on a certain day).

Web page

Document in HTML format.

Word processor

Program for creating letters, reports, books etc. (e.g. WordPad, Microsoft Word).

Work memory

The memory (RAM) in the computer. The size is given in megabytes.

WWW

World Wide Web, part of the Internet, through which text and pictures can be retrieved with a browser.

XLS

File name extension for Excel files.

599

607